Endorsements for
Billions at Play

"It is an honor to provide the foreword for this book. I agree with the points made—and with Ayuk's case for the critical role that OPEC will play in helping African oil producers achieve a much-deserved voice in the petroleum industry. Yes, one could argue that Ayuk is a dreamer. However, he has taken the time to develop a detailed roadmap for realizing that dream. It's up to each of us to take the time to read it and to play a part in making his dream of petroleum-fueled economic growth, stability, and improved quality of life happen for Africa."

— Mohammad Sanusi Barkindo,
OPEC Secretary General

"In the chapter entitled *Abundant, Accessible, Affordable: The 'Golden Age' of Natural Gas Shines in Africa,* Ayuk correctly identifies the benefits of natural gas, especially as the world looks for ways to lower CO_2 emissions."

—Jeff Goodrich,
Former CEO of OneLNG

"The answer to Africa's utility woes can be found in Ayuk's book. For example, not everyone is willing to assert that Africa will never achieve its full potential if it cannot power its industries, services, or households. Ayuk's chapter isn't all doom and gloom, [however,] Ayuk calls it like it is."

—Dr. Thabo Kgogo,
Former CEO of Efora Energy Limited

"NJ Ayuk is right to call upon African governments to do their share in making Africa appealing to American exploration and production companies. I hope American companies will see that Africa still has a lot to offer in terms of economic returns."

—H. Daniel Hogan,
CEO and General Manager of
Lukoil International Upstream West

"Ayuk sees the irony in oil and gas produced in Africa being sent away to be refined, then returned as finished products that Africans pay a premium for. Africa is exporting raw materials it could be refining and processing, if it only had the capabilities, but not everyone is willing to admit that with the level of candor Ayuk does."

—Bruce Falkenstein,
Joint Operations Manager,
License Management & Compliance for LUKOIL

"NJ Ayuk is a champion of African commerce, and that's clear in his new book. In chapter 9, he presents an unvarnished view of corruption's negative effect on Africa's business environment. His message is something anyone who is doing business there, or wants to, should hear."

—Sergio Pugliese,
President for Angola African Energy Chamber

"Ayuk sees opportunity all around him, and he realizes that appropriate development will solve many of the continent's challenges, including power generation."

—Ann Norman,
Pioneer Energy's General Manager for Sub-Saharan Africa

"Ayuk goes beyond acknowledging this cycle of mismanagement and corruption. He also gives us ideas for breaking it. I can see how some of his ideas for oil money revenue will be considered controversial, but I hope, at least, that they trigger productive dialogue. We can't continue as we are."

— Akere Muna,
Former Vice Chairman of Transparency International

Billions at Play

The Future of African Energy and Doing Deals

NJ Ayuk

Made for Success
PUBLISHING

Made for Success Publishing
P.O. Box 1775 Issaquah, WA 98027
www.MadeForSuccessPublishing.com

Distributed by Made for Success Publishing

First Printing

Library of Congress Cataloging-in-Publication data
Ayuk, NJ
> Billions at Play: The Future of African Energy and Doing Deals
>> p. cm.

> LCCN: 2020949307
> 978-1-64146-559-5 (*hardback*)
> 978-1-64146-560-1 (*paperback*)
> 978-1-64146-561-8 (*ebook*)
> 978-1-64146-562-5 (*audiobook*)

Printed in the USA and the UK

For further information contact Made for Success Publishing
+14255266480 or email service@madeforsuccess.net

Contents

FOREWORD

The late Nelson Mandela famously said, "A winner is a dreamer who never gives up."

NJ Ayuk is precisely the type of dreamer Mr. Mandela was speaking about.

In this book, Ayuk lays out his commitment to putting African countries on the path to a prosperous future. The key, Ayuk tells us, is a concerted effort by African leaders, businesses, and individuals to ensure that the continent realizes the full potential of its vast petroleum wealth.

As the CEO of a thriving pan-African law group known for its oil and gas expertise, Ayuk is somewhat of an expert on this topic. His industry insights and talent as a deal-maker have earned the respect and trust of OPEC member countries—along with opportunities to negotiate on our organization's behalf.

What's more, Ayuk has invested his own time and resources into showing the way: He started by founding the African Energy Chamber and co-writing *Big Barrels: African Oil and Gas and the Quest for Prosperity*, a book that showcases African countries that are successfully harnessing their petroleum resources.

In this book, Ayuk builds on what he started in *Big Barrels*, encouraging Africans to use their continent's petroleum resources to seize control of their own destinies.

Perhaps most importantly, though, the book does not shy away from potentially controversial ideas. Although he dreams of African oil success, he is fully aware of the obstacles to that success and makes a strong case for bringing more women into the industry, particularly executive roles. Ayuk also takes African governments and companies to task in the areas where they fall short, from the unfair distribution of oil wealth to poor governance that violates the people of Africa.

Ayuk is straightforward in his assessment of Africa's inefficient power grid and the ineffective leadership of its energy companies, advocating for the unbundling of utilities as a way for the continent to take control of its future. In addition, he calls for a cultural shift that will enable oil and gas companies to transition to energy businesses that will invest in renewables in Africa.

He also addresses the very real problem of gas flaring in my native country, Nigeria, where natural gas could be harnessed to provide long-overdue access to reliable electricity for large segments of the population.

In his latest edition of *Billions at Play*, Ayuk frankly describes the devastating impact the COVID-19 pandemic has had on Africa's economy, from ravaged government budgets to postponed licensing rounds. Once again, he calls upon African governments to do their part to safeguard Africa's vital oil and gas industry and ensure its success. As always, Ayuk doesn't shy away from Africa's challenges. Instead, he urges leaders and decision-makers to get to work addressing them—and provides specific ideas to help them succeed.

It is an honor to provide the foreword for this book. I agree with the points made—and with Ayuk's case for the critical role that OPEC will play in helping African oil producers achieve a much-deserved voice in the petroleum industry.

Yes, one could argue that Ayuk is a dreamer. However, he has taken the time to develop a detailed roadmap for realizing that dream. It's up to each of us to take the time to read it and to play a part in making his dream of petroleum-fueled economic growth, stability, and improved quality of life happen for Africa.

OPEC Secretary General
Mohammad Sanusi Barkindo

ABBREVIATION KEY

bbl: barrels of oil

bbl/d: barrels per day

bbo: billion barrels of oil

bboe: billion barrels of oil equivalent (refers to crude oil and natural gas. The measurement of gas in the unit of barrel is based on the approximate energy released by burning one barrel of crude oil.)

bcm: billion cubic meters

bscf: billion standard cubic feet of gas

E&P: exploration and production

IOC: international oil company

LNG: liquified natural gas

mmbo: million barrels of oil

mmboe: million barrels of oil equivalent

mmbTU: million British thermal units

mscf: million standard cubic feet

mscf/d: million standard cubic feet per day

mt/y: million metric tonnes per year

NGO: non-governmental organization

NOC: national oil company

pb: per barrel

toe: tonnes of oil equivalent

tcf: trillion cubic feet

downstream = refining and petrochemicals industries

midstream = storage and transportation; pipelines

upstream = exploration and production

*Unless otherwise noted, all dollar amounts listed throughout the manuscript are in USD.

1

IT'S HIGH TIME FOR AFRICAN OIL AND GAS TO FUEL A BETTER FUTURE FOR AFRICANS

I~N APRIL 2020, THE ATMOSPHERE~ in northern Colorado was tense. Yes, the COVID-19 pandemic certainly was part of it. But in an area known for its prolific oil and gas industry, there also were concerns about the petroleum industry downturn. Rigs were sitting idle. Oil and gas people were being laid off.

I am not trying to minimize anyone's difficulties, but from a big-picture perspective, there also was—and still is—a glimmer of hope. Communities throughout northern Colorado have built strong economies and diversified over time, putting them in a better position to weather the current storm.

In fact, northern Colorado is an outstanding picture of oil and gas supporting economic growth, job creation, and increased opportunities. In Aurora, Colorado, for instance, revenue and economic activity generated by the petroleum industry made it possible to develop the nearby Colorado Air and Space Port and Gaylord Rockies Resort & Convention Center, among other projects.

I realize that COVID-19 is impacting the world economy, and, as I said, this is still a difficult time for northern Colorado. But the economic diversification there, rooted in the area's petroleum industry, will likely play a huge role in minimizing economic damage and easing recovery after the pandemic.

When I completed the first edition of this book in 2019, I asked why oil and gas success stories should be limited to the United States. "It's time to see the same results in African communities," I wrote. I stand behind those words, but now, with the world facing major health and economic crises, I have something to add: Why shouldn't African countries benefit from the kind of resiliency and diversification we're seeing in northern Colorado and other U.S. communities? The answer to both questions is the same: There is no good reason why Africa can't achieve the same things. And our oil and gas resources can help us get there. They can help us recover more quickly from tough times and lay the foundation for prosperity and a better quality of life during times of growth.

To some degree, it has already started.

One promising example is happening about an hour east of Lagos, Nigeria, where the construction site of a $12 billion oil refinery and petrochemical plant has become a multicultural hub of sorts.[1] More than 7,000 workers from Nigeria, India, and other countries have worked on this project, and the refinery is expected to go online in early 2021.

The man behind this project, Nigerian business magnate Aliko Dangote, predicts that once complete, the refinery will process 650,000 bbl/d and create thousands of jobs. Already, 900 Nigerian engineers are being trained in India for permanent positions at the refinery, and even more jobs will be created when Dangote's multinational industrial conglomerate, Dangote Group, moves forward with plans to build a port, jetty, power plants, and roads there.

If everything comes together as planned, the refinery complex has great potential to diversify and strengthen Nigeria's economy, spur knowledge and technology transfers, attract lucrative foreign investment opportunities, and put an end to Nigeria's dependency on petroleum exports.[2]

It's an audacious project and a powerful example of the oil and gas (O&G) industry's power to create a brighter future for Africa. And it's one of many promising O&G-related developments taking place across the continent.

As of this writing:

- The Alen Monetization Project offshore Equatorial Guinea, which will ensure stable gas supply to Equatorial Guinea's liquid natural gas (LNG) and downstream revenue-generating infrastructure, is on track to start in 2021. The project was launched by Noble Energy and has since been purchased by U.S. oil and gas multinational, Chevron Corporation, which has been successfully leading natural gas commercialization efforts in Nigeria for decades. Chevron also operates the world's largest liquid petroleum gas (LPG) floating production storage and offloading (FPSO) vessel in Angola, which turns previously flared gas into cleaner fuels.

- Somalia opened its first-ever licensing round in August 2020 for up to seven exploration blocks. "COVID-19 will not last forever," Somali Petroleum Authority Chairman and CEO Ibrahim Ali Hussein said. "Oil companies will be budgeting for Somali exploration."

- Democratic Republic of Congo President Félix Antoine Tshisekedi has asked government officials to fast-track legal processes and permits that will allow the valorization of natural gas produced onshore by European oil and gas company, Perenco. This move will open the door to investments in gas monetization and facilitate much-needed gas-to-power initiatives.

- The DeepSea Stavanger oil and gas drill rig recently arrived in Cape Town, South Africa, to drill the Luiperd prospect in Block 11B/12B off the Mossel Bay coast, Western Cape for Total SA and its partners. "The arrival of the drill rig, following the recent successful Brulpadda discovery, reaffirms confidence in South Africa as an investment destination of choice for the exploration of oil and gas," Minister of Mineral Resources and Energy Gwede Mantashe said. "This is despite the negative impact of the COVID-19 pandemic on economies around the world."

- At least 68 U.S. companies have agreed to supply equipment and services for engineering, procurement, and construction of a $23-billion two-train liquefied natural gas (LNG) processing plant project in Mozambique. The Mozambique Area 1 LNG Project, owned by Total Exploration and Production, is expected to develop an initial 18 trillion cubic feet of natural gas by 2024.

- The Lake Albert Development Project is moving forward again now that Uganda's government and investment partners Total, Tullow Oil, and China National Offshore Oil Corporation have resolved a long-standing capital gains tax dispute. The project includes exploration and production activities along with the construction of the 1,443-kilometer East Africa Crude Oil Pipeline beginning in 2021 and an oil refinery. The two oilfields on the shores of Lake Albert contain approximately six billion barrels of oil.

Despite these achievements, I've heard the nay-sayers enough to know how they'll respond to so much "good news": *You are being overly optimistic. What about the petroleum downturn and the pandemic?*

My response would be, first, that volatility has been a reality in the oil and gas industry from its earliest days, so the current low prices aren't something that hasn't been lived through before. Downturns do not negate petroleum resources' value to Africans. As for the pandemic: There is no question that it is a horrific global disaster and tragedy. But it will not be permanent.

Meanwhile, we still have reasons to be hopeful about Africa's petroleum industry. As executive chairman of the African Energy Chamber, I've found that increasing numbers of governments have been open to working with the chamber during this time, and so have companies. That opens the door to dialogue and joint efforts to find common solutions. The chamber also has released specific measures that we believe will help Africa's oil and gas industry recover from the pandemic. They are included in this book.

I'm familiar with arguments made before the pandemic as well: *Oil and gas have yet to solve Africa's problems, and in fact, only causes more problems. What about Africa's corruption and political instability? What about the lack of infrastructure?*

But it is high time to leave this unproductive negativity in the past.

It's quite easy for someone to say Africans don't fit the mold of oil and gas entrepreneurs—we have proven that we just have to break the mold and fight for an oil industry that works for every African. We're all familiar with Africa's challenges, and we're aware of Africa's perceived resource curse. Too often, our natural resources create wealth for foreign investors and a select group of African elites. At the same time, everyday people fail to benefit or—even worse—suffer the effects: instability, conflict, and environmental damage.

But this is what everyone refuses to talk about—that the curse is reversible. If African governments, businesses, and organizations manage Africa's oil and gas revenues wisely, we can make meaningful changes across the continent. We can replace instability with good governance, economic growth, and better opportunities for everyday Africans. Oil can work for everybody. It can create positive outcomes, and it can transition economies. We all have an obligation to support reliable companies that are investing and doing good work, encourage those that are timid, and warn those who still think business must be done like in the good old days.

I'm not being idealistic. You can find plenty of examples of natural resources contributing to meaningful changes for the better, both in Africa and in other parts of the world.

The following are two of my favorite recent examples.

Capitalizing on Copper in Chile

Chile is one of the largest copper producers in the world: It controls more than 20 percent of the world's copper reserves and is responsible for 11 percent of the total global production. And, in June 2017, a delegation of Chilean government leaders and business representatives arrived in Addis Ababa, the capital of Ethiopia, with an invaluable gift. They came to tell African leaders how their country built their highly successful copper mining industry—and avoided the damaging effects of the resource curse.

During a series of round-table discussions coordinated by the African Minerals Development Centre (AMDC), the Chilean delegates shared insights and best practices from their copper mining industry with representatives from Ethiopia, Ghana, Guinea, and Zambia. The sessions provided an opportunity to learn how Chile successfully:

- Developed and maintains a thriving copper supply chain.

- Encourages cooperation between the government and private sectors.

- Incentivizes innovation among local suppliers.

Not only is Chile known for the success of its copper industry, but it's also recognized for consistent economic growth during the last several decades. According to the World Bank, Chile is one of the most prosperous and economically stable countries in Latin America.[3]

Chile can thank strategic government policy for the success of the copper mining industry and the strength of the economy. "The local authorities have reinvested the income from the mining industry into other industries to make the local economy more competitive and diversified," wrote Martina Mistikova in a blog for Biz Latin Hub. "In the last 20 years, Chile transformed its infrastructure using public-private partnerships. Thanks to improved connectivity and the subscription and signature of free-trade agreements with more than 64 countries, Chile ranked 33rd among 138 countries in the Global Competitiveness Index for 2016-2017."[4]

The South American country has also benefited from the government's commitment to transparency. "Information on both operations and revenues is published regularly by the Finance Ministry, along with comprehensive looks at royalties, taxes, mining export values and production volumes," wrote Sean Durns in an article for Global Risk Insights. "The Chilean Commission on Copper and the Mining Ministry further publish information on a regular basis, which includes environmental assessments and licensing petitions."[5]

Not only that, but Chile's government has developed regulations to protect the environment and address the interests of indigenous groups in relation to copper mining activities.[6]

Versions of all of these practices can be put in place in Africa. The fact that African and Chilean leaders have met to discuss them is extremely encouraging. That kind of open dialogue and willingness to learn from others is exactly what we need to maximize the value of Africa's natural resources.

And, of course, we also can look within Africa for practices to emulate.

Bright Ideas in Botswana

For Botswana, 1966 was a time of giddy highs and discouraging lows. On one hand, the landlocked country in southern Africa gained its independence from Great Britain that year. On the other, Botswana was one of the poorest countries in the world.[7] For the next several years, about 60 percent of government expenditures relied on international development assistance, and Botswana's per capita income was just $70 a year (Compare that to $3,960 in the United States, $570 in South Africa, and $4,290 in Zimbabwe that year[8]). Agriculture—mostly cattle farming—represented 40 percent of Botswana's gross domestic product (GDP), and the country had about 19 kilometers of paved roads.

But fast forward several decades, and Botswana was completely transformed.

"By 2007 Botswana had 7,000 kilometers of paved roads, and per capita income had risen to about $6,100, making Botswana an upper middle-income country comparable to Chile or Argentina," wrote *Botswana's Success: Good Policies, Good Governance, and Good Luck* author Michael Lewin. "Its success is also evident in other measures of human development."

Development assistance had shrunk to less than three percent of the government budget, Lewin added, and major strides had been made in infrastructure and education.

What caused such a significant transformation? It was fueled by Botswana's wealth of diamonds, but the engine behind the country's growth and stability has been the government's carefully planned fiscal policies and good governance.

First of all, Botswana has made economic diversification a priority, instead of choosing to rely on diamond revenue. Most recently, the government has been creating hubs intended to foster growth, the use of technology, and entrepreneurial opportunities in industries from agriculture to health. One of the newest of them, Botswana's Innovation Hub, is developing a Science and Technology Park intended to grow Botswana's information and communication technology (ICT) sector.[9] Another example, the recently approved Education Hub, is the government's response to mismatches between skills development in Botswana and market needs. The hub will be focused on developing quality education and research training programs.[10]

Diversification is one piece of the puzzle in Botswana. Another is its wise approach to fiscal policies. Rather than going on government "spending sprees" when the diamond money was flowing, Botswana developed policies that called for moderate spending during economic boom times. That, in turn, allowed expenditures to continue during economic downcycles. The country's spending has been guided by National Development plans, approved by parliament in six-year cycles. Planning is done by committees that include members of civil society in addition to government representatives—and decisions are reviewed by the House of Chiefs, which represents Botswana's principal tribes.[11]

Generally, much of government spending has been focused on education, health, social assistance, and public infrastructure—all of which bolster the quality of life for everyday people while contributing to stability and a nurturing environment for economic growth.

Another key strategy in Botswana? Saving and investing revenue. By doing so, Botswana has a means of stabilizing the economy during downturns and making sure that future generations benefit from the country's wealth, long after natural resources have been depleted.

I understand that every country is different, but Botswana's practices remain solid examples for other African nations to customize and build upon.

Don't Give up on Oil and Gas

People ask me all the time why I'm convinced that petroleum resources are key to a better future for Africa in light of the mismanagement, exploitation, and conflict associated with African oil and gas production over the years. But I firmly believe that ignoring the continent's massive petroleum resources is not the key to avoiding the resource curse—the answer is using our resources strategically.

Think about it: As of 2017, Africa's proven natural gas reserves totaled 503.3 trillion cubic feet (tcf)[12] and proven crude oil reserves that year exceeded 126 billion barrels of oil (bbo).[13] And because Africa remains largely underexplored, the potential for vast, undiscovered petroleum reserves is well worth considering. In 2016, the U.S. Geological Survey estimated that there were 41 bbo and 319 tcf of gas waiting to be discovered in sub-Saharan Africa.[14] I'm convinced that we're going to see more significant discoveries, especially with increased usage of exploration and production (E&P) technologies like directional drilling and reservoir simulation.

Petroleum resources have always represented opportunity for Africans. Again, the problem has been a failure to leverage those resources wisely, to fully develop and capitalize on their value chain, and to protect the interests of everyday Africans where oil and gas revenue is concerned. Though this has been the pattern up to now, it's not too late to reject what hasn't worked, embrace what does, and fuel a stronger economy, increased stability, and improved quality of life for Africans.

As I write this book, the oil and gas market is seeing a rebound. The industry is in a much different place than when João Gaspar Marques and I wrote *Big Barrels: African Oil and Gas and the Quest for Prosperity*.

But this rebound is meaningless if we don't do the right thing; if we don't work to fix Africa's challenges instead of harping on what's wrong.

So, how do we use oil and gas to transform our continent? For starters, we stop limiting our focus on the extraction and sale of crude oil.

Instead, we create opportunities for the upstream, midstream, and downstream sectors of the oil and gas industry. We need to move away from rhetoric to relevance, symbols to substance, limousine populism, and charisma to character that provides pragmatic, common-sense solutions to many who expect more from Africa's oil and gas and other natural resources.

We capitalize on our natural gas resources to address Africa's widespread electricity shortfalls, which not only will transform the lives of individual Africans, but also will open the door for more efficient and productive African companies and international investors with greater capacity to grow, profit, and contribute to economic and social development.

And while we're at it, we put the work and regulatory frameworks in place to successfully unbundle our oversized, overburdened utilities so they can consistently and reliably deliver electricity.

We create more opportunities for African women in the oil and gas industry. It's a win-win: Women have a great deal to offer, and good jobs for women contribute to a more stable, more economically vital Africa.

We insist upon good governance and policies that create an enabling environment for oil and gas companies—and make it practical for those companies to create meaningful opportunities for individual Africans, companies, and communities.

We join forces to strategically address challenges on the horizon. We can't stick our heads in the sand when it comes to factors that could impact our oil and gas industry. What's happening in Louisiana isn't an isolated incident. The United States has more recoverable oil reserves than any other country in the world and is now an energy exporter.[15] President Trump has been putting constant pressure on

OPEC to maintain low oil prices. African leaders and businesses need to take steps now—from economic diversification to monetizing our petroleum value chains—to keep our countries' economies stable if the U.S. creates an oil glut and prices plummet again.[16]

At the same time, we do the work necessary to create the kind of environment that will continue to attract American investors and companies, which remain vitally important to Africa's oil and gas sector.

Next, we implement clear and consistent strategies for the needed energy transition. The oil and gas industry is here to stay for a long time to come, not only in Africa but throughout the world. While the issue of climate change is pressing and imminent—and must be addressed by stakeholders in every industry around the globe—the complete eradication of oil and gas is unachievable. Indeed, most people don't understand how interwoven the oil and gas industry is in our everyday life, with oil and gas used in everything from the electricity production that lights the world to the fertilizers that feed the world. Petroleum is a key component in an untold number of products, the phone you use to call your mom to the dentures in your mouth, and the tires on your car. The top climate experts aren't calling for a halt in oil and gas production but are instead calling for a sustainable energy transition. In this context, Africa is in an ideal place to lead the charge in creating a sustainable oil and gas industry, while also creating a leading renewable energy sector. The renewable energy potential is essentially unlimited, and the leapfrog technologies developed on the continent are lighting the way forward for renewables around the world.

To be successful, we must be honest and move rapidly to establish stable regulatory frameworks, innovative business environments capable of attracting investment, and strong political commitment to an energy transition. It is also important to understand that this change is not going to be easy, as most countries still witness ongoing political conflicts and a strong dependency on legacy fossil-fuel based power generation infrastructure that might restrict opportunities to develop the conditions for energy transition faster than our western counterparts.

Above all, we look to ourselves for solutions. We learn to negotiate petroleum E&P deals that benefit everyday Africans as much as government leaders. We demand new models for managing petroleum revenue that spread the wealth equitably. And we stop seeing ourselves as victims in need of foreign aid and guidance.

It is critical to know your worth and the value you bring into any oil and gas deals. Many Africans have always been shy or scared to seek value for what they bring to the table. It's a bad idea. I know my worth. I know what I bring to the table, and I am not ashamed to demand proper compensation. I don't like politicians regulating compensation. We have to learn to let market forces determine some things in the oil industry.

Africans are more than capable of making our continent successful.

Let's get started.

2

IT'S UP TO AFRICANS
TO FIX AFRICA

W AR-TORN SUDAN HAS BEEN the site of a years-long civil conflict. In the 1970s, vast oil reserves were discovered in the southern part of the country. Meanwhile, pipelines and refineries were appearing in the northern region, perhaps as an attempt to prevent secession.[1] The two regions of the country could not agree on how to "share" oil revenues, causing in-fighting and an eventual split in 2011 into two separate nations. To this day, South Sudan remains one of Africa's least developed countries.[2]

But even here, we see rays of hope.

In mid-2017, my company—Centurion Law Group—successfully facilitated one of the biggest and most difficult deals in African oil and gas to date in South Sudan. We worked with Nigeria's Oranto Petroleum and the South Sudanese government to open the door for Oranto to explore for oil in South Sudan's Block B3. The resulting exploration and production sharing agreement (EPSA) enabled Oranto's comprehensive exploration and long-term development to begin immediately.

Shortly after that landmark deal, Centurion Law Group entered into a strategic alliance with a South Sudanese law firm, Awatkeer Law Chambers, in Juba.[3] Awatkeer's local network and Centurion's pan-African reach means we can train South Sudanese attorneys on using our legal technology platforms to better serve businesses, the government, and non-governmental organizations (NGOs) in South Sudan, particularly in matters involving energy law.

This agreement was a significant development because Oranto's EPSA is the first to be signed in South Sudan since 2012. This EPSA is a testament to the government's strengthened commitment to nationwide economic revival through investments in utilities and infrastructure, particularly in the oil and gas sector. More importantly, it signals a renewed hope: If we can succeed here, we can succeed everywhere on the continent.

I have helped both private companies and African governments alike take proven steps in the oil and gas industry to improve African economies and help everyday Africans live better lives by harnessing the influence of our natural resources. So, I know that we Africans can overcome significant obstacles to help ourselves. I'm optimistic that our successes can be contagious.

At the time of this writing, some 400 delegates had recently returned home from South Sudan Oil & Power 2018.[4] Attendees gathered to discuss (and, rightly, celebrate) the growth of exploration activities, the resumption of oil production in the region, and the ongoing enhancements to regional infrastructure and security in operational areas. This second annual conference of oil and gas professionals represents the contagious nature of success: Open dialogue among government delegations, diplomats from abroad, and private sector representatives is fostering conversations that will lead to a stronger Africa.

But I also know that accomplishing this goal takes work—a lot of work—and requires the initiative and cooperation of Africans—all

Africans. I call on you to step up. We must all shoulder the responsibility of working to improve Africa. It's not an onus, but an honor.

Handouts Keep People Down

There's an adage that goes something like this: *Give a man a fish and you feed him for a day. Teach a man to fish, and he'll feed himself for a lifetime.*

Charity has its place. It's hard to watch someone flounder, especially when we can help lift them back up. Monetary aid is a quick fix that can stave off hunger, help someone keep their home, or pay for urgent medical care. But this generosity, however well-intentioned, can be misdirected. And once the gift has been used up, there is nothing left.

For too long, well-meaning foreign entities have stepped in to provide aid to Africa—but, in doing so, they have inadvertently stepped on our toes. In some instances, they did more harm than good. Many charitable and nonprofit endeavors are designed by donor nations and foreign institutions that don't sufficiently understand what the recipient country or community really needs or how it operates.

This is also often the case with for-profit companies. It's quite common for multinational companies to offer an extra benefit or two to sweeten their deal with host countries. But these "benefits" typically reflect the same lack of understanding—particularly in African countries.

I recently heard the story of a foreign oil company trying to curry favor with a tribe. The company's executives approached the tribe's chief to ask what his people needed. The chief proposed a hospital; the execs agreed. It sounded like a win-win: The tribe would get necessary improvements in healthcare, and the oil company would foster goodwill by addressing the most pressing needs of the tribe.

The problem was, a hospital was not actually the community's most pressing need. The chief had merely suggested the first thing that came to mind. While it was true that people in the tribe were getting sick, it wasn't due to a lack of access to medical care. It was because they were drinking contaminated water. The tribe didn't need a hospital; they needed a proper water supply.

But, of course, the oil executives didn't know that. And they didn't spend any time doing additional research or consulting with the local government. They just moved forward and built the hospital. Once complete, the building sadly lay vacant: There were no doctors to staff it or beds to accommodate patients. It was locked up and fenced in, no good to anyone.

I like to give these execs the benefit of the doubt; I like to believe that the company actually tried to do the right thing and find out what the locals needed—but they neglected an essential step in their due diligence. They talked with one person and didn't validate his request or determine the logistics.

Good intentions only get you so far. In reality, good intentions must be backed up by hard work, due diligence, and solid execution to have an impact.

You can't simply throw money into a community and expect positive outcomes. But, in some cases, this is what is happening. We've heard stories of companies going out and tossing out bags of money from a boat. Neighbors fought each other over the cash until it was seized by gangs, leaving the community with nothing but ill will.

And while first-world governments and international charity organizations would argue with me, I consider many of their efforts in exactly the same light: They may be well-intentioned, but they are essentially throwing out sacks full of money.

William Easterly, an economics professor at New York University, co-director of NYU's Development Research Institute, and nonresident fellow of the Center for Global Development, has called African aid "One of the scandals of our generation." Easterly argued at a debate back in 2007, "Money meant for the most desperate people in the world is simply not reaching them: $600 billion in aid to Africa over the past 45 years, and over that time period there's basically been zero rise in living standards."[5]

Zambian global economist Dambisa Moyo has research that supports this point. "Aid has been and continues to be an unmitigated political, economic and humanitarian disaster for most parts of the developing world," she wrote in her book, *Dead Aid*.[6] Africa has been the recipient of more than $1 trillion in aid over the past 50 years—but all this charity seems to have just exacerbated poverty. During the peak of Western aid from 1970 to 1998, Moyo reported, poverty in Africa actually rose—from 11 percent to 66 percent.

The problem with charity is that it can become a crutch. The longer people receive contributions, the more they rely on them—and the less motivated they might be to put forth extra effort toward self-reliance. And, as Moyo bluntly pointed out, "Aid has never created a job."

Such is the case in Africa. If you've read my book, *Big Barrels*, you might remember a discussion about this. My research for that book uncovered analysis that shows aid-dependent countries are less capable now of rising out of poverty than they were 30 years ago.

Reliance on others is a hindrance. And aid, however well-intentioned, often comes with a price.

Let's consider loans. Sure, loans are intended to be paid back rather than simply gifted out of generosity. But loans foster attachments that can be just as detrimental as the crutch of charity. When payment comes due, countries that have racked up too many loans are unable to pay off their debts.

This is definitely the situation across sub-Saharan Africa, where the Overseas Development Institute (ODI) classified almost 40 percent of those countries "in danger of slipping into a major debt crisis" as of October 2018 and named eight nations—Chad, Mozambique, Republic of Congo, São Tomé e Príncipe, South Sudan, Sudan, The Gambia, and Zimbabwe—that are already in debt distress.[7]

"Although borrowing is often seen as a prerequisite for growth, unsustainable debt poses significant risks to global commitments to end extreme poverty, including the Sustainable Development Goals (SDGs). Unsustainable debt burdens compel governments to spend more on debt servicing and less on education, health, and infrastructure," ODI authors Shakira Mustapha and Annalisa Prizzon wrote. "High debt also creates uncertainty, deterring investment and innovation, and has a negative impact on economic growth. A poorly managed debt crisis would not only undermine progress towards the SDGs, but it could also reverse the development progress made over the past decade."

While we are grateful for the decades of financial support, we need to learn to stand on our own—to fish for ourselves, as it were. The days of our reliance on foreign investors and outside aid must come to an end if we Africans are to make meaningful improvements in our homelands.

Collaboration Is Critical to Africa's Future

Let's look at some startling geography: Africa, the second-largest continent after Asia, is five times the size of Europe. But its coastline is only a quarter as long, and 16 of its countries are landlocked. This severely hampers international trade.

In their study "Geography and Economic Development" for the National Bureau for Economic Research, John Gallup, Jeffrey Sachs, and Andrew Mellinger pointed out that "Coastal countries generally have higher incomes than do landlocked counties. Indeed, none of the 29 landlocked countries outside of Europe enjoys a high per capita income."[8]

Does this mean that economic development in landlocked African nations is impossible?

Absolutely not. But it requires a dedication to cooperation. Africa is a sum of her parts; if one of her nations falls, the rest also suffer. But if we rise together, supporting each other and considering one another's successes our own, our strength is unlimited. We're already seeing signs of such support, from the 17 nations bordering the Gulf of Guinea joining forces to enhance the maritime safety and security of their region to 4 East African countries teaming up to increase agricultural productivity and growth through scientific advancements.

Success breeds success. But it also takes the collective labors of all stakeholders: the African governments, the African companies and investors, and the organizations striving to establish the continent's rightful place in the world of 21st-century commerce.

The Role of African Governments

Let's talk about the government. What is its responsibility in achieving successful economic growth?

The ODI infographic, "Financing the End of Extreme Poverty," claims, "Growth alone can halve poverty. Investing in health, education, and social protection could do the rest."[9]

Yes, many African nations are small economies, where increasing growth rates and expanding revenues will be a challenge. But, as Indermit Gill and Kenan Karakülah pointed out in a piece they wrote for the Brookings Institute, "Increasing tax revenues is something that almost all of the subcontinent's governments can do by themselves."[10]

Meanwhile, Gill and Karakülah believe, as I do, that the larger African economies have the ability to expand their own economies and spur plenty of positive growth—even across borders: "There are some countries that can do this on their own. With more than half of the region's economic output, Nigeria and South Africa control not just their own destinies but also those of their neighbors."

I would add that large countries that prioritize cooperation among federal, provincial, and municipal governments are the ones most likely to successfully generate growth. Look at Nigeria and South Africa. Has a strong central government helped them yet?

The Nigerian government controls the vast majority of the nation's resources—and, therefore, the power—leaving the weaker municipal governments poorly funded, inefficient, and all but powerless to handle local issues. Every level of government should have sufficient resources to complete the projects under its jurisdiction. But that's not happening—the levels aren't cooperating, and everyone is suffering the consequences. This has actually held back development, especially in creating value and building infrastructure.

Meanwhile, South Africa's 1996 Constitution identifies its three bodies of government (national, provincial, and local) as "spheres" rather than levels to connote interdependence instead of dependence. While great in theory, this effort toward deconcentration has been hampered by the lack of an adequate policy framework. An unclear delegation of responsibilities often means that the sphere expected to execute an activity doesn't have the capacity to deliver.

As South Africa shows us, the key elements needed here are strong, clear, enforceable regulations. We need to improve our regulatory policies to create effective and noncomplex master plans. At the same time, let the private sector work. While a strong central government is good for stability, a more decentralized policy will enable local communities to work effectively, employing local expertise whenever possible.

"Countries with better policy frameworks exhibit higher efficiency of investment," the World Bank explained.[11] "A country's institutions may create incentives for investment and technology adoption and the opportunity for workers to accumulate human capital, thereby facilitating higher growth over the longer term. Weak institutions, by contrast, may encourage rent-seeking activities and corruption, leading to less productive activities; discourage firm investment and human capital accumulation; and lead to worse growth outcomes."

With this in mind, the most impressive example of strides toward a positive business environment might be Rwanda. This is, after all, a country with basically no natural resources—but, nonetheless, they built something amazing.

In spring 1994, the world watched the manmade genocide of almost one million ethnic Tutsis and moderate Hutus perpetrated by ethnic Hutus. In most western cities, people wondered: How did this happen? How could we let this happen? Even after the killing spree ended, the country was in utter despair and on the verge of collapse.[12] And yet, the last two decades have brought an amazing economic turnaround because the government worked to position itself as an attractive destination for business ventures. They focused on elements to draw investors, from improved infrastructure and transportation services to intra-regional trade and security to enhanced healthcare services. Most importantly, they introduced an efficient bureaucracy. This is really something that most African countries could proudly emulate. With the right leadership, every country can be a success story.

I see two major regulatory changes African governments can implement immediately to promote investment.

The first is the sanctity of contracts. Investors want to know, unequivocally, that their agreements will be respected and that they will see the end result of their financial obligation. The second is the ease of doing business. African leaders must take an active role in both of these elements by taking a hard look at their tax framework. We cannot create suitable business environments or create investment opportunities if we aren't ensuring that people will yield the right dividends after their hard work. We need to show the benefits of the investments while we prepare ourselves to meet the market dynamics because integration without preparation will only lead to frustration.

The Role of African Businesses and Investors

The free market works well, not because the private sector is made of saints—many business people I have met are just as self-serving as politicians—but because of competition. Without this crucial element inherent in the free market, there is no guarantee that the resources the private sector employs will, in fact, be used efficiently.

We Africans must build better organizations and run better businesses. The private sector must partner with the government to create jobs and grow domestic opportunities. African businesses have to understand that it is about delivery and getting the job done: All the glamour does not count if there's no return on investment.

I don't mean that business people should be greedy cut-throats, only out to make a big profit. But a country's success hinges a lot on its businesses succeeding. Business owners should consider a two-fold obligation: They need to make a profit to keep their shop afloat and support the prosperity of their community.

One solid way to make a profit is by investing in a company rather than making a direct engagement.

When I first started my company, I had the benefit of partnering with an American law firm, Greenberg Traurig, under the leadership of its Africa Chair, Jude Kearney. They didn't just offer me cash on deals. They offered to invest in our people and help me build my workforce alongside that of our clients. I thought that was an interesting model, one that I hadn't considered. It really shaped my company and gave us a lot more to work on than a simple handout would have. In the process, I enhanced my Western education even more and instilled good business ethics and skills into my staff, while also emphasizing African values.

Businesses can succeed in Africa by empowering communities. Building solid organizations with solid human resources and establishing strong networks *in* Africa and *within* Africa will allow the partners to create opportunities that tap into unlimited resources.

I've already lamented foreign handouts. But that's certainly not to say that foreign business affiliations are unwise. On the contrary: Foreign partners are essential to Africa's growth. They can teach us the transferrable skills we need to push ahead. For me, personally, my American education and my American partnership gave me the chance to believe in myself.

But capital only works in an enabling environment.

The best partners for African companies are the investors who want to transfer technology and empower Africans to use—and improve—it. Simply put, we are not going to develop Africa without technology.

We need investors who show that they want to fully participate with us by coming in and building long-term sustainable businesses that last and make a profit, create jobs, and further development.

On the contrary, investors who still see Africa as a place to throw sacks full of money (literally and figuratively) are going to have a hard time.

Everyday Africans today frown at the "aid model" because they know that aid has led to corruption, mismanagement, theft, and—worst of all—animosity among Africans.

The Role of Pan-African Organizations

Nations across the continent have woken up. We've realized the truth behind the concept of strength in numbers. Cooperation and collaboration among neighbors and across borders are promoting African self-reliance.

We are uniting for positive change.

This is happening to groups like the Investment Climate Facility for Africa (ICF) and other independent organizations that foster initiatives that make it easier to do business. ICF, in particular, makes it possible for companies to "Register, pay their taxes, solve commercial disputes, clear goods through customs, and so much more, in a quick, simple and transparent manner. This simplification and efficiency is helping to speed up economic growth, ultimately changing the lives of millions of Africans."

As ICF Co-Chair and former President of the Republic of Tanzania H.E. Benjamin Mkapa explained, "ICF was set up to prove that investment climate reforms can be done quickly, using little resources while creating great impact for the private sector, governments, and countries in general. We have done this. We have shown that it is possible. Now it is up to African countries to follow the example set by ICF and to pursue greater investment climate reforms that will spur Africa's development and unleash the entrepreneurial spirit of its people."[13]

Likewise, the African Development Bank (AfDB) Group bolsters African economies by helping its 54 regional member countries and 26 non-regional (non-African) member countries achieve sustainable economic development and social progress. By helping African countries—individually and collectively—invest public and private capital and financing projects run either by the government or the private sector, this multilateral development bank is attacking its main target of poverty across the continent. This means that the AfDB doesn't just provide monetary assistance. To support development efforts, regional member countries receive policy advice and technical assistance as needed.

With its connection to and understanding of the continent, the bank is in a unique position to help its members most effectively. The AfDB website (www.afdb.org) explains, "The admission of non-regional members in 1982 gave the AfDB additional means that enabled it to contribute to the economic and social development of its regional member countries through low-interest loans. With a larger membership, the institution was endowed with greater expertise, the credibility of its partners, and access to markets in its non-regional member countries. The AfDB enjoys triple-A ratings from all the main international rating agencies. However, the AfDB maintains an African character derived from its geography and ownership structure. It exclusively covers Africa. It is also headquartered in Africa, and its president is always African."

That, I think, is key: Africans must unite *in* Africa, *with* Africans, *for* Africa.

That's not to say that we need to rule out international involvement entirely. The AfDB exemplifies the value in a larger constituency with a broader reach and greater access to funds. Such is also the case with the "Great Green Wall." Without external support of multiple non-profit organizations and international agencies like the World Bank and the United Nations, some 20 African countries may never have teamed up to battle hunger and strengthen their economies. But they did so on African terms.

The Great Green Wall for the Sahara and the Sahel Initiative (GGWSSI) was a pan-African program launched by the African Union (AU) in 2007 to reverse land degradation and desertification in the Sahel—the semi-arid belt that spans 5,400 kilometers

(3,360 miles) from the Atlantic Ocean in the west to the Red Sea in the east—and Sahara regions. The initiative started as a massive tree-planting project that was to result in a wall of trees—15 kilometers (9 miles) wide and 7,775 kilometers (4,831 miles) long—stretching from Senegal in the west to Djibouti in the east. While the wall was deemed impractical, the land protection campaign has evolved into something new.

"Slowly, the idea of a Great Green Wall has changed into a program centered around indigenous land use techniques, not planting a forest on the edge of a desert," Mohamed Bakarr, the lead environmental specialist for Global Environment Facility, told Smithsonian Magazine.[14] "We moved the vision of the Great Green Wall from one that was impractical to one that was practical. It is not necessarily a physical wall, but rather a mosaic of land use practices that ultimately will meet the expectations of a wall. It has been transformed into a metaphorical thing."

Across the continent, all Africans must advocate for better business practices and good governance. This should not be left to Western companies or foreign institutions. We welcome help, but we have to lead this. We can no longer be passive bystanders when it comes to fighting for policies that will encourage investment, create jobs, and bring prosperity to Africa's countries and its people.

So, let's learn to fish—and teach each other what we learn.

3

A PLACE AT THE TABLE: AFRICA AND OPEC

WHEN EQUATORIAL GUINEA JOINED OPEC in 2017, it was like taking a seat at the global equivalent of the adults' table. The nation—Africa's fourth-largest oil producer that year[1]—would finally have a say when decisions affecting the world's oil economy, and its own destiny, were made.

OPEC members control more than 40 percent of the world's oil production, some 39.4 million bbl/d in 2017.[2] Of that, Equatorial Guinea's output is just a small fraction, about 195,000 bbl/d.[3] But oil's value to the national economy can't be understated: It accounts for 80 percent of Equatorial Guinea's total exports and 90 percent of government revenues.[4] With OPEC determined to see prices settle in what they call a range comfortable and acceptable for all market players, just being part of the conversation—being heard—is of considerable significance for Equatorial Guinea.

"It gives us a voice," Gabriel Mbaga Obiang Lima, Equatorial Guinea's Minister of Mines and Hydrocarbons, told S&P Global Platts in a 2019 interview. "We do have the belief that joining OPEC has been a good thing. It has definitely provided us with information that otherwise we would not have had, but also joining OPEC and joining this new initiative has achieved what we wanted, which was to stabilize the oil price. Any new ideas that will maintain this stabilization will be welcomed by the government."

The initiative Lima referred to is OPEC's landmark Declaration of Cooperation, which members agreed to in 2016, and OPEC recently extended. I think it's safe to say that the agreement's production cuts rescued the oil industry from collapse, boosted interest in African oil investment, and returned economic security to oil-independent nations, many of which are in Africa. And it's unlikely those achievements would have occurred without Africa's participation, something OPEC Secretary General Dr. Mohammad Barkindo acknowledges.

At a gathering of oil producers in Malabo, Equatorial Guinea, in April 2019, Barkindo credited Africa with moving the Declaration forward. He reminded the audience that more than one-third of the 24 countries working together under the negotiated framework are from Africa, and that African nations comprise half of OPEC's membership. The numbers, he said, "Underscore the vital role this great continent plays within OPEC, within the Declaration of Cooperation, and within the global oil industry."[5]

With 130 billion barrels of proven crude oil reserves—a figure that is 50 percent higher than the total at the end of the 1990s—and proven natural gas reserves doubling since the mid-1980s, Africa represents a frontier filled with promise, he added.

"It is irrefutable evidence of the petroleum potential of Africa, the exciting and abundant opportunities, and the role that this industry can play in unleashing tremendous economic development and prosperity across the continent," Barkindo said.

The Africa-driven Declaration is already having an effect on the continent as a whole. When the oil market is in crisis, the path to dignity and prosperity is closed off to many African families. It leaves many Africans, particularly those without advanced degrees, to chart their own course where clear and attainable paths to a meaningful and prosperous life once existed. But when the market is stable, the benefits extend across all nations, even those without their own petroleum resources, as we'll see when we talk about OPEC's aid programs.

As for Equatorial Guinea, it now anticipates a significant increase in offshore drilling, and its expectations are well-founded. In recent years, the country has secured $2.4 billion in foreign investment,[6] and 10 exploration wells are planned.[7] The country believes these discoveries will not only reverse a recent production decline but may also lead to a five-fold production increase by 2025—proving that OPEC membership can be a powerful force for transformation.

Growing Numbers, Adding Strength

But beyond the material effect on markets and investment, the Declaration of Cooperation also demonstrated something else: the importance of taking a unified stand.

In fact, unity underpins everything OPEC does. OPEC speaks for the common interests of its members, but it also takes their individual needs and opinions seriously and advocates on their behalf. For his part, Barkindo repeatedly encourages the continent's countries to build alliances to make the most of their hydrocarbon resources, whether they are OPEC members or not. Barkindo has proven himself to be the leader and the champion OPEC needs at this time, with withering attacks coming from some in Washington's executive and legislative branch of government. His ability to manage the exit of Qatar, handle the issues around Iran and Libya, Venezuela, Saudi Arabia, and bring Russia on board has been revolutionary. I have had an opportunity to watch him close up. He has been remarkably cool under fire, refreshingly articulate, and demonstratively intelligent; he has shown he has the savviness to build coalitions and keep a difficult organization together. This kind of common sense and charismatic leadership needs to be cherished in Africa and worldwide.

I am still amazed by his humility and breathtakingly well-executed drive to bring Russia and others to make a deal to rescue the oil industry, which greatly benefited African economies. Listening to his skeptics and taking the blistering attacks from many, he has stayed committed to the goals of OPEC and fights daily for OPEC in the face of a hurricane.

In OPEC, the notion of strength in numbers is very real. The organization says that every new member adds to the group's stability and strengthens members' commitment to one another. Different perspectives create a rich culture where colleagues can learn from one another, anticipate and respond to the complexity of today's oil markets, and, ultimately, influence prices. OPEC also has said that new members bring fresh insights into regional social, economic, and political developments. Above all, OPEC is evidence of what careful stewardship of oil and gas riches can achieve, particularly within a complex global framework.

Equatorial Guinea isn't the only newcomer to recognize the appeal of OPEC membership: Gabon rejoined the group in 2016 after a long hiatus, and, at Lima's urging, Republic of Congo came aboard in 2018. They bring the number of African OPEC members to seven, half of the organization's total of fourteen.

With Africa being one of the world's remaining oil and gas frontiers, where big discoveries are still possible, it's no wonder the balance is shifting: Adding African nations to its roster means OPEC has more control over the world's energy output and the increased political capital that comes with it.

That's just one part of the equation. As we all know, the Middle East has been the heart of OPEC's dominion since the start. But with reservoirs there maturing and production declining, expanding its geographic range is one way OPEC can bring its overall production profile into equilibrium. When OPEC allies with African producers, it's like they're taking out a market share insurance policy, with even small producers adding incrementally to OPEC's dominance.

To open the door to nations like Equatorial Guinea, Republic of Congo, and Gabon, OPEC needed to rethink its membership strategy and get rid of its long-held production quota. For years, only countries that produced a minimum of 500,000 bbl/d could even dream of OPEC membership. That doesn't mean all producers who qualified became part of the group: The United States isn't ever likely to join, and Russia—which set aside its animosity toward de facto OPEC chief Saudi Arabia to participate in the historic, price-stabilizing production cuts of 2017—remains independent as well.

Now, with the production standard out of the way, OPEC is being even more aggressive in its membership bid, extending invitations based on potential rather than just history. For evidence, we only have to look at the December 2018 meeting in Vienna, where OPEC asked several small Africa producers to sit in. For Chad, Ghana, Cameroon, Mauritania, and Côte d'Ivoire—which together pump out only about 600,000 bbl/d—and Uganda, which has yet to begin production, this may be a sign that membership is on the way.[8]

And while their addition would benefit OPEC, it would help the continent even more. To be taken seriously in OPEC—to have more negotiating effectiveness within the organization—Africa needs more representation. It's really rather simple—the more African members, the higher the total production they account for, the more likely they will be heard. If we want to increase the influence Africa has within OPEC and improve our profile in the world oil economy, more African nations need to join in.

Friends in the Right Places

When President Vladimir Putin agreed to cut Russian oil production in 2017 to align with OPEC's goals, it was another significant step in an increasingly valuable partnership between the two parties. With daily oil output hovering around 11.34 million bbl/d,[9] to suggest Russia is anything less than a global powerhouse is laughable. And there's no joking when it comes to Russia throwing around its considerable weight: The December 2018 extension of price-boosting production cuts might never have happened without Russia's promises—as well as its ability to hammer out a deal that would stop Saudi Arabia and Iran from quarreling and satisfy their demands.

It wasn't the only time Russia has come to OPEC's aid. In the mere three years it has been allied with OPEC, Russia has helped the group through tough times, including price instability, regime changes in member countries, and the usual internecine bickering—not to mention criticism from America's tweeter-in-chief. But the benefits are hardly one-sided: Russia can now exert previously untold influence over the world's massive oil markets and, by extension, the Middle East.

There's speculation that Russia could be on the verge of formalizing its relationship with OPEC. But whether that happens or not, its affiliation with the group is excellent news for African producers. After all, if you are measured by the company you keep, being on Russia's side is the right place, indeed.

If You Want to Go Far, Go Together

An increasingly large bloc in OPEC isn't the only measure of Africa's emergence on the global oil and gas stage, nor is it the first time the continent's producers have banded together for a common goal. That honor goes to the group now known as the African Petroleum

Producers' Organization (APPO), which was established in Lagos in 1987.

APPO's goal is to maximize the economic benefits of petroleum activities through the cooperation of its 18 member countries: Algeria, Angola, Benin, Cameroon, Chad, Democratic Republic of Congo, Republic of Congo, Côte d'Ivoire, Egypt, Gabon, Ghana, Equatorial Guinea, Libya, Mauritania, Niger, Nigeria, South Africa, and Sudan. APPO provides everything from technological to workforce support for exploration, production, and refining.

It also supports OPEC's efforts to stabilize prices, even if that means capping production. After all, the two groups have many members in common, and with what Barkindo calls the intensification of OPEC's engagement with Africa, collaboration between OPEC and APPO seems almost instinctual.

In fact, the value of their partnership was top of mind when Barkindo spoke at the APPO CAPE VII Congress and Exhibition in Equatorial Guinea in April 2019.

"It can often appear that our industry is subject to forces beyond our control," he said. "Geopolitical events, natural catastrophes, technological breakthroughs or other critical uncertainties: We are all aware of the impact they can have. However, as Equatorial Guinea, APPO, OPEC and the Declaration of Cooperation shows, there is another force alive and well in our industry. This is the desire of producers, consumers, and investors to have sustainable stability in the oil market. This force thrives in the hearts and minds of decision-makers who know that collaboration and teamwork remain the most effective problem-solving techniques this industry or indeed any industry knows.

"This force can lead us out of any darkness and into the light," he continued. "It is based on the principles of transparency, fairness, equity and respect among nations."

Barkindo concluded his address with one of his favorite African proverbs: "If you want to go quickly, go alone. If you want to go far, go together."

To me, nothing speaks of cooperation more than that.

The Unknown Effect of NOPEC

Throughout the years I spent as an undergraduate and law school student in the U.S., one of the things I truly admired was American ingenuity. I loved following news stories about U.S. startups that scraped together enough money to go overseas, explored for oil, and, despite overwhelming odds, achieved success.

These companies were creating opportunities both for Americans and the people in their host countries. It was the American Dream playing out before my eyes. There is no doubt in my mind that those stories inspired my career trajectory in Africa, where I have had a chance to advise many African governments on oil matters and improving relations with one another.

Needless to say, it is disheartening to see a country like the United States, which is responsible for innovation, simultaneously proposing legislation that undermines innovation in places overseas. And that is just one of the unintended consequences the proposed No Oil Producing and Exporting Cartels Act (NOPEC) could have. In the end, the U.S. House of Representatives bill could likely produce the opposite result of the business ventures that inspired me as a student: It would lead to fewer opportunities for Americans and for the countries they partner with.

Equatorial Guinea is the fifth OPEC member from sub-Saharan Africa—and OPEC's smallest producer. But even before the ink was dry on Equatorial Guinea's membership card, Minister of Mines and Hydrocarbons Gabriel Mbaga Obiang Lima was making ambitious plans. His goal is to see oil production increase to around 300,000 bbl/d by 2020, which would represent a return to pre-2014 market crash levels. Longer term, he'd like to see production reach 500,000 bbl/d by 2025.

One unknown that may stand in the way of such progress is NOPEC. The legislation, which is pending in the United States at the time of this writing, would allow the United States Department of Justice to sue a foreign crude producer for coordinating production and manipulating price, citing antitrust violations. Foreign companies would be stripped of their sovereign immunity protections.

The legislation is not new: It was first introduced in 2000, and former presidents George W. Bush and Barack Obama both opposed it. President Trump, however, could support it. After all, he has used his Twitter platform repeatedly to blame OPEC for artificially driving up the price of oil.

American frustration with OPEC is understandable. Because it has historically controlled as much as 80 percent of the world's oil production, OPEC has been able to influence the market, and the U.S. has been forced to live with the consequences.

But attempting to take OPEC down with punishing lawsuits is not in America's best interest. In 2007, when a nearly identical version of NOPEC was under consideration, the U.S. Office of Management and Budget warned that legal action against OPEC and its members could result in oil supply disruptions. Instead of lowering gasoline prices, the lawsuits likely would cause prices to surge upward. Treasury Secretary Henry Paulson said that the mere passage of NOPEC would threaten foreign investment in the U.S.: OPEC nations might withdraw assets to prevent them from being seized.

Those weren't unreasonable claims, and the same risks hold today.

OPEC has already warned the United States that if the legislation goes through, the organization will "stop working." In other words, the production cuts now in place would disappear, and OPEC nations would begin pumping as much oil as they can. The price would fall, which could have serious consequences for American shale producers who require a certain level to break-even.[10]

NOPEC would put foreign investments in the U.S. oil and gas sector, from exploration projects to infrastructure, at risk, too.

For example, earlier this month, UAE-based Gulftainer received the U.S. government's go-ahead to operate the Port of Wilmington in Delaware, a fully serviced deepwater port and marine terminal, for the next 50 years. Gulftainer already has announced plans to develop the port's cargo terminal capabilities and enhance its overall productivity. How likely are more deals like this after NOPEC?

America's lost partnership and investment opportunities could extend beyond OPEC members. Non-OPEC members may wonder if the precedent set by NOPEC puts them in legal jeopardy, especially in a litigious country like the U.S. Other countries may think twice before partnering or investing in U.S. oil and gas projects to protect their own relationships with OPEC nations.

Then there's the matter of U.S. oil and gas companies that operate overseas. Foreign countries may begin restricting their access or ordering them to leave altogether. Not only would these lost opportunities affect E&P multinationals like ExxonMobil, VAALCO Energy, Chevron, Murphy, Anadarko Petroleum Corporation, Apache Corporation, Marathon Oil, Occidental Petroleum, Noble Energy, Kosmos Energy, but oilfield services providers like Halliburton, Schlumberger, Stewart & Stevenson, McDermott International, MODEC, Nalco Champion, National Oilwell Varco, Oceaneering International Inc., Precision Drilling, Weatherford International, and Baker Hughes could be hurt.

Any of these scenarios could damage the U.S. economy in the form of fewer jobs, reduced oil supplies, and higher gasoline prices.

Of course, I cannot help but consider NOPEC's potential to harm my home continent. America's renewed interest in anti-OPEC legislation comes at a time when African involvement and influence in OPEC is at an all-time high.

Equatorial Guinea and Gabon became members of OPEC in 2016 and 2017, respectively. When the Republic of Congo joined OPEC in June 2018, it increased the number of African nations in OPEC to seven—compared to six from the Middle East—and gave the African continent unprecedented dominance in the organization, at least in terms of membership.

This shift could be seismic in terms of African growth and stability.

For too many years, the presence of oil in African nations has been more of a curse than a blessing, contributing to the wealth of foreign investors while indigenous populations endure socioeconomic hardship and political unrest.

Today, a new generation of Africans is stepping forward in countries throughout the continent. They are looking to themselves to make positive changes in their communities through entrepreneurship and technological innovations with their American partners. Those efforts to create a stronger, more stable continent must include the strategic capitalization of natural resources like oil. And the opportunity tap into the resources and influence of a major organization like OPEC and the African Energy Chamber—as a large, united voice—could be just the boost African producers need.

But if NOPEC were to pass, a moment of opportunity would be replaced with further instability in Africa, as much needed American investment dries up. While Africa is on the verge of a bright new future, African nations and cities easily could swing in the direction of greater crime and bloody conflicts: scenarios that could even result in American troops and dollars being called in to fix them.

Much of Africa is changing for the better. Policy that pushes Africa toward civil unrest flies in the face of American ideals.

America needs OPEC countries in Africa and the Middle-East to assist with the Arab-Israeli peace process, fighting Boko Haram and Al-Shabaab rebels, and promoting American values. Litigating against these countries will make trial lawyers like me very rich but put American national security and economic interest on a collision course.

America has a legacy of creating opportunity. Criminalizing OPEC won't get at the root causes of increased American gasoline prices, and instead, will only inflict economic harm domestically and internationally. Overall, this would introduce unpredictability, volatility, and the kind of boom and bust cycles that OPEC has worked so hard to avoid. There's no wondering why the American petroleum industry is against NOPEC. It's bad for everyone all around.

Membership and Its Rewards

Understanding why OPEC is interested in Africa is one thing. But aside from much-needed market clout, increased global prominence, and enhanced opportunity to coordinate with other global oil producers—which are admittedly huge advantages—what else do African nations gain by joining OPEC?

One potentially overlooked benefit of access to OPEC is access to information. When oil prices dropped beginning in 2014, many smaller producers were caught off guard. This was largely because they lacked the market insight to understand the potential effect of American shale or the eventual repercussions of oversupply. For OPEC members, the days of being blindsided are over. And while recent history shows that membership can't completely protect producers from global swings, it does offer an opportunity to participate in a thoughtful, coordinated response built upon relationships, dialogue, and well-founded research.

What's more, OPEC members can seek and share information with others who have experience being successful and, perhaps, just as important, being unsuccessful. There is a huge reservoir of lessons learned that operators can exploit and expand upon as they develop their growth strategy.

OPEC membership can even help finance that strategy by opening the door to direct foreign investment, including Middle Eastern countries with substantial sovereign wealth to spread around. Obviously, an influx of capital can accelerate exploration, development, and production—which we hope will generate revenue that trickles into the economy as a whole. But even the mere act of qualifying for capital can be beneficial, especially as it requires rigorous reporting, which is something many African producers struggle with. As a matter of fact, being in OPEC is an exercise in compliance and reporting: The organization upholds extremely strong standards for both. Many times, the reports wind up in the hands of Wall Street financial institutions, where they can improve a country's credit rating and, in turn, the prospects for financing new projects.

Funding Real Change

If status, stability, information, partnerships, and regulatory discipline were the only things OPEC offered, to some, that might be enough.

But that would be overlooking one of the organization's flagship programs: the OPEC Fund for International Development (OFID).

A finance institution established in 1976, OFID promotes financial cooperation between OPEC member states and developing countries in Africa, Asia, Latin America and the Caribbean, and Europe—

whether they are members or not. Aimed primarily at bolstering socioeconomic development, under their "united against poverty" flag, the fund provides everything from loans and balance of payments support to grants for humanitarian emergency relief.

Over nearly 50 years, the fund has provided assistance for initiatives in nine focus areas: energy, agriculture, education, financial services, health, telecommunications, water and sanitation, industry, and transportation. Among the most recent beneficiaries are four "partner" countries:

- Burkina Faso, which received $19 million to upgrade a 94-kilometer (58-mile) stretch of road that will improve trade between rural areas and the capital city of Ouagadougou. The project is also expected to enhance access to social services for a quarter of a million people.

- Ethiopia, which will use the $22 million it received for road improvements in a region where agriculture is a primary income source. Nearly three-quarters of a million people will have improved access to social services and marketplaces.

- Guinea, for a project expected to help alleviate poverty and enhance food security for more than 450,000 people. The country received $25 million for its Family Farming, Resilience and Markets in Upper and Middle Guinea Program.

- Malawi, which received $15 million earmarked for its Shire Valley Transformation Program. Expected to help about 56,000 families, the program provides irrigation, drainage, and wetlands management to improve agricultural productivity.[11]

It's worth mentioning that none of these nations is currently an OPEC member; in fact, Burkina Faso doesn't even have oil or natural gas reserves, although the other three are in various stages of exploration or early production.

Looking at the projects OFID supports, it's easy to see how their approach differs from the typical Western way of providing aid, which often involves throwing money at a problem and hoping for the best. Yes, conventional capitalism has achieved miracles—there's no denying it—and building a school or setting up a food bank have their place. But OFID is more interested in creating enabling infrastructure—roads that connect people to markets and water management that overcomes yield-limiting factors and increases crop production—to help raise people out of poverty.

Like other investors, OPEC is concerned about a "return"—but not in the usual interest-bearing or revenue-building sense. OFID funds are directed only toward programs that are sustainable and likely to grow. They want to see that the programs they support yield real change, real results, with outcomes measured not only by the number of people serviced but how far they've come. At the end of the day, it's OPEC's reputation on the line: If a project fails, conditions deteriorate rather than improve, and people suffer, OPEC will have to take the hit. To avoid that risk, their research and oversight are thorough and complete.

Who Will Be Next?

The OPEC of today is a far cry from the decades when the only African members were long-time producers Algeria, Libya, and Nigeria—countries whose combined output was dwarfed by that of OPEC heavy-hitters Saudi Arabia, Iraq, and Iran.

Even though they aren't members, both Sudan and South Sudan participated in the group's effort to prop up prices through production cuts. Actually, South Sudan, the world's newest nation, is considering membership, and OPEC is likely to welcome it with open arms. Although the country's output has suffered as the result of security concerns and political violence, its 1.5 billion barrels of proven reserves—the third-largest total in sub-Saharan Africa—make it a key OPEC candidate.

As I mentioned, Uganda is also mulling OPEC membership, even though production there isn't planned to commence until 2022. Although Uganda won't be accepted until it starts producing, it will be a good strategic move for the country, as it will be able to learn from others who followed a similar path, right from the start.

And it appears that African representation within OPEC is nowhere near cresting: As Mozambique, Kenya, Senegal, and Mauritania enter the oil economy, joining OPEC might not be far behind.

This makes perfect sense, of course. As I told Footprint to Africa in 2018, African nations cannot afford to not be at the negotiating table when the great decisions about their future are made.[12]

At the same time, OPEC will benefit from the rise in African political voices. An enhanced sector outlook, coupled with new discoveries and strong leadership by younger and more capable leaders, is rapidly attracting the interest of investors across the world.

Toward a Stronger, More Stable Industry

Many people look at African nations and think they are too small or too fragile to have a role in OPEC. And it's true that most of them don't have the reserve size or wealth funds of the historic OPEC members. When there's market volatility or a breakdown in talks that will create economic volatility, they will suffer the most. If the group agrees on production cuts, Saudi Arabia can withhold 400,000 bbl/d and manage, while most African countries would go bankrupt and fall into economic recession. It's also important to understand that the fundamentals and dynamics are different between OPEC's Middle East leaders and Africa. While the Saudis can produce a barrel of oil for $7, it costs most African countries $30 to $50. Even the contracts differ: Saudis have service contracts where everyone works for them, while African countries have production sharing contracts where investors need to recover their money. Only by keeping the investors happy can those oil economies continue to grow.

Yet, when all is said and done, I believe that OPEC and Africa can work together to create a stronger, more stable oil and gas industry.

It will take time. African countries are not going to see a lot more power within OPEC until they start producing more. At its core, this is a numbers game. You have to explore more. You have to produce more. A great example is the United States, which is better able to raise its voice today after becoming one of the largest producers of petroleum and a net exporter.

For Africa, having a place at the table is half the job. There's value in knowing OPEC colleagues who started small transformed themselves into powerhouses. It changes your thinking. You start seeing big things and believing in them. There's no mountain you can't climb.

An African at the Helm

Having a voice doesn't always mean hitting the same note as everyone else, of course. In every group, there's potential for discord. Members often have contradictory goals, which can make it hard to find common ground.

Since 2016, credit for orchestrating OPEC—and minimizing conflict—goes to Secretary General Mohammad Sanusi Barkindo.

Barkindo's rise from the small Nigerian town of Yola to OPEC leadership exemplifies how someone can come from a small place and do great things.

Barkindo has significant industry experience: He was managing director of Nigeria's national oil company NNPC and also served as

Nigeria's national representative for OPEC. Since 1991, Barkindo has headed Nigeria's technical delegation to UN climate negotiations.

In addition to his professional achievements and academic credentials—he was educated in Africa, the United States, and Britain, where he earned a postgraduate diploma from Oxford—Barkindo is a master at fostering collaboration. In fact, the biggest deal that OPEC put together in recent years was the Declaration of Cooperation that brought resource-rich Russia together with OPEC members and allies to rescue the oil market. This was no easy task: When you look at the countries involved, you see all kinds of characters. Not everyone gets along, regardless of shared heritage, national proximity, or common goals—and the recent departure of Qatar from the OPEC rolls is a telling example.

Producing just 600,000 bbl/d, Qatar ranked near the bottom of OPEC's production in 2018: It was number 11, in fact. However, the Arab nation, which joined OPEC nearly 60 years ago, in 1961, is the world's largest exporter of liquefied natural gas (LNG). It also has the world's third-largest natural gas reserves, behind only Russia and Iran.[13]

Qatar's oil minister, Saad Sherida Al-Kaabi, told *The National*—which is published in the United Arab Emirates—that the country was withdrawing from OPEC to produce unfettered amounts of oil and focus on its plans to increase LNG to 110 million tonnes per year from the current 77 million tonnes per day.[14] However, it's interesting to note that Qatar has been in a diplomatic crisis since a Saudi-led coalition severed ties with the country over its alleged support of terrorism, making its retreat from OPEC seem less about oil than other things.

That isn't the only conflict Barkindo has dealt with during his tenure as OPEC chief. He's had to broker peace between Iran and Iraq, whose on-again/off-again relationship is legendary. Libya has issues. In short, it can be a real challenge to make this union work. But, Barkindo maintains his cool, mediates like the pro he is, and pulls together a forceful agenda. The potential for Africa to thrive under his leadership is tremendous.

4

EMPOWERING WOMEN FOR A STRONGER, HEALTHIER OIL AND GAS INDUSTRY

In 2014, actress and celebrity Emma Watson addressed the United Nations on gender equality. In launching the UN's HeForShe global campaign, Watson called on *both* men and women to fight for gender equality.

"The more I've spoken about feminism, the more I have realized that fighting for women's rights has too often become synonymous with man hating," Watson said. "If there is one thing I know for certain, it is that this has to stop. For the record, feminism, by definition, is the belief that men and women should have equal rights and opportunities."[1]

Watson could not be more right—feminism is about equality of the sexes, an issue that obviously should concern both men and women. The need to care about this topic is so obvious that I'm shocked when I'm questioned on my fervent support for women in energy. Even more, I'm saddened that I often feel I have to defend my right to care about this issue because I'm a man.

In this chapter, I want to make it clear that leaving women behind is a detriment to good business and society as a whole. Here, I hope to properly illustrate that women are *vital* for the success of Africa's oil and gas sector.

Gender Inequality in Energy and Africa

The energy sector is notorious for its struggle to attract female employees. Women in the oil and gas industry face an array of challenges—inadequate (or nonexistent) maternity leave, a lack of female mentors, pay inequality, higher rates of sexual harassment, and a working culture that can devalue women and femininity as a whole. A 2018 study by the University of Massachusetts,[2] for example, found that oil and gas had the highest rate of sexual harassment charges of any industry in the United States.

It is no wonder, then, that women make up so little of the global energy sector. Women represented about 22 percent of its global workforce in 2017, and participation dropped to 17 percent at senior and executive-level roles. Only 1 percent of the CEOs in oil and gas were women.[3] What's more, in many cases, the women who work in this field earn less than their male counterparts. A study released at the 2016 World Economic Forum, "The Future of Jobs," reported a 32 percent pay gap in the oil and gas industry globally.[4]

Africa is no exception. While it has been difficult to find hard data on female participation in Africa's oil and gas industry, anecdotal evidence shows that women are vastly underrepresented. I believe this is unacceptable, short-sighted, and, frankly, a real stumbling block to African countries that want to realize the full socioeconomic benefits that a thriving oil and gas industry can provide. If you truly want your nation to thrive, why wouldn't you do everything in your power to help half of your population participate in one of your most lucrative industries?

The United Nations Development Programme (UNDP) has described sub-Saharan Africa as one of the most gender-unequal regions in the world, largely due to "perceptions, attitudes, and historic gender roles." More women have limited access to health care, education, and economic opportunities here than anywhere else.[5] The lack of economic opportunities alone costs the countries of sub-Saharan Africa a combined total of $95 billion in lost productivity annually, UNDP estimates. The oil and gas industry has real potential to start turning this situation around, but with gender inequality pervading this sector, the beneficial economic impacts are curtailed.

I believe most men in oil and gas still don't get it when it comes to equality in the industry. We are quick to talk about diversity. However, our work environments are still mostly male. When you speak with men, they tell you that we have to hire, promote, and give contracts to women based only on merit. Well, of course, we do! What's the problem? Are they suggesting that there would be plenty of women working in oil and gas if there were only more qualified candidates? Are they implying that advocates for a diverse oil and gas sector are more concerned with setting and meeting quotas than in doing what's best for the industry? Neither suggestion is accurate. What is true is that we should be harnessing the oil and gas industry's tremendous potential to help everyday Africans, male *and* female.

The African Natural Resources Center and African Development Bank addressed the industry's potential to help African women in their 2017 "Women's economic empowerment in oil and gas industries in Africa" report. "Given that there is a large gender gap in gross national product (GNP) per capita in all surveyed African countries, women stand to gain more from economic empowerment and boosting of their incomes, be it through formal (oil and gas) sector employment or entrepreneurship," the report stated.

But, the report went on to say, that's not what we're seeing. African men are getting the majority of oil and gas jobs, compensation, and business opportunities. African women, meanwhile, rarely see those benefits—but they still have to share the risks and costs associated with the industry, from displacement to economic impacts. And because women often are on shakier economic ground than men in Africa, they are actually more vulnerable to these risks.

Consider this: Farming is a major income-generating activity for African women—but when oil and gas pipelines are built, they are often built over that farmland. In addition to displacing women's sole source of income, these changes to the environment also make it increasingly difficult for women to access simple day-to-day necessities. As Wangari Maathai, Africa's first female Nobel Peace Prize winner, famously said, "In Kenya, women are the first victims of environmental degradation, because they are the ones who walk for hours looking for water, who fetch firewood, who provide food for their families."[6]

And when oil companies offer economic compensation to households affected by their activities, the money typically goes to the male head of the household.

The oil and gas industry is missing a golden opportunity to empower women by partnering with and purchasing from female entrepreneurs, who could provide a vast range of services and goods—from logistics to engineering to food services. Female entrepreneurship rates in sub-Saharan Africa are the highest in the world, according to Global Entrepreneurship Monitor's "Women's Entrepreneurship 2016-17 Report." Nearly 26 percent of the adult female population in Africa is involved in early-stage entrepreneurial activity. But one of the most glaring examples of the oil and gas gender gap is the industry's failure to work with local female-owned micro, small, and medium-sized enterprises (SMEs) as suppliers, service providers, and partners.[7]

Guidance certainly is available for companies that are willing to work with female-owned SMEs. For example, BSR, a global non-profit business network and consultancy dedicated to sustainability, recently released a video with practical steps that companies can take to promote gender equality in supply chains. The guidelines are not focused on the oil and gas industry, but they can be applied there.

"As a company, you can act by integrating a gender lens into your supply chain strategy, supplier codes of conduct, due diligence approach, and sourcing practices," said Magali Barraja, manager at BSR, and Dominic Kotas, a BSR communications associate, in an article promoting the video. "Taking these actions is a solid first step to ensuring that women workers are visible, the specific challenges they face are better identified, and remediation measures are being designed with gender specificities in mind."[8]

Leading the Way

To be blunt, the oil and gas industry's failure to create more opportunities for women is a travesty. Women have a mighty role to play in this sector, particularly as leaders. In fact, those who have achieved executive status have been hugely successful and impactful. You would think that the industry would learn a thing or two from the positive examples that female oil and gas leaders are setting. Their achievements should be generating excitement and inspiring more companies to look to female talent to fill managerial and executive roles.

Let's look at Catherine Uju Ifejika, chairperson and CEO of Nigeria-based Britannia-U Group.

When Uju Ifejika was working as a junior counsel at Texaco Petroleum in the 1980s, the young attorney would have been shocked if someone told her she'd later be described as "Africa's most successful female oil tycoon." Or as one of the richest women on the continent. Or as the founder of the first indigenous petroleum industry E&P company in Nigeria to be headed by a Nigerian woman.

In the early days of her career, Uju Ifejika was simply trying to build a successful legal career in a fast-paced, high-pressure setting. She never set out to break new ground for women or shift from practicing law to running a major oil and gas company. But today, as president and CEO of Brittania-U, Uju Ifejika is an important role model for women.

She credits her rise to power, to some degree, to sheer determination.

"I'm not a geologist and I have never worked in exploration and production," she said during an interview with Fascinating Nigeria. "The only thing I know is how to take something that is nothing and create something out of it that you can see and appreciate. . . Not being an engineer or a geologist was immaterial. Today, I speak the language of the geologist, I can interpret the maps, and when they bring in technical things we look at them together—because I was able to rise above my fear level."[9]

Her company—which is involved in E&P, petroleum engineering, data consulting, importation of refined products, shipping, vessel operation, and subsurface engineering activities—regularly partners with other indigenous businesses, contributing to economic stability. They have also trained more than 25 people from host communities to be certified marine engineers and currently provide full-time employment for more than 20 community residents, along with nine others as contract staff.

While Uju Ifejika's drive and accomplishments are inspiring—in part because examples of women holding executive leadership roles in the oil and gas industry are rare—women succeeding in this sphere should not be a rarity.

Indeed, there are concrete steps the industry and African countries can take to ensure women have an active stake in this industry.

Taking Steps

I'm convinced that empowering women through the oil and gas industry would have far-reaching socioeconomic benefits.

"Women are often the linchpins of their communities, playing key roles in ensuring the health, nutrition, education and security of those around them," stated "Oil and Gas Extraction Industry in East Africa: An African Feminist Perspective." The 2014 paper was released by Akina Mama wa Afrika (AMwA), a regional Pan-African women's organization based in Kampala, Uganda.

I couldn't agree with them more.

Companies, in particular, have a lot to gain by creating opportunities for women, including improved public perceptions, a stabilizing role on the African communities where they work and live, and an expanded talent pool at a time when the oil and gas industry is grappling with serious skills shortages.

So how can the sector better empower women? Making a strategic effort to recruit, hire, and retain them—across all levels—would make a tremendous difference.

First, companies can work with the government to eliminate barriers that make working in the industry difficult for females. It's telling that, so far, only four countries in Africa have ratified the International Labor Union's Convention No. 183, which provides guaranteed paid maternity leave, ensures breaks for breastfeeding and/or pumping, and protects women from discrimination.

Additionally, a study by the International Labor Union found that even in those African countries that require companies to provide paid maternity leave, the laws are rarely enforced, with only an estimated 10 percent of women continuing to receive salaries while on leave.

This issue needs to be immediately addressed by both governments and the private sector. I urge governments to create responsible, sustainable laws to protect women in the workplace. Looking to countries on the continent that have already created successful maternity leave protections—like Rwanda, which provides for 12 weeks off, fully paid, and South Africa, which requires 4 months of leave—is a good start.

Companies, too, have a role to play here. And there are tangible benefits for stepping up. My company, for example, has changed its maternity leave policy over the years to become more and more generous. We now offer up to 12 months of paid leave for the primary caregiver and 3 months for the secondary caregiver, while also making payments to pensions and insurance plans. This policy, one of the most competitive in the world, creates not only a positive outcome for families and society, but also for our company and our clients. Our maternity leave policy has helped with retention, especially of highly skilled employees with specific expertise, and has therefore reduced turnover costs for Centurion. We have seen an increase in worker productivity and an improvement in employee loyalty and morale. This allows us to compete with larger firms.

Crucial in the success of these policies, however, is creating a positive environment and encouraging families to make use of the benefit. The availability of leave is irrelevant if female employees are afraid to use it.

At the entry level, companies can and should promote the wide range of jobs they offer to women, support educational programs, and make it a priority to increase the numbers and visibility of female role models within the company.

At the mid-career level, companies should make it a priority to provide women the same opportunities as men and provide sponsors who can guide and advocate for the women under their wings.

And at the senior leadership level, companies should make it a priority to have women in these positions and provide support to help them succeed.[10] Targeting hiring policies are a clear path forward here.

Those are the kinds of practices in place at Kenya-based East African Breweries Ltd. (EABL), where more than 45 percent of its board of directors are women—a huge jump from a decade earlier when women made up only 16 percent of the company's board. That change is the result of company hiring policy, said Eric Kiniti, EABL's corporate relations director. "Before hiring at the senior management level, we ask that there must be a female candidate in all our short lists," Kiniti said. "And if there isn't, we ask why."

Global management consulting firm McKinsey & Company recommends four administrative goals to foster gender diversity, including female leadership, in companies:

- Make gender diversity a high board and CEO priority.

- Communicate relevant gender diversity policies to employees.

- Confront limiting attitudes toward women in the workplace.

- Implement a fact-based gender diversity strategy (use metrics and data to understand women's contributions to the company).[11]

Of course, once these or similar policies are in place, they must be followed. In Africa, that's not always the case. South Africa, for example, actually requires gender equity in state-owned institutions by law, but women only constitute 33 percent of the employees in those institutions.

Katy Heidenreich is the author of *The Oil Industry's Best Kept Secret: A Book Full of Inspiration and Advice.* She points out that achieving a more gender-inclusive workforce will take more than simply welcoming women. It will also require a strategic effort to attract them to oil and gas in the first place. The industry needs to combat the idea that oil and gas is a man's world and show women the rewarding, lucrative careers available to them.

Take offshore assignments, for example. Why shouldn't more women pursue them?

"Life offshore is a different world," Lindsey Gordon, a female petroleum engineer with BP, told Offshore Technology. "The platforms and FPSOs (floating production storage and offloading) are amazing feats of engineering. The camaraderie is second to none, which is important when you're together for weeks at a time. To round it off, I get to take a helicopter to work."[12]

Women also need to see that balancing work and family is doable. Caroline Gill, a lead geologist at Shell UK, described in Heidenreich's book what works for her and her geologist husband.

"As a couple, we both have the flexibility to work at home, and we can pick up any outstanding work once our children are in bed. It's totally an equal partnership—we both do our fair share. Even when we're working long hours, it doesn't impact on family life."

In an article for LinkedIn, "Women in Energy: Oiling the Wheels of Talent," Rolake Akinkugbe, FBN Capital's Head of Energy and Natural Resources, points out that technology could play a role in helping women balance work and family responsibilities. "As digitalization advances, it may be possible for more types of roles in the industry to be carried out remotely, making it easier for women who seek flexibility to sustain careers in the industry over a longer period," she said.

As for recruiting women, Akinkugbe said, bringing successful females in the industry to the attention of other women will carry a lot of weight. "The importance of visible representation cannot be overemphasized; women tend to be inspired by other women pursuing high-ranking careers in the oil industry, because of its historical dominant macho image. The less gender diversity there is at technical and senior levels of the industry, the less other women are likely to see themselves pursuing careers in oil and gas, and consequently, firms will find it even more difficult to recruit women. The reverse is also true."

Another key to building gender diversity momentum is giving more women the authority to make hiring policy. An encouraging example in this area is Eunice Ntobedzi, a director of Sandico Botswana, an energy services company. She employs women engineers in the development of energy projects in Botswana. Ntobedzi also works to close the gender gap through the Botswana International University of Science & Technology, which encourages women to support sustainable development in their country.[13] Talk about a win-win: These efforts help empower women and support vital efforts to bring power to everyday Africans.

Oil and gas companies in Africa should follow Ntobedzi's lead, not only in her hiring practices, but also in her commitment to supporting women's training opportunities. Those are just a few of the things that international mining company Asanko Gold Inc. has promised to do through its new Asanko Women in Mining Botae Pa (Good Purpose) in Ghana, West Africa. The initiative's projects will include promoting careers in the mining sector for women and offering professional development, mentoring, networking, and community programs that focus on the needs of women and girls in the areas of education, health, and finances.[14] If only more extractives-industry companies, oil and gas businesses, in particular, would do the same.

Women in government are also driving dialogue and new initiatives, including the first lady of the Republic of Angola, Ana Dias Lourenço. An economist, government minister, longstanding chair of the Southern African Development Community, and former World Bank governor, Lourenço is participating in top-level discussions on gender equality at the United Nations.

Irene Nafuna Muloni, the Cabinet Minister for Energy and Minerals in the Ugandan Cabinet, is urging for more female involvement in the energy sector. In fact, Uganda requires women to be considered part of new development activities in the industry.

Education: Long-Term Investments

Some argue Africa will not be able to address the gender gap in a meaningful way without changing cultural norms and perceptions—and that kind of change must begin with family education programs, which could be offered by governments, schools, businesses, and NGOs.

"An enabling environment has to be created at every level of society, starting within households," wrote Gerald Chirinda, executive director of Tapiwa Capital, a company that focuses on building sustainable enterprises in Zimbabwe. "It is important for parents to invest their time and be intentional in positively influencing and encouraging their daughters. It is equally important to teach boys the importance of respecting, honoring and empowering women."[15]

I agree with Chirinda, but I believe girls also need educational opportunities that give them the necessary science, technology, engineering, and math (STEM) foundation to take lucrative positions in oil and gas. We're starting to see examples of educational programs like these. One is the African Science Academy (ASA), a Ghana-based secondary school for girls that specializes in advanced math and physics. Students are recruited from throughout the continent, and scholarships are available to cover students' tuition and travels. No qualified African girl is turned away for inability to pay, the academy claims. And ASA's top achievers get to attend a week-long study program at Oxford or Cambridge universities in the United Kingdom, which opens the door to even more educational opportunities.[16]

In many cases, nonprofit organizations are taking the lead when it comes to creating educational opportunities for African girls. Take the nonprofit Working to Advance STEM Education for African Women (WAAW). The organization was founded by Unoma Okorafor of Nigeria, who recently wrote about its mission for www.indiegogo.com: "In the next ten years, thousands of people throughout Africa will be impacted deeply by technology changes in our world . . . For Kenya and Nigeria to compete around the world our girls need to learn skills such as the basics of robotics, setting up multiple kinds of energy systems, coding, and the foundations of our modern scientific world."[17]

WAAW operates STEM camps for teenage girls throughout Africa, along with STEM teacher training, weekend and after-school coding clubs, and mentoring, among other programs. It's time for others, including businesses, public-private partnerships, and governments, to follow their example.

Putting Policies in Place

In fact, governments have a *huge* role to play in paving the way for more women to benefit from oil and gas industry opportunities. That should start with local content policies that address women specifically.

These policies should include mandates to:

- Provide certain percentages of local women paid positions.

- Work with women-owned suppliers and sub-contractors.

- Require suppliers and subcontractors to employ women.

- Create education and training opportunities, including STEM studies, for women and girls.

- Ensure that women and men receive equal compensation, whether it's wages, community programs, or property royalties.

- Provide for sustainable, adequate maternity leave, and protections for leave when immediate family members are ill and require care.

Foreign companies would probably be more receptive to increased local content required if governments offered them carrots, and not just the stick. Why not offer tax incentives for hiring local women, subcontracting with—and buying supplies from—women-owned SMEs? Or provide incentives for offering maternity leave?

In addition to creating and enforcing local content laws, governments can help women through policies that create a more enabling environment for SMEs linked to the oil and gas industry. The International Labour Office, in "Inclusive Business Practices in Africa's Extractive Industries," recommends:

- Simplifying business registration and licensing procedures.

- Streamlining tax policies and administration.

- Facilitating access to finance, especially micro-credit for start-ups.

- Improving land titles, registers, and administration.

- Simplifying and accelerating access to commercial courts and alternative dispute resolution resources.

- Improving access to market information.

We also need legislation that protects and enables women: laws that protect women from sexual harassment and protect their right to work.

Africa, as a whole, has shockingly poor protections for women facing sexual harassment or assault. In South Africa, for example, 1 in 3 women is raped in her lifetime; 4 out of 10 married women in Central and West Africa were married before their 18th birthday, and 40 to 60 percent of women in North Africa say they've experienced street-based sexual harassment. This is unacceptable, and strong laws need to be put in place—and enforced—to protect women now.

We also need laws that ensure equal pay for equal work. At the end of the day, women don't pay less for milk than men. They don't pay less for rent. They shouldn't be working for lower wages than men.

Non-Government Organizations: Moving in the Right Direction

While I hope to see more efforts by businesses to help women better leverage oil and gas opportunities in the very near future, I am encouraged by the growing number of organizations making strides in this area. One of these organizations, TheBoardroom Africa, connects highly qualified, peer-endorsed female leaders with African companies seeking to fill board of director positions, including in the oil and gas sector. The organization was founded by Marcia Ashong of Ghana, whose professional background includes upstream oil and gas law, project management, consulting, and business development. She runs the program with co-founder Tasmin Jones, a social entrepreneur based in London.

"We need to dispel the myth that there aren't enough qualified women out there ready to take on board leadership," Ashong said. "By building the leading network of board-ready women we have already started to break down this myth, but more importantly we are working closely with the business community and key influencers through thought leadership to raise awareness on the benefits of diversity at the top."[18]

Another organization, the Association for Women in Extractives and Energy in Kenya, works to provide women with opportunities for equitable professional and economic development in Kenya's extractives industry, including the oil, gas, and mining sectors.

A relatively new organization, the African Women Energy Entrepreneurs Framework, was conceived as a result of the workshop on Women Entrepreneurs and Sustainable Energy (WESE) at the African Ministerial Conference in Libreville, Gabon, in June 2017.

The organization's objectives, among others, include:

- Ensuring gender-responsive policies and all-inclusive participation in the realm of renewable energy and entrepreneurship.

- Fostering partnerships between regional blocs, governments, the private sector, and civil society at the regional, national, and local levels.

- Integrating coordination and knowledge management in strengthening the capacities of national and local governments, women's cooperatives and associations, and women entrepreneurs themselves.

- Enhancing access to finance and markets for women energy entrepreneurs.

- All of these organizations have the potential to create meaningful opportunities for women, but they're only one piece of the puzzle.

Bringing more women into the industry, and giving them the tools to succeed, should be a priority across the board in Africa. Employers, government, educators, and organizations all need to do their part.

We have everything to gain from a thriving oil and gas industry. And with more women in this sector, it's better positioned to soar.

WEX Africa: Showing How It's Done

Oguto Okudo refuses to let it distract her when colleagues at SpringRock Energy Kenya refer to her as "Little Girl" or when she receives emails addressing her as "Mr. Okudo."

She knows that in Kenya—and much of the African continent—her role as country manager for an energy company makes her a rarity. For every success story like hers, there are thousands of African women whose economic prospects are bleak at best. So, rather than getting irritated at the slights and false assumptions she encounters on the job, Okudo has been working to help other African women enter and thrive in her field. The organization she founded in 2011, Women in Energy and Extractives Africa (WEX Africa), is taking aim at gender disparity in the oil, gas, and energy sectors.

WEX Africa provides women with access to information and personal development training, promotes the energy and extractive sector as a career choice for women, and informs industry decision-makers of the challenges and opportunities for women in their companies. Okudo sees the organization's work as a win-win for women and for the communities where they live. "Women are change catalysts," she told *Daily Nation* in 2018. "When you tap into their full potential, you are able to have more inclusive economic developments while improving living conditions for all in the society."[19]

I'm extremely impressed with the approach WEX Africa takes to address the wide spectrum of needs African women have today. The organization has developed programs to target four specific "spheres," each for a different population group.

Sphere 1 comprises women who are directly affected by exploration in their communities. WEX Africa considers this their target population and strives to serve as their advocate and present their needs to local leaders and businesses. "We understand that the impact of energy and extractive operations are not gender neutral," their website says.

Sphere 2 is made up of women embarking on entry into the industry and those already in it. WEX Africa strives to help women in this sphere by notifying women about opportunities, informing industry decision-makers of challenges, helping women obtain necessary licenses, and getting the word out about the organization as a resource.

WEX Africa serves Sphere 3, young women and girls, through educational programs, including the "Kitabu si Taabu" campaign, which encourages young girls around the globe to go to school. The organization also has customized learning and STEM programs for young girls in extractive and energy-impacted communities with literacy rates among women as low as three percent.

The organization's Sphere 4 comprises women engaged in business in the value chain. WEX Africa strives to serve them by urging leaders to create a supportive environment and encouraging women to get involved in this sector. The organization also inspires knowledge and opportunity sharing among female entrepreneurs.

What an excellent role model, not only for other organizations, but also for governments and businesses. Clearly, it is possible to develop programs that offer meaningful support and assistance for women, programs that will allow them to capitalize on the many opportunities that exist in oil and gas.

At the end of the day, we need to empower more African women to benefit from the oil and gas industry, whether we're talking about opportunities for boots on the ground jobs at drill sites, professional positions, leadership roles, or business prospects for women-owned enterprises.

As actress Emma Watson said during her speech to the United Nations: "I am inviting you to step forward to be seen, and to ask yourselves, 'If not me, who? If not now, when?'"

Setting the Stage

Here are just a few examples of female oil and gas leaders—women who are, hopefully, setting the stage for others to follow.

FBN Capital's Head of Energy and Natural Resources Rolake Akinkugbe, of Nigeria, was named Best African Oil & Gas Analyst of the Year in late 2018 for her commitment to the industry, her knowledge, and her valuable analysis.[20] Akinkugbe serves on the Economic Advisory Board for the Office of the Vice President in Nigeria. She is a frequent media commentator; writes about natural resources in Africa; is a monthly reviewer of global news headlines on BBC World News, and is a conference presenter on energy, natural resources, and investment. Not only that, but she also runs a public speaking training initiative, VoxArticl8™, and is the founder of InaTidé, a social enterprise that sources both finance and technical expertise for off-grid, sustainable energy projects in sub-Saharan Africa.[21]

Elizabeth Rogo is the founder and CEO of Tsavo Oilfield Services, a Kenya-based energy consultancy serving the oil and gas, geothermal, and mining sectors in East Africa. In addition to her professional commitments, Rogo mentors young professionals in the energy sector and is a sought-after presenter on gender diversity and local content in the oil and gas industry.[22]

Dr. Amy Jadesimi, physician and CEO of Nigerian logistics company, LADOL, recently received the Oil and Gas Leading Women award at the Foreign Investment Network (FIN) and Federal Ministry of Petroleum Resources Honorary Patrons Dinner and Awards Night during the Nigeria International Petroleum Summit 2019, in Abuja.

She was also named the Young CEO of the Year by the African Leadership Forum, a Young Global Leader by the World Economic Forum (WEF), and an Archbishop Tutu Fellow for her work to reduce maternal mortality. She has also been named as a Rising Talent by the Women's Forum for Economy and Society, one of 20 Youngest Power Women in Africa by Forbes, and was listed among the Top 25 Africans to Watch by the *Financial Times*.[23]

Althea E. Sherman is the interim president/CEO of the National Oil Company of Liberia (NOCAL). She also served as the company's COO and, as an attorney, has more than 20 years of legal and business experience with major U.S. corporations, including Oracle Corporation, AT&T, and Verizon Communications.[24]

In Equatorial Guinea, Mercedes Eworo Milam earned widespread respect when she held the role of director general of Hydrocarbons of the Ministry of Mines, Industry and Energy. In fact, in 2014, she was recognized for her outstanding work in ensuring the sustainable development of the country's oil and gas sector when she received the Woman of the Year award at the Oil and Gas Awards. She was credited with maintaining a firm balance as hydrocarbons director, encouraging oil companies to invest and giving them the confidence to operate. She ensured that women were hired and considered for jobs, training, and promotions, and awarded contracts.[25]

5

ABUNDANT, ACCESSIBLE, AFFORDABLE: THE "GOLDEN AGE" OF NATURAL GAS SHINES IN AFRICA

"Are we entering a Golden Age of Gas?"

This was the question the Paris-based International Energy Agency (IEA) posed in 2011[1]—a question the agency answered with a resounding "Yes." Their outlook was positive for a number of reasons, not the least of which is that there's an awful lot of the resource to go around, in terms of both distribution and volume. There are natural gas basins on six of the seven continents, excluding only Antarctica, and the report's authors estimated that the total amount of commercially recoverable reserves—back then, this was about 193.8 trillion barrels—could sustain production levels for 250 years.

The IEA noted that, in addition to being plentiful, natural gas is cleaner burning than other fossil fuels and cheaper for consumers. Over time, the agency predicted, natural gas could become a transport fuel, reduce the use of coal and nuclear energy, and drastically cut pollution and greenhouse gases. By 2035, they projected, global demand will grow by 55 percent, and natural gas will account for 25 percent of world energy, a significantly larger share of the global mix than ever.

Although prices have wavered slightly since this 2011 pronouncement, the optimism was not misplaced. Natural gas can achieve all of those things and more. Natural gas occupies a special place in the energy world, standing at the nexus of economy and environment. It's abundant, accessible, and affordable. And because it provides the most energy per unit of carbon emission among fossil fuels, it bridges the gap for those not quite ready to kick the hydrocarbon habit but interested in a more climate-friendly form of fuel.

And the luster of this Golden Age of Gas extends well into Africa. So much so, in fact, that many industry experts consider the continent to be its new frontier. With descriptions such as "a prime mover,"[2] "the new oil for Africa,"[3] and the key to "transformative change"[4] on the continent, I believe that we will see natural gas playing a crucial role in Africa's economic future.

Sparking Social Change in Africa

For too many in Africa, the amenities of "modern life" remain beyond reach. Even as urbanization expands, and with it, the attendant demand for lights, appliances, and digital devices, great swaths of Africa plunge into near or total darkness come nightfall. More than 620 million sub-Saharan Africans—or a full two-thirds of the population—live without access to any electricity at all. And that number is actually rising. While the IEA projects that one billion people will gain access to electricity in Africa by 2040, including 950 million in the sub-Saharan region, explosive population growth is expected to sink more and more people into a powerless abyss.

As IEA notes, "the remaining global population without electricity access becomes increasingly concentrated in sub-Saharan Africa—

this figure reaches 75 percent in 2040, compared with half today."[5] Incidentally, this is the only place in the world where lack of access is getting worse, not better.

This is not a problem related to an absence of conveniences or lack of luxuries. It's a very real public health issue. In the Democratic Republic of Congo, for instance, remote village clinics are so far off the grid that only solar power is available to light the way for medical care. Solar, of course, can't be relied on for consistent baseload power, so when there's no sun, very few services can be delivered.

Ghana, on the other hand, represents the kind of medical advances that can occur when electricity reaches more people. Well-lit, well-powered health facilities are actually driving demand for health services, with more women coming into facilities to give birth with a skilled birth attendant. In addition, the nation's more reliable power grid has translated into better cold supply chains that keep essential childhood vaccines safe and may even help prevent the continent's next Ebola outbreak.

But expanded access to reliable electricity would do more than improve Africans' quality of life: it would also wean sub-Saharan Africa from its dependence on biomass for energy. Some 730 million people rely on fuelwood, charcoal, agricultural waste, or even animal dung for cooking. Burning biomass produces a potentially harmful, particulate-laden smoke, and burning it indoors—as millions of people do—concentrates the smoke and fumes to the point where inhaling them is as toxic as smoking two packs of cigarettes a day.[6] Researchers link exposure to indoor air pollution from biomass to the premature deaths of about 1.3 million people worldwide every year.[7]

On the continent, we can look to North Africa as a model of electrification success—90 percent of the region's population has electricity connections. And even despite the rather grim outlook in sub-Saharan Africa, we do see some pockets of progress, particularly in Nigeria, Ethiopia, Tanzania, and Kenya. From 2000 to 2018, Kenya increased its power access rate by 65 percentage points to 73 percent and is targeting universal access by 2022. Ethiopia provided power to 5 percent of its population in 2000. The access rate is now 45 percent with a target for universal access by 2025.[8]

Growing Interest in Gas-Fired Power

We know that Africa's electricity troubles are formidable, adding to and amplifying severe economic, societal, health, and human development woes. But I've seen the glimmer of hope. By strategically exploiting the continent's new natural gas discoveries to produce electricity—"gas-to-power," as it's known—investors and producers can help Africa reduce imports, grow exports, expand access to electricity, improve its economy, and fund social development.

Natural gas is also seen as a step toward a low-carbon, sustainable world that relies exclusively on renewable resources. In light of increasing environmental pressures to reduce greenhouse emissions, cleaner (and increasingly affordable) natural gas has stepped into the spotlight to replace coal as the most attractive alternative for generating electricity. For transportation and power production, natural gas produces less CO_2 emissions than diesel, gasoline, or coal. For electricity generation, natural gas-fired power plants can be integrated with renewable sources like wind and solar.[9]

Aside from the green benefits of gas-fired generation, gas-to-power has financial pluses: Facilities are typically less expensive and faster to build than coal or nuclear plants, and natural gas is so efficient that just a small volume generates a lot of electricity.

Natural gas has been the leading fuel for electricity generation since 2015, after sitting in the number two spot (behind coal) for decades.[10] Russia, Japan, and Taiwan have the top five gas-fired power plants in the world.[11] And as a result of major offshore gas discoveries, Africa has a keen opportunity to participate more fully in the gas-to-power movement today.

Africa has certain economic advantages when it comes to extracting natural gas, including relatively open access and generally attractive leasing terms. The continent's lower cost structure has been attractive to a wide range of investors, including majors, independents, and national oil companies. Although resources are not divided equally—more than 92 percent of the continent's total gas reserves are concentrated in four nations: Nigeria, Algeria, Egypt, and Libya—prospects are promising across the continent, from the coast of Mauritania to the waters off Mozambique.

In other words, the potential is there. And some governments across the continent are already exploiting it.

According to the World Bank,[12] Nigeria alone has enough discovered gas to generate more than 80 GW of power for 30 years. Nigeria's Roadmap for Power Sector Reform sets a goal of 20 GW of generation capacity by 2020, and most of this capacity will be gas-fired. Discoveries offshore Ghana, Namibia, and Côte d'Ivoire are expected to yield enough gas to meet current electricity demand for more than 50 years, while Cameroon, Republic of Congo, Mauritania, and Gabon have enough discovered gas equivalent for more than 100 years. A super-major-scale discovery offshore Senegal and Mauritania holds an estimated additional 450 bcm of gas.[13] Not only could some of it be converted to electricity, the finding prompted Senegal's energy minister to say he foresees energy self-sufficiency for his nation, with the possibility of it becoming a net gas exporter very real.

Those aren't the only advances, however. In addition:

- South Africa's Department of Energy gas-to-power program was developed to facilitate the construction of gas distribution infrastructure.[14]

- Natural gas-fired thermal plants sustain 50 percent of the sub-Saharan region's grid-connected capacity. The International Renewable Energy Agency (IRENA) says that more than 90 percent of capacity comes from Nigeria, Ghana, and Côte d'Ivoire. Angola is currently developing 400 MW of gas-fired power plants.

- Mozambique's development of its Coral gas field brought in more than 70 percent of its $11 billion gross domestic product in 2016, and the reserves will fulfill the energy needs for itself and its neighbors.[15]

- Cameroon has experienced recent successes with floating LNG offshore platforms. It also introduced technological improvements that could further reduce the cost of production and make natural gas even more competitive for power generation.

Despite the progress, African producers all across the continent are, unfortunately, still making a grave mistake: handicapping themselves and Africa as a whole by continuing to flare off gas. Instead of wasting this precious resource, we should be capturing it and using it to build our manufacturing base.

We need to come to a universal understanding: We can't run industries by generators. Gas-to-power will help us use the gas to create a diversified, industrialized economy.

Re-Evaluating Priorities

In an article published in 2018, I posed this question: *Why would a country in West Africa choose to import expensive diesel from refineries in*

Texas for its power stations, when it could use its own cheaper resources, or those of a gas-producing neighbor, to power its economy? [16]

Fulfilling the needs of Africans first is vitally important. What would be even better? Fulfilling our needs with our own resources. The domestic market within our continental borders must not be overlooked any longer. Once we've taken care of ourselves, then we can discuss exports. But let's try to be cognizant of where those exports are headed.

Historically, the continent hasn't developed its energy resources to bring power to the people—instead, the focus has been on supporting other nations through exports. Consider OPEC member Nigeria, which ships 40 percent of its oil to the United States, or Ghana, where the largest single export is fuel going to the European Union. In fact, two out of every three dollars put into the sub-Saharan energy sector since 2000 have been committed to the development of resources for export.

With the sub-Saharan region expected to produce 175 bcm of natural gas per year by 2040, natural gas could have continent-wide influence, supplementing Africa's hydropower resources and replacing coal and liquid fuels (and biomass) for power. But that can happen only if Africa keeps some of its natural gas riches to itself.

I agree with H.E. Gabriel Mbaga Obiang Lima, Minister of Mines, Industry and Energy in Equatorial Guinea, who recently told me, "We must provide for our citizens, who need to be able to power their cars, their homes and their businesses. To this end, it is cheaper to create an industry by which we can use our own gas, as opposed to exporting our gas as LNG and then being forced to import fuel for domestic use. There is great value in both export and domestic use of gas in a diverse and strong economy."

Equatorial Guinea is one of the largest oil and gas markets in sub-Saharan Africa. And with an impressive resumé that includes service in the oil and gas sector since 1997, Lima understands the vital role that hydrocarbons play in domestic revenue. Prior to taking on his current post, he was minister delegate, vice minister, Secretary of State for Mines and Hydrocarbons, government representative in the Equity of the State in production-sharing contracts, and presidential adviser of hydrocarbons. In addition, he has served as a board member of three national companies: Sonagas, SEGESA, and GEPetrol.

"While there is certainly a demand for our products to be exported globally, there is also a great need for the downstream sectors to be developed in Africa and for these resources to be used at home, as refined products, fertilizers, petrochemicals, and in power generation," said Lima, whose goal is to create a positive environment for national and international oil and gas companies, while ensuring that local residents benefit from those efforts. "This leads to more stability, diversification, better quality of work, and more jobs for our people."

Lima's points about natural gas align closely with those of Guillaume Doane, the CEO of Africa Oil & Power. As the organizer of high-level investment conferences focused on the African energy industries, he has his finger on the pulse of the sector. In fact, he cites Equatorial Guinea as an exemplary model of the "Africa First" movement that calls for African countries maximizing local beneficiation of their natural resources.

"Equatorial Guinea, in so many ways, has set an example and demonstrated a leadership position on the importance of utilizing its natural resources for the benefit of its own people and neighbors. Its use of natural gas for LNG exports, for gas-to-power facilities, for compressed natural gas, and, further down the road, on exciting industry and petrochemical projects, provides a reference point for the rest of the continent," Doane told me in a recent interview. "Furthermore, Equatorial Guinea has established something of a template for how African countries holding a wealth of natural gas can share their resources and work with their African neighbors on building gas import infrastructure."

We should also realize that the global export market might not be the "cash cow" that it once was. The market is oversaturated due to factors such as the United States shale boom, increased Middle Eastern production, and Australia's significant LNG export investments. African producers used to look toward the United States and European countries as solid buyers. Not so much anymore.

I believe that this is actually a blessing in disguise. Using locally sourced (or at least continentally sourced) natural gas can help curb our costly imports of refined oil products from abroad. Forcing our energy producers to look "inside the box" (within Africa, that is) can be the impetus needed to foster vibrant intra-African energy trading. And strong economic ties can promote political alliances and create a strong internal market.

So, let's forget about trying to compete with the world's major energy producers over international contracts and focus instead on our regional market. That's simply more realistic—and more important for the economic health and future prosperity of our continent.

Consider Tanzania: Currently, at least 50 percent of the power generated from natural gas is being used by the Tanzania Electric Supply Company (TANESCO), with the rest going for industrial heating, petrochemical feedstock, and cooking and vehicle fuel. Its natural gas production is effectively slashing its dependence on energy imports— saving upwards of $7.4 billion between 2004 and 2015, according to the Tanzania Petroleum Development Corporation (TDPC). Those funds have been funneled into projects that might have otherwise been put on hold, such as the development of a fertilizer plant that will have an installed capacity to produce 2,200 and 3,850 metric tons of ammonia and urea per day, respectively. That project is creating up to 5,000 long-term jobs—and improving the country's economy for generations.[17]

Tanzania's strong regional economy will also improve relations among countries and create a robust internal market for African industries, African businesses, and African people. Once its domestic natural gas system is fully developed, Tanzania intends to export some of the electricity it produces—but only as far as neighboring Kenya.[18]

I applaud the work of a consortium headed by South African independent SacOil in championing a 2,600-kilometer (1,615-mile), large-diameter natural gas pipeline from the Rovuma basin in northern Mozambique to Gauteng Province, where both Johannesburg and Pretoria are located. Dr. Thabo Kgogo, Interim CEO of SacOil, told the magazine ESI Africa that the project will "improve Africa's energy infrastructure landscape, support economic growth, increase the international competitiveness of southern African economies, create jobs and improve living standards."[19]

And, really, that is what's at the heart of the natural gas opportunity in Africa. Yes, investors from all over the world recognize the economic potential of tapping into uncharted resources. But, as the continent's energy industry grows, I believe that it is the people of Africa who must, and will, benefit the most.

But don't just take my word for it—consider these choice words from the Fourth China-WTO Accessions Roundtable in Nairobi in December 2015: "We believe that tackling barriers to intra-African trade can have disproportionate, positive effects on the poorest people. This makes greater African trade integration central to our own goal of ending poverty by 2030, and to the aspirations of African governments and communities."[20]

Ambitions Rise With More LNG

Would you believe that Africa is actually the site of the world's first commercial LNG liquefaction plant? It might be hard to imagine, given that the continent is behind much of the producing world when it comes to LNG, but a plant in Arzew, Algeria, came online in 1964.[21]

Unfortunately, the resource didn't quite take off in the beginning. But that's changing.

LNG is becoming a priority for Africa's emerging natural gas sector. This odorless, colorless, non-toxic, non-corrosive natural gas (predominantly methane with some portion of ethane) has been cooled to liquid form for ease of storage or transport—often by barge—to locations where pipelines are not practical or economical to build. Once LNG arrives at its destination, it is re-gasified and distributed, typically via pipeline.

"There is evidence throughout the continent that natural gas—more specifically, LNG—might be the answer, both to boost the African energy sector and to help individual countries improve their situations," Guillaume Doane pointed out in our interview. "Africa has a large, vibrant and young population whose demand for cheap and reliable energy is growing faster than any other part of the world. African countries should be able to depend on one another for the supply of that energy. Fulfilling this promise requires courageous leaders who have the will to do what is necessary to ensure that no country on the continent is left behind in the quest for prosperity and energy security."

Possibly one of the best examples Doane sees is Nigeria, which has a strong legacy as a long-time producer and exporter of LNG: "With the continent's largest gas reserves, Nigeria is now positioning itself as also one of the biggest producers of natural gas for domestic use. It is taking a serious look at reducing gas flaring and utilizing its resources for power generation and local industry."

As part of its goal of reducing the carbon intensity of its economy, South Africa is also undertaking an ambitious LNG-to-power project. The nation is currently in the bidding process to develop, finance, construct, and operate a 3,000 MW LNG-to-power plant. Regulatory delays and technical difficulties have caused a lag, but South Africa plans to use vessels offshore to receive, convert, and store the LNG it imports. Eskom, South Africa's power utility, agreed to purchase the electricity generated by the plant.

Africa Oil & Power says that financing and development structures are make-or-break factors for LNG-to-power projects. That's one reason South Africa (and others) have included floating storage and regasification facilities (FSRF) in their plans. At $300 to 500 million to build, these vessels cost about half as much as an onshore import terminal. In addition to reducing CAPEX, FSRF take only about two years to bring online, which means they shorten the overall project timeline considerably.

Elsewhere, Morocco is also considering the development of LNG import infrastructure, while Egypt has chartered two floating vessels for LNG storage. Investors in Ghana are considering funding a 1,300 MW LNG-to-power plant, which would lessen that country's dependence on the often-unreliable West African Gas Pipeline.

Maybe most exciting of all is that the advancements aren't just localized to nations with huge reserves.

In recent years, as LNG supply has increased and prices have fallen, LNG-to-power has been more broadly considered as an alternative solution for power generation. Since 2015, developments in LNG-to-power technologies have been a boon to African countries that lack their own supply of natural gas or don't have an import pipeline in place. Among them is Mozambique, which has plans in place to develop 10 LNG trains that would consume about 70 percent of the current discovered resource base, according to the World Bank.

I'm encouraged by the outlook for LNG on our continent: Industry consultant Douglas-Westwood predicted that global spending on

LNG facilities would rise by 88 percent by 2019, with $193 billion spent on liquefaction and shipping.[22]

Such industry growth represents a great opportunity for African countries with natural gas reserves, benefits that could easily extend to those countries' people.

Gabriel Mbaga Obiang Lima agrees: "Investing in domestic gas use industrializes the country: it creates new industries, diversifies the economy, and creates much-needed jobs."

Or, as the authors of "East Africa—Opportunities and Challenges for LNG in a New Frontier Region" noted, the income that deep-water LNG developments can generate for government—from job creation and taxes paid by employees to increased spending within local economies—could, in turn, drive even more employment and taxation.

"During the construction phase of an LNG project there could be 3,500 to 5,000 people directly engaged in building the plant; of these, some 80 percent would be skilled technicians to professional staff," they wrote.[23]

What's Standing in Our Way?

Such benefits could be compounded if several important stakeholders would lead the charge in promoting intra-African trading. As I've mentioned in Chapter 3's discussion of collaboration, it is vital for governments, indigenous companies, and continental consortia to band together. And we absolutely need African oil and gas traders, power producers, and industrialists to get on board.

Trading companies buy futures on the commodity market and lock in good prices for their customers, typically the refineries, utilities, or large office complexes with lots of spending power. To get the best deals for these customers, traders must keep their ears to the ground and not their heads in the sand. As a result, the traders have built sophisticated networks. They figured out long ago the importance of cross-border cooperation, and there is something to learn from them and their experiences.

Unfortunately, these traders can occasionally put a stranglehold on the market. We need to create a platform that requires some volume of natural gas to be set aside for African power projects. This is an absolute necessity for the sweeping industrialization required to gain the continent's competitive edge in the global economy.

In my estimation, small-scale LNG is the solution.

The bad news is that this means breaking the iron-clad hold of the energy traders who control LNG trading. Overwhelmingly, the traders are against small-scale LNG because that would cut into their sales to preferred buyers in Europe, Asia, and America. Instead, they would need to find alternative funding schemes to pay for their equity in LNG or other gas projects.

Africa's timeworn energy export strategy, perpetuated by our strong energy traders, is perhaps the biggest hold-up in gas-to-power development. We need policies that promote intra-Africa trading. True, some progress is being made with the Continental Free Trade Area (CFTA), which would increase intra-African trade by 52 percent by 2022, remove tariffs on 90 percent of goods, and eliminate unnecessary delays at border posts and other hindrances to successful intra-African trading. Until very recently, red tape held up the ratification of this critical intra-Africa free trade agreement: It only took effect with the signatures from 22 of the 55 African Union members. The hesitancy of some of our nations proves the point that exporting to potentially better-paying markets is a greater priority to some than building up our domestic base. In April 2019, The Gambia became the 22nd country to sign the CFTA, allowing the initiative to move ahead.

Guillaume Doane believes that successful intra-African energy trading also is being held back by the lack of infrastructure and investment capital: "Africa has less oil and gas export infrastructure than any other region in the world. The continent needs more pipelines and more export/import facilities that would enable trade," he said.

For smaller countries, the entire idea of developing appropriate gas-to-power infrastructure may seem forbidding. Because gas-fired plants are so efficient, they consume very low volumes of gas, which can make related gathering and inland transportation projects uneconomic. Creating a gas-to-power network doesn't always make sense on a nation-by-nation basis; there just aren't the economies of scale to support it, at least in terms of building the required upstream and midstream infrastructure.

But the fact is, even among the smallest economies, opportunity abounds.

Regional cross-border power cooperatives, with intra-regional generation hubs that also meet energy demands in neighboring countries, could be the answer across the continent. Host countries rich in natural gas could increase export revenues and develop crucial infrastructure, while their importing neighbors would have the electricity they need without having to build their own generating facilities. Everyone benefits!

"We believe this is an extremely viable solution for Africa: Countries with reliable access to fuels like LNG or propane can install enough generating capacity to meet their national needs as well as excess capacity that can be wheeled across the grid into neighboring power pool countries," APR Energy's Regional Sales Director Colm Quinn told *African Review*.[24]

To be fair, I should point out that Africa's natural gas consumption is still small compared to the rest of the world—just 109.8 billion cubic meters (bcm), approximately 3,849 bscf, or 3.4 percent of the global total in 2011. To put it into perspective, it takes Africans a year to use as much electricity as Americans do in just three days,[25] and average per-capita electricity consumption in the sub-Saharan regions is not enough to continuously power a single 50-watt light bulb.[26] But the volume is growing. The continent's gas consumption is rising about six percent a year, fueled by increased economic activity, infrastructure investments, and domestic price subsidies.

One chief obstacle to overcome in converting ample stores of natural gas into electricity is a lack of adequate gas transportation infrastructure to link fields with gas-to-power plants. Currently, aside from coastal Nigeria, there's virtually no gas pipeline infrastructure in sub-Saharan Africa.

But that might be changing as Nigeria negotiates to bring its gas resources to the continent's coastal countries.

The Trans-Saharan Gas Pipeline project, which will travel from the Nigerian border 841 kilometers (522 miles) to Algeria then 2,303 kilometers (1,431 miles) within the Algeria Gas Infrastructure pipeline, was finally approved in January 2017, some 8 years after the original agreement between Algeria and Nigeria was signed.[27] And Nigeria's Infrastructure Concession Regulatory Commission (ICRC) is working to develop an offshore gas pipeline that will link Nigeria with Morocco and eventually benefit 11 sub-Saharan West African nations: Benin, Togo, Ghana, Côte d'Ivoire, Liberia, Sierra Leone, Guinea, Guinea-Bissau, The Gambia, Senegal, and Mauritania. The Trans-Saharan Gas Pipeline is expected to have very low per-unit transportation costs and should carry enough gas to generate 5,000 MW of electricity. As a result of new gas resources in Nigeria and Ghana, the West African Gas Pipeline Company (WAPCo) says it would expand capacity from 170 mcf per day to 315 mcf per day.[28]

Banding Together

I'm not the only one with the desire for an energy-independent Africa—where African resources are used for the development of

African nations and all her people, where all Africans have access to electricity generated in their homeland, and where all African nations cooperate to spur industrial development and create jobs.

In fact, 18 nations from all regions of the continent believe so much in the importance of banding together that they created the African Petroleum Producers Organization (APPO). What began in 1987 as a collaboration among a select few African oil-producing powerhouses has doubled in size and expanded to include smaller producers as well. The most recent entrant was Niger in 2012, whose fledgling industry holds boundless promise.

The efforts to organize were led by Nigeria—along with cohorts Algeria, Angola, Benin, Cameroon, Republic of Congo, Gabon, and Libya—to begin moving toward energy independence, sustainable development, and economic diversification in Africa through cooperation in hydrocarbon research and technology.

To fulfill its mission, APPO set out these objectives:

- Member Countries' Cooperation: Increase cooperation among member countries and other global institutions in various sectors of the hydrocarbon industry.

- African Energy Development: Develop regional markets and coordinate pan-continental energy integration strategies.

- High-Level Studies and Partnerships: Provide education about the major challenges in the African energy sector.

- Socioeconomic Development: Promote economic development and market diversity by focusing on local procurement, employment, and gender diversification in the energy industry.

- Environmental Protection: Engage environmental protection and management policies.

- International Best Practices: Adopt international best practices.

- Organizational Visibility: Establish leadership energy matters within and beyond Africa.

Likewise, almost five years ago, Africa Oil & Power (AOP) came on the scene with much the same focus. In fact, Guillaume Doane co-founded the group as a platform to bring together "an elite class of ministers and senior-level government officials and top executives of private sector companies spanning the energy value chain, including upstream, downstream, engineering, construction, services, consulting, power generation, legal and finance." The organization holds a series of government-endorsed country-specific conferences, as well as an annual all-Africa event, to promote networking and high-level discussion on all the issues concerning the African energy space.

A strong advocate of the "Africa First" movement in support of African countries maximizing their natural resources for the benefit and betterment of their people, AOP's mission is to:

- Enable investment in the African energy industry, the world's most underexplored, underdeveloped, and overlooked region.

- Empower indigenous companies on the continent by promoting leadership, national content, technology, and entrepreneurship.
- Create engaging content experiences for the industry's biggest power brokers.

I love the missions of these associations. But so far, it's still not enough: APPO only accounts for a third of African countries, and AOP targets the elite dealmakers. We need to see more collaboration.

All African states have to put skin in the game. The big countries like Nigeria have to step up and show leadership—just like they did in getting APPO off and running. The energy companies need to bring in good lawyers and advisors who understand the market. And we all need to talk to each other and learn from one another.

That's the kind of collaboration and advocacy I had in mind when I co-founded the African Energy Chamber (AEC) in early 2018.

The AEC initiative promotes opportunities for growth and expansion of indigenous African companies across the continent, from personnel training to community partnerships to relationship building. Within a short period, we have become the voice of the oil and gas sector in Africa. Our ultimate goal is to see African companies grow and take the lead in the development of their continent.

The AEC is the continent's voice for ongoing change and progress in the African energy industry. From the robust regulatory reforms of Angola to the interest of the Republic of Congo in OPEC to the impressive local content strides taken by South Sudan, the AEC stands firmly with the re-emergence of Africa's energy industry.[29]

I remain active with the chamber today and serve as its executive chairman, speaking and writing regularly on its behalf. In addition, several key colleagues who helped form the group still participate actively in our work. We are all deeply committed and believe strongly in our collaboration.

We know that our efforts are already making a difference.

In less than a year of existence, the group helped Equatorial Guinea—one of the continent's biggest LNG exporters—execute memoranda of understanding that facilitated an LNG sales agreement with Ghana and negotiated LNG supply and construction of transport infrastructure with Burkina Faso. I expect that these concrete examples are just the start.

Another promising cooperative effort is LNG2Africa. This initiative brokers deals in the private sector, leading to inter-African sales and purchase agreements and creating opportunities for the development of this industry across the continent.

Perhaps more importantly, the initiative promotes collaboration and the sharing of knowledge among producers and consumers to facilitate best practices and foster infrastructure development. As the LNG2Africa website explains, "Through LNG2Africa, beneficiaries across the LNG value chain will exchange knowledge and data and will commission technical studies for the construction of regasification and LNG storage terminals and transportation infrastructure, either by pipeline or LNG carrier."

Initiatives such as APPO, Africa Oil & Power, and LNG2Africa are helping establish a voice for our continent. Africa will yet affirm the IEA's rhetorical question and prove that it is, indeed, the Golden Age of Natural Gas—and that natural gas will spur our own Golden Age of prosperity and achievement.

I'm confident that, if we work together to make sure that we use African gas for Africa first, Africa will indeed fill up our coffers.

6

MONETIZING NATURAL RESOURCES: SUCCESSES, LESSONS, AND RISKS

NIGERIA IS RESOURCE RICH and energy poor.

The country ranks sixth in the world in oil production, tenth in proven oil reserves, and eighth in proven natural gas reserves. Still, it has failed to use its potential energy to keep the lights on, get people moving, or power the economy.

Instead, oil is being exported, and gas is being wasted. Electricity is sporadic in many parts of Nigeria—at best, a dependable supply is available only about 40 percent of the day. What can you expect when you're producing only 4 GW of functioning power capacity for a country of nearly 200 million? Will flipping a switch illuminate the darkness or start a motor whirring? There's no guarantee.

The people—42 percent of them impoverished—remain grid-locked without adequate transportation fuel.

The industrial base is sedentary, not just because it lacks production feedstock but also because it's impossible to grow reliable businesses on generators when the power goes out. How can the country hope to attract foreign investment without electricity? Imagine you're a Silicon Valley chip producer, and you're considering taking advantage of the nation's human capital to operate a manufacturing facility here. When there's no electricity for the better part of the day, what do you do? Buy fuel and pass the cost along to your customers? What sane consumer would buy an expensive product when there are cheaper alternatives from countries with 24/7 electricity supply?

The bigger question is: How can a smart nation have so much, but do so little with it?

One problem is that Nigeria is hardly harnessing its natural gas resources at all. Less than 17 percent of the country's 193 tcf proved reserves are being put into service. About 184 tcf is considered "stranded," meaning it cannot be delivered economically to market. But even worse, because the country lacks adequate infrastructure, such as pipelines and storage facilities, more than half of the natural gas associated with crude oil production—some 63 percent—is routinely flared, or burned off, every single day.

In a very real sense, wealth that could be trickling down to the pocketbooks of Nigeria's people is going up in a veritable vapor cloud.

Flaring: A Lose-Lose for Africa

Although the practice has long been part and parcel of hydrocarbon production, flaring is wasteful, harmful to the environment, dangerous to people and animals nearby—and it's been banned in Nigeria for more than 30 years. However, you'd never guess it by how much flaring goes on: about 700 mcf per day and climbing. That's no petty amount, by the way. It is equivalent to roughly one-quarter of the current power consumption of the entire continent.[1] Prefer a hard currency comparison? Nigeria loses $18 million daily from flaring.

Though more than 65 percent of government revenue is from oil,[2] it is estimated that about $2.5 billion is lost annually through gas flaring.

The federal government cracks down on flaring from time to time, but to little effect. The gas flare penalty of $.03 per mscf isn't enough to discourage oil and gas companies that find flaring an inexpensive alternative to other disposal methods. As proof, consider that flared gas rose from 244.84 bscf in 2016 to 287.59 bscf in 2017, an increase of about 18 percent. Now there's a new plan to end gas flaring in Nigeria by 2020, but experts are pessimistic it will succeed. The incentives aren't there, they say, and neither is the infrastructure, regulatory framework, or legislative heft to support it.[3]

Unfortunately, this isn't just a Nigerian story. Across the continent, gas is stranded or flared. Only ten percent of Africa's gas reserves are monetized.

But what if, instead of leaving natural gas in the ground or burning it off, we could capture, store, transport, and use it? Just imagine: Africa could produce dry gas for local consumption or turn it into electricity, as discussed in Chapter 5. We could convert it into exportable LNG, a process that has made gas fungible in many other producing nations. We'd have a steady feedstock supply for manufacturing and an effective source of electricity for commercial and residential use. Create jobs and develop local expertise. Reduce pollution. And be able to leverage our on-the-ground global energy experience to benefit ourselves, not just add profits to a Western company's financial statement.

As the world depends more and more on natural gas—demand is expected to grow by as much as 40 percent by 2030—the economic implications of monetizing our gas reserves are staggering.

To accelerate the pace of development and keep more money from going up in smoke, we have to learn from countries that were once in the same place Nigeria is now.

The lessons start now. And we don't have far to go to find them.

Equatorial Guinea Capitalizes on LNG

As I've noted, one of the main challenges for monetizing natural gas is that it requires extensive infrastructure—something that's currently in short supply in many parts of Africa. But it doesn't have to be that way. For one thing, the development of LNG has made it easier to bring stranded gas to market—LNG takes up less space, is more economical to transport across large distances, and can be stored in larger quantities.

On the continent, one country that is taking advantage of that fact is Equatorial Guinea.

Equatorial Guinea entered the energy sector when large crude oil reserves were discovered in 1996. By 2016, it was one of Africa's largest oil producers. Like everyone else in the oil business, though, the country has been sorely affected by market volatility, especially as oil accounts for 90 percent of the government's revenue.[4]

With 1.3 tcf of proven natural gas reserves—a mere fraction of Nigeria's total—Equatorial Guinea is using the promise of LNG and condensates to diversify away from the volatility of its oil-heavy revenue base and bring prosperity to its people. The country has already made substantial progress toward those goals, and their work shows what can happen when government and major energy companies work together for the good of the populace.

In 2018, for example, Equatorial Guinea signed an agreement with Noble Energy—a Fortune 1000 company from Texas—that is expected to make the country the gas nexus of the eastern Gulf of Guinea. The contract set the framework for the development of natural gas from the offshore Alen field and outlined the high-level commercial terms for Alen natural gas to be supplied to the Punta Europa gas complex, AMPCO methanol plant, and Equatorial Guinea LNG plant.[5] The agreement also includes the construction of a gas pipeline that will run 65 kilometers from the field to the processing plants.[6]

At the same time, the government announced it will build what it is calling a natural gas megahub at Punta Europa, helping the country become a significant player in the global LNG exports market. The project is expected to bring in $2 billion in revenues. But it's not just big business—it's an unprecedented opportunity for the country's citizens. Minister of Mines and Hydrocarbons H.E Gabriel Mbaga Obiang Lima believes the project will create 3,000 direct and indirect jobs. He is determined, too, that local companies will be part of the value chain.

As if that weren't enough, Equatorial Guinea also inked a deal with Togo to facilitate LNG trade between the two countries. The agreement is part of the LNG2Africa initiative, which is dedicated to linking African gas to Africa first. According to press reports, Togo will study the import and regasification of LNG and its use for power generation.[7] A similar agreement between Equatorial Guinea and Burkina Faso may be in the works.

And, I must mention, if you look upward, you won't see much gas flaring. Instead, the unused gas production is now reinjected to aid oil production.

That's progress. But what about the other plans underway? Are they likely to lead to Equatorial Guinea achieving its goals? All signs point to success. The country has these critical factors in place:

- Access to finance
- Infrastructure
- Intellectual capital
- A sound legislative framework with government support for the industry to encourage investment
- Cooperation

Not so coincidentally, those are the same elements at work in places like Qatar and Trinidad and Tobago—where monetizing natural gas has become somewhat of an art form.

Qatar's Quest for World Domination

Qatar is so tiny one writer said it was small enough to fit in your pocket.[8] Yet the Arab nation has the world's largest gas reserves—872 tcf, or about 4 times the total of Nigeria's—and the planet's highest GDP, thanks largely to oil production. It's hardly content to rest upon these considerable laurels, however, declaring its intention to be the "Gas Capital of the World."

It doesn't appear to have far to go.

Since 1949, when what is now the industrial city of Umm Said was established as a tanker terminal, major oil and gas companies have put down roots there. The city has also been the incubator for homegrown businesses, including natural gas feedstock users Qatar Fertilizer Company—which is the world's largest single-site producer of ammonia and urea—and Qatar Petrochemical Company. The world's largest gas-to-liquid (GTL) plants are in Qatar, and with Qatargas operating 14 LNG plants, the country supplies more LNG than anyone else.[9]

As part of Qatar's quest for world gas domination, it is expanding its LNG capacity by further developing the North Field natural gas, which already accounts for nearly all its gas production. With a target completion date of 2024, the project is expected to bring in $40 billion in additional export revenue, while income from LNG sales are projected to leave the government with a budget surplus of $44 billion.[10] That extra cash will be earmarked for Qatar's sovereign wealth fund.

Learn From the Master: Trinidad and Tobago

If Qatar's abundant natural gas resources make replicating their example seem impossible, taking a look at Trinidad and Tobago may be more instructive.

The twin-island nation off the coast of Venezuela contains less than 1 percent of known global reserves of natural gas, about 16 tcf—or less than one-tenth of what Nigeria holds. Despite this, it has become the world's leading exporter of two gas-based products—ammonia and methanol—and is among the top 5 exporting countries of LNG. This is particularly impressive considering its LNG business didn't kick off until 1991, and its game-changing LNG Train 4, which has a capacity of 5.2 million metric tonnes per annum, has only been online since 2005.[11]

How did it achieve so much with so little in such a short amount of time?

Much of the credit belongs to the government, which jump-started the energy sector in the 1970s through equity investment—although it benefited from a bit of luck when those efforts came on the heels of the Arab oil embargo. The supply restrictions sent the price of oil soaring, at least by 70s standards, from $3 per barrel in 1972 to $12 per barrel 2 years later. With well-timed new discoveries off Trinidad's east coast, the country had a sudden revenue windfall, money the government invested wisely in initiatives to improve the state's social and economic well-being. That included the construction of the Point Lisas Industrial Estate, which was designed to accommodate industries that used islands' natural gas as feedstock.[12]

Investment was just one part of the government's strategy, however.

Through policy actions, it vigorously promoted E&P, attracting a variety of investors to develop its gas reserves. Other policies facilitated the development of a petrochemical industry, leading to the growth of its giant methanol and ammonia export business.

What's more, the country has never been shy about riding herd over its hydrocarbon resources. After buying Shell's operations in 1974, the government began to steward the nation's reserves even more actively, nearly to the point of nationalizing the entire sector. While it initially stopped short of that step, it devised a plan to assert more control over both oil and gas production through its "Third Way" policies—a centrist agenda that subsequently led to the creation of the National Gas Company and the eventual monetization of the country's abundant supplies of natural gas. The government later put a plan in place to further shift away from oil, promote competition to attract new business (and enhance the state's share of the profits), and privatize local industry.

More recently, the government has segued from an investor role to a more regulatory position. Typically, it divests itself of interests when its involvement is no longer considered strategic—in other words, when its place can be filled by foreign investors. However, there's no question that the government's early equity position and hands-on involvement created the framework for how Trinidad and Tobago's energy resources would create wealth for its people—a foundation that's standing strong today.

With the government determined to see the islands achieve developed nation status by 2020, revenues from hydrocarbon development are being used to support five priorities: developing innovative people, nurturing a caring society, governing effectively, enabling competitive businesses, and investing in a sound infrastructure and environment. Much like Equatorial Guinea and Togo, Trinidad is looking to its neighbors for help achieving its ambitions. In 2018, Trinidad signed an agreement with Venezuela to import and process its natural gas, specifically that coming from the offshore Dragon

Field. The deal will close any domestic supply gap that Trinidad might experience, and we only have to look back to the period from 2013 to 2016 to see why this is important: Low availability forced the Atlantic LNG plant to reduce its output, squeezing revenues. The pace will also ensure that Venezuela can process and monetize its currently stranded natural gas field. In short, it's a win-win for both countries.

Where's the Win-Win for Africa?

It's not a pipe dream to think that Africa can benefit from its natural resources in the same way Qatar and Trinidad are—the experience of Equatorial Guinea shows it's possible. Africa has been called the next frontier in the oil and gas industry, largely on the strength of our natural gas reserves, including an estimated 100 tcf discovered in Mozambique and Tanzania. As I told Forbes magazine late in 2018, Africa's LNG export volumes are about to rise dramatically with involvement by Gazprom in Cameroon, Fortuna in Equatorial Guinea, Anadarko, and ExxonMobil in Mozambique, and Total in Tanzania. Even Nigeria is moving in the right direction: They are working harder to reduce flaring and have a new LNG train coming online.

I'm happy to say that good policies are coming, and some heavy-handed regulations are being rolled back. That will help Africa better control her own future.

But that's only part of the equation. To truly keep this frontier from becoming a wasteland, it will take effective and transparent leadership. The average man or woman has no idea if they are getting a fair deal from the exploration of their country's natural resources. Do most Nigerians know one reason they don't have electric power on demand is because the state-owned oil company is flaring the generating source? Can you imagine the outrage if they did? Their resources, their riches disappearing before their eyes.

Sadly, lack of transparency is just part of the problem. Mismanagement, corruption, abysmal rule of law, poor protection of investment, lack of human resources, and absent or crumbling infrastructure also plague Africa—preventing us from turning opportunity into prosperity. We are not doing all we can to enable exploration: As I explained in Forbes, there is no doubt that Nigeria's much-delayed Petroleum Industry Bill has slowed exploration activity in onshore and offshore areas and, most important, gas monetization.[13]

As the examples I cited suggest, there are certain things in common among countries that have successfully monetized their natural gas resources. It's not really possible to boil everything down to a simple list of dos and don'ts, but some of the more productive factors are:

- Taking a market-led approach, focused on efficiency in the flows of capital, goods, and ideas.

- Maximizing oil investor confidence in the rule of law, the enforcement of contracts, and the protection of labor rights.

- Encouraging mutually beneficial partnerships between multinational and indigenous oil and gas companies.

- State entities need to ensure that they have a participating share in all future gas projects.

- Retaining production in kind for use in the domestic market or trading abroad.

- Taking a greater role in decision making and more active participation in operations.

- Devising a favorable legislative framework.

- Developing a fair structure of taxation, royalties, levies, and bonuses.[14]

- Linking markets, including domestic consumption.

- Promoting security and stability to protect foreign and domestic investment.

We can put gas to work to create a more profitable environment for business, meet our energy needs, and capitalize on the potential it represents for our future. We can be both resource rich and energy rich—and I mean that in terms of human energy as well as keeping the lights on.

We Can't Slow Down Now

The past 20 years have been a rollercoaster for Africa's oil and gas production. In 2000, the continent produced almost 8 million bbl/d; by 2010, it topped 10 million bbl/d. While many thought this upward trend could continue, 2017 saw yields drop back to the 8 million mark.

This 20-year up-and-down cycle coincided with oil prices. The high global oil prices, exceeding $100 per barrel on average between 2000 and 2014, created huge revenues for oil producers on the continent. The earnings also spurred some serious exploration activities in heretofore largely unexplored areas, making it all the more difficult for producers to adjust when average prices sank to $50 per barrel. Accustomed to higher earnings and the resulting freedom to try new things, they reacted by trimming their exploratory efforts and focusing instead on the known plays.

It's understandable that industry players want to staunch the bleeding, but cutting down exploration is the exact opposite of what is needed to maintain and grow a robust sector.

We've always known that the oil and gas market is volatile. It's a high-risk, high-reward field. But it seems that many of us forgot this (or chose not to plan for the ride) during the glut at the onset of this century. A lot of our colleagues decided to cut and run with whatever profits they had left, rather than dig in and pursue new yields.

I worry now that we are not seeing the warning signs of a greater fall to come because we are not looking at the fundamentals.

Exploration Is a Must!

In 2018, the number of oil and gas rigs in Africa reached a three-year high, according to Baker Hughes.[15] So clearly, E&P is still alive and well as I write this book, but I'd hate to see rates plummet the next time oil prices drop.

Case in point: The oil price crash we saw in 2014 became a deterrent to high-cost, high-risk oil and gas exploration. Across the continent, we need an enabling environment that encourages continued—and enhanced—E&P.

"Without major exploration and production, the oil-dependent economies of West Africa, in particular, are on a fast-track to terminal production decline," Oxford Energy Forum analysts James McCullagh and Virendra Chauhan wrote, "The production profiles will be all the more disconcerting for future governments given the continued lack of economic diversification in many countries."[16]

Currently, national oil companies are the "weakest link" when it comes to driving E&P forward.

Equatorial Guinea's Gabriel Mbaga Obiang Lima put it bluntly: "Africa's national oil companies are in a coma: No recommendations, no suggestions, no speaking up and trying to find solutions. They just produce less, have less revenue, and complain more."

It's time to wake up!

Fostering Foreign Investment

The African petroleum market continues to represent tremendous opportunities for foreign producers.

Just ask Nyonga Fofang, Managing Director of the private equity firm Bambili Group, which has pan-African investments and clients. An alumnus of Harvard University, Fofang's career spans more than 20 years, including Wall Street, international capital markets, and service on the board of Standard Chartered Bank. He has spoken about significant growth potential in Africa's petroleum market despite the likelihood of continued volatility.

"The frontier exploration areas in Africa are generating a lot of buzz, and for good reason," Fofang told Africa Oil & Power in 2018. "Countries like Namibia and Uganda, which have seen recent discoveries of oil and gas, are ripe for investors. In addition to positive exploration potential, the countries offer stable regulatory frameworks for investors. On the east coast, Tanzania and Mozambique are still creating a lot of excitement from mega gas finds. The development of these fields and the implications for LNG exports and gas-to-power programs in southern Africa are game changing. These areas and others will provide significant opportunities."[17]

Fofang has called upon African leaders and businesses to do more to encourage investors to capitalize on these opportunities.

"We would like to see more investment in infrastructure, energy, agriculture and health," he said in 2017. "Given the strategic importance of some of these areas, this would require public-private partnership models."[18]

I strongly agree with my friend: We should be charming investors with better incentives for exploration. Let's consider a few pathways that help drive strong, consistent E&P activity.

- **Visionary leadership.** We need leaders who will make it attractive for African producers to seek out new resource pockets. Their ability to resolve cross-border disputes is key. Our leadership must start being more pragmatic. And this means making some difficult decisions that might not be popular among the wealthy power players, as you'll see below.

- **Removing regulatory bottlenecks.** There is no reason to wait for many years just to get approvals to begin production from a field. This is horrible. Many companies would rather invest in commercially viable fields in the United States where they can get a good return on investment than wait for decades for regulatory approvals in Africa.

- **Smaller plays.** We need to make the license maps smaller to attract small players. Breaking up the blocks into smaller sections will give the independents a competitive edge and ultimately benefit the entire industry. Encourage (or require) the large producers to relinquish some of the areas they are not exploring to small players.

- **Stronger fiscal framework.** We need to change the fiscal framework to support the needs of marginal plays. We need better regulations, not more of them. And increasing taxes on oil companies and service companies at this time does not help. Instead, we need better fiscal terms like breaks on value-added taxes and import duties.

- **Local content.** Oil and gas producers in Africa must unequivocally look to Africans for both labor and leadership. And African producers must continue to expand cross-border transactions that keep African resources on the continent.

- **Regional content.** Speaking of cross-border transactions and keeping resources on the continent, we should think about expanding our definition of local content to take other African countries into account. Certainly, it makes sense for every African state to work towards the goal of making sure that home-grown entrepreneurs play a role in oil and gas development, either directly or indirectly. But no single country can do it all. When we have a need we can't meet on our own, we should look close to home—to neighboring and nearby states—before we turn to foreign suppliers. (I'll talk more about this in Chapter 9.)

Pushing Production

Given its expansive energy industry, production discussions often focus on Nigeria. Its many successful legacy fields have consistently produced vast quantities of oil. But even here amid the tried-and-true, new frontiers await for exploration opportunities, with offshore discoveries at depths of 1,000–1,500m.[19] In fact, recent exploration of Nigeria's offshore Owowo field revealed 1 bbo, spurring the Nigerian National Petroleum Corporation (NNPC) to implore investors to amp up their exploration in this mostly untested yet clearly prolific play. The NNPC sees $48 billion in investment opportunities for capital projects within the country's oil and gas industry.[20]

The prospects aren't limited to this energy powerhouse. The entire continent is seeing a surge in capital expenditure in the sector: Some $194 billion has already been allocated for E&P at 93 upcoming oil and gas fields through 2025.

A number of other countries have also been taking steps to show their commitment to the fundamentals of E&P—and I hope that many more will follow their lead.

Angola: This petroleum powerhouse is a seasoned industry giant. Commercial production began as far back as the mid-1950s, and oil overtook coffee as the country's leading export in 1973. But since reaching an all-time high production level of almost 2 million bbl/d in March 2010—almost vying with Nigeria for the top spot—Angola's industry has been sagging.[21] In 2018, production levels averaged 1.55 million bbl/d; in March 2019, the figure was even lower, at 1.37 million bbl/d[22]—although this is still impressive enough to garner the second-highest spot in sub-Saharan Africa.

The production decline resulted from aging fields and shy investors; neither of those factors is surprising. But given that the country sits atop 9 bbo of proven oil resources and 11 tcf of proven natural gas reserves, the government is attuned to the potential for significant economic growth a booming petroleum sector could bring—with good governance.

Since taking office in 2017, Angolan President João Lourenço has been making major changes to the country's oil sector. In May 2018, he introduced reform measures to renew interest in development areas that have been suspended due to low yields, with specific targets to boost production by opening marginal fields to African independents. By December 2018, several new laws to encourage E&P were on the books.

This included a Natural Gas Regulatory Framework, the country's first law regulating natural gas exploration, production, monetization, and commercialization, providing guidance and offering more attractive tax rates to encourage investors. The reform measures also streamline the regulations to better facilitate foreign investors' entry into the nation's oil sector. One of the most important regulatory changes was the creation of an independent regulator, the National Agency for Petroleum, Gas, and Biofuels, which took over the management of Angola's oil and gas concessions. Previously, state oil company Sonangol had that responsibility. Now Sonangol will function solely as an E&P company. The change was a smart move: Foreign companies most likely will appreciate the opportunity to work with a neutral entity and the improved business environment they can now experience in Angola.[23]

In 2019, Angola continued its efforts to bring foreign E&P companies back to the country by announcing plans to auction nine blocks in the Namibe basin and selling parts of Sonangol.[24]

Republic of Congo: In the face of the global oil and gas slowdown, Minister of Hydrocarbons Jean-Marc Thystère Tchicaya affirmed his country's determination in late 2018 to "develop our mining sector to ensure the renewal of our reserves of liquid and gaseous hydrocarbons."[25]

As sub-Saharan Africa's third-largest oil producer, with an output of 333,000 bbl/d in 2018, the Republic of Congo has spent the past several years on a crusade to promote its energy investment opportunities. Most notably, in 2016, the nation reformed its hydrocarbon regulations to encourage operators to expand their E&P efforts. The government also decreased royalties for natural gas operations in frontier zones from 15 percent to 12 percent. The new regulations also removed cost transfers between permits and allowed international exploration companies to import certain goods and equipment tax-free.

Another method of promoting the development of the industry is to encourage exploration of shallow-water offshore plays. Licensing for ten offshore blocks in the shallow Coastal Basin were expected to be evaluated in September 2019. Companies that pledge their support of the national oil company SNPC's regional 3D seismic project, covering 5,000 square kilometers of the Peu Profond area of the Congo Shelf, will receive early consideration.

The government also wisely introduced a new policy to ensure stability. Even if lawmakers later amend the country's fiscal regime, any signed production-sharing contracts will be upheld. This stability policy ensures that the overall economic equilibrium of the contract will be maintained.

Equatorial Guinea: Fields in Equatorial Guinea are facing the natural decline in production that comes with age. But although investment will likely decrease every year, E&P activity should show a slight increase. This is expected, in part, because of the late-2018 introduction of 11 new oil and gas wells to be drilled over the next year, at a total planned investment of $2.4 billion.

Low investment in exploration could be the new norm; gone are the days of one dollar in six or seven going to exploration. Despite this trend, we're seeing a modest uptick in Equatoguinean drilling activity. Lima said that the country has taken advantage of the slowdown by using the time to review and improve its policies.

"We have been busy in the downturn, working to improve our regulatory environment and attract new investment to the sector," he said. "Now that the oil price is at a sustainable level, activity in the oil and gas sector is set to take off at an unprecedented pace."[26]

Lima explained that his country's oil industry didn't simply stand passively by during the price crash; rather, they went straight to the global power players to begin dialogue, create alliances, and learn as much as possible about pricing and market strategies. They even became a full member of OPEC in May 2017.

Lima believes that a key difference with Equatorial Guinea's energy sector—and the secret of its success—is that they take the best practices of other African producers and adapt them to fit the local environment. The Ministry of Mines and Hydrocarbons has embraced the notion that the oil and gas industry is lightning-fast to transform, which means they understand the need for flexibility with regulations and planning.

In fact, the Ministry is so committed to improving the sector that it named 2019 "The Year of Energy." This campaign emphasizes the country's dedication to its energy industry, from strengthening regional oil and gas partnerships to investing in sustainable in-country growth.

And the country remains dedicated to home-grown efforts. In July 2018, the Ministry ordered operators to cancel all contracts with Canada's CHC Helicopters because of the company's noncompliance with local content regulations. As Lima explained, "These laws are in place to protect and promote local industry, create jobs for citizens, promote the sustainable development of our country, and we are aggressively monitoring and enforcing the compliance of these requirements."[27]

Later in the year, Lima issued a mandate to operators to suspend operations with some multinational oil service companies for their failure "to work within the confines of our very flexible and pragmatic local content regulations that are market driven and ensure that both investors and our citizens benefit." The Ministry made it clear that it will continue to actively monitor the compliance of all service companies and issue further suspensions as found.

Gabon: Gabon has been producing oil for more than 50 years. Its peak production in the early 2000s reached 370,000 bbl/d, and it remains one of the top 5 producers in sub-Saharan Africa. To counter the natural decline of its mature fields, the government has looked to offshore resources, where some 70 percent of the country's reserves are expected to be found.

The country has also reworked its hydrocarbon code. A significant change eliminates the corporate income tax for producing oil companies. Royalties are now set at 5 percent for oil and 2 percent for gas, and the state's share of profits dropped from 55 percent to 50 percent in conventional zones and from 50 percent to 45 percent in deepwater areas.[28] In addition, cost recovery limits increased from 65 percent to 70 percent for conventional oil zones and from 75 percent to 80 percent for deepwater oil; limits for natural gas rose from 65 percent to 75 percent for conventional and from 75 percent to 90 percent for deepwater.

The Ministry of Petroleum and Hydrocarbons hopes these initiatives will revitalize operators' interest in its 12th offshore licensing round of 11 shallow and 23 deepwater blocks, which opened in November 2018.

At the same time, Gabon has also been focusing on supporting smaller local independents while increasing employment opportunities and training for nationals. The revised code established a special economic zone to make sure the infrastructure promotes in-country efforts.

"The existence of this special economic zone is very important to support the industries that will build up around oil and gas exploration . . . A strong economic base will arise from these areas," Minister of Petroleum and Hydrocarbons Pascal Houangni Ambouroue said in March 2018. "A part of that is ensuring that there are enough skilled workers, and so training is now playing a key role in Gabon. We are putting in every effort to make sure we have the process in place to ensure that our workers are up to date with the modern trends in the oil and gas industry."[29]

Kenya: Exploration in Kenya can be traced back as far as the 1950s, but there were no commercially viable discoveries until 2012. That's when the South Lokichar Basin revealed 750 million barrels of recoverable oil. These days, Kenya appears to be making further strides toward boosting E&P.

Taking a huge leap forward, President Uhuru Kenyatta signed the Kenyan Petroleum Exploration Development and Production Bill in March 2019.[30] The passage marks a significant milestone. In addition to strengthening the country's comprehensive contracting, exploration, development, and production framework, one of the bill's main provisions is to earmark 25 percent of the revenue from all oil and gas produced in the country for county and local governments. This is being accomplished through a trust fund managed by a board of trustees established by the local leadership.

In addition, the Kenyan government entered into an agreement with the Kenya Joint Venture, whose constituents are Tullow Oil Kenya BV, Africa Oil Kenya BV, and Total Oil, to develop a pipeline to link Kenyan oil fields with the international market. The 820-kilometer Lamu-Lokichar Crude Oil Pipeline is set to come online in 2022. An environmental study concluded at the end of 2018, and feasibility studies are currently underway.

Unfortunately, early 2019 ushered in some disappointing news about multiple multinationals, including Hunting Alpha, Africa Oil, and Royal Dutch Shell limiting Kenyan operations (or pulling out of Kenya entirely) due to perceived "subdued" levels of productivity and "modest activity forecast for East Africa in the medium-term."[31]

Here's hoping that the March 2019 bill will help turn that around. Perhaps a glimmer of hope is that while Royal Dutch Shell relinquished two blocks where it had been exploring, it actually acquired new exploration licenses in other markets.

Cameroon: Cameroon's outlook in early 2018 was discouraging: Only one company responded to Cameroon's latest licensing round. Eight blocks were up for grabs in the Rio del Rey and Douala/Kribi-Campo (DKC) basins,[32] and Perenco was the only company to respond. But even here, we've seen some promising developments on the E&P front.

Cameroon's NOC, Société Nationale des Hydrocarbures (SNH), and the local subsidiary of Perenco signed a Production Sharing Agreement for oil exploration in the Bomana block in February 2019. The field covers 22.75 square kilometers in the Rio del Rey basin, an eastern extension of the prolific Niger Delta Basin.[33]

Victoria Oil & Gas announced in June 2018 that there is more natural gas in its Logbaba gas and condensate field than originally thought. The company now says the proven and probable reserves there total 309 billion standard cubic feet, which is up 52 percent from its previous estimate[34] and should support a production rate of 90 mscf/d for 10 years.

In addition, an appraisal campaign in the offshore Etinde Field was deemed a success in October 2018.[35] Another offshore project is moving forward, too: as of this writing, Tower Resources was preparing to begin drilling at the Thali project.[36]

Cameroon lawmakers also are reviewing a new petroleum code with the possibility of it becoming law in 2019.

Successful Mergers That Breed Cooperation

The exploration success rate in African has dropped from some 40 percent to 35 percent over the past decade. The decline has highlighted the importance of acquisitions as an alternative, albeit generally more expensive, way to build resources. Oil and gas players on the continent should consider mergers with service companies to better enable them to tie profitable acquisitions to an exploration component.

Something I find particularly promising is that, from 2017 to 2018, intraregional cross-border deals from all sectors tripled (in terms of aggregate value) from $418 million to $1,292 million.[37]

This is a great sign of African cooperation—the teamwork we surely need but still sorely lack across the board.

We need to continue with efforts like that, and anything else we can realistically do, to continue driving E&P.

As Minister Lima said, complacency is our enemy.

"For many years, we have been enjoying having a 'wagon in the train' and just looking at the world from our comfortable seats built upon good prices and production levels," he said. "The crisis (of 2014) made us realize that geopolitics and interacting with our environment matter. From this moment, we can choose to be the victims of changing currents, or we can decide to change and do something about it."

Lima goes so far as to encourage the concept of an "African oil basket" where all producers on the continent would bundle their crude to boost its overall value and give Africa's producers more leverage on the world stage. Similar to the OPEC Reference Basket (ORB), this bundle would set a benchmark oil price based on the average of prices for all the blends produced on African soil.

Lima says all energy ministers must participate in industry events and learn from each other.

"The more the interrelationship, the better. We have got to know each other much better, and we are nowadays definitely talking more than before," he said. "We need to move away from our worry that we can't do it. We need to lose the fear that we cannot operate. There is a learning curve, and we need to start learning."

7

JOB CREATION: MAKING OUR OWN MULTIPLIER EFFECT

In 2017, the International Growth Centre (IGC) published a study[1] showing that Mozambique has gained quite a lot from Anadarko Petroleum's discovery of large natural gas deposits in the Rovuma Basin. For example, the discovery has led to the creation of 10,000 new jobs between 2010 and 2013. It has also captured the interest of international oil companies (IOCs), which has, in turn, attracted companies working in other sectors. As a result, the total amount of foreign direct investment (FDI) moving into the country rose by billions of dollars each year, with $9 billion worth of FDI reported in 2014 alone.

And the benefits don't stop there: The additional inflows created even more new jobs, with census data indicating that the number of FDI-related positions had risen to nearly 131,500 as of 2014. What's more, each FDI-related position generates, on average, another 6.2 openings in the same sector and the same area.

The study's conclusion? The Rovuma Basin gas discoveries may have given rise to nearly 1 million jobs in Mozambique. This is wonderful news, given that the total number of jobs in the country is only around 9.5 million!

But there's a catch.

Mozambique didn't exactly generate those 1 million new positions by itself. IOCs brought in expatriate staff. In turn, the expatriates needed local goods and services. They established connections with Mozambican firms so that they could get them, and their actions caused the multiplier effect to kick in.

So, what's the lesson here? Do these numbers demonstrate that FDI is Africa's primary target and that every country on the continent ought to aspire to attract outside investors?

I hope not. Instead, I think that Mozambique's example should inspire Africans to create their own multiplier effect. I believe it can help us understand that IOCs such as Anadarko and Royal Dutch Shell are not the only entities that can help spread the gains made by the oil and gas industry into other sectors of the economy.

This is not to say that African countries should spurn the idea of working with major foreign companies. Not at all! We can't succeed with zero input from outside. Corporate giants can help us acquire the skills, technology, and corporate cultural norms we need to maximize our success. But they aren't the only source of value.

It ought to start with us.

More specifically, it ought to start with small and medium-sized enterprises (SMEs).

Starting Small (and Medium-Sized)

Currently, the majority of everyday Africans work for SMEs. They work for tiny mom-and-pop shops, for mid-sized companies, and every type of operation in between. These enterprises may be small compared to, say, Shell, but they do have certain advantages over multinational titans. They interact more directly with customers, and they have a better grasp of what will work—and what will *not* work—in local markets.

In many cases, SMEs have an even better understanding than government agencies and state-owned companies of what their clients truly want and need. They are also more nimble than government-run institutions because they do not have to navigate quite as many bureaucratic obstacles when they decide they would rather work with a local partner or a contractor than complete a job on their own.

This is true across the board, in multiple sectors of the economy. In upstream oil and gas operations, for example, a mid-sized Angolan firm that is extracting 1,000 bbl/d of petroleum from a marginal field may be able to hire an emergency cleanup crew relatively easily, without having to navigate the multi-layered bureaucratic barriers that govern access to Sonangol's human resources department. In the oilfield services industry, the deputy director of a small Nigerian marine engineering company may be more likely to know where she can rent extra boats on an irregular basis than her counterpart at a European conglomerate.

In the realm of transport, the district manager of a mid-sized Chadian trucking company may have access to the same maps and GPS equipment as his counterpart at an international operator serving half the continent—and far more knowledge about where to find a mechanic for emergency repair jobs on back roads near the border with Sudan. In retail food sales, the owners of a mom-and-pop general store serving work camps near Uganda's Lake Albert oilfields may be able to use family networks in the Democratic Republic of Congo to secure extra supplies of a coveted item quickly, rather than waiting for the next corporate convoy to arrive. In the area of technology services, web designers working for a scrappy start-up firm in Accra may know more about the cheapest way to secure wireless internet service than anyone in a major foreign tech company's Ghanaian office.

More Rules, or Better Conditions?

So, what can African governments do to support the capabilities of such companies? How can they make the most of these African entrepreneurs' detailed knowledge about local markets and the ability to respond quickly to changing conditions? Should they pass laws designed to beef up local content requirements in a bid to ensure that African SMEs receive a share of FDI inflows?

The short answer: No, they should not. Rather, the goal should be to make local content rules unnecessary.

One of the main reasons local content laws exist in Africa is that African governments want the local oil and gas sector to create more jobs. That is, they want to reap some benefit from their decision to let their subsurface resources be extracted and sent to market.

This is logical. But frankly, African SMEs are better at job creation than larger entities. They don't depend on foreign workers, as the IOCs do all too often. Instead, they typically hire locals. Therefore, African governments ought to take steps that allow as many SMEs as possible to succeed.

Local content regulations can help create a level playing field for local SMEs in the beginning phases of oil and gas development, but they ought to be phased out in the long term. Once African companies gain the skills, technology, and personnel they need to outperform foreign investors and to create new jobs consistently, they should not need local content rules anymore. Instead, they will benefit more from the confidence that they are operating in an environment where the government supports entrepreneurship, enforces laws consistently, upholds contracts, protects property rights, collects taxes and fees in a transparent manner, discourages corruption, supports education and training programs, and so on.

Borrower Beware

Another thing governments can do to help SMEs is to make sufficient investments in infrastructure. After all, small and medium-sized companies need pipelines, roads, and utility connections, too. But infrastructure programs are complicated and expensive—and difficult to finance. China's government has offered assistance on this front, and many African leaders have gladly accepted. Some of them may have done so out of sheer exuberance at the thought of gaining access to billions of dollars' worth of credits from a lender that does not demand political reform as a prerequisite for handing over cash.[2]

It is worth noting, though, that this type of investment in infrastructure is counterproductive in some ways. More specifically, it limits African countries' ability to create new jobs. It makes the disbursement of loan funds contingent on commitments to award construction and modernization contracts to state-owned Chinese companies, even though these firms typically bring in their own workers and avoid hiring locals. Additionally, these investments sometimes carry unfavorable terms, such as the use of commodities as collateral (or even payment).

Africa's oil and gas-producing states don't need funds that are offered under such conditions. Instead, they need opportunities to team up with commercial lenders with an appetite for risk—and no small amount of patience. They need to form relationships with lending institutions that are willing to give borrowers time to develop their assets and reach the point of being able to support themselves and generate enough revenue to repay their creditors without excessive discomfort.

If African governments can meet all these targets, African SMEs will be free to keep growing and evolving. They will have an incentive to stretch the boundaries of the multiplier effect—to move into all the sectors that can provide support to oil and gas development, including (in no particular order) engineering, banking and financial services, commodities trading, logistics and transportation, legal services, construction, manufacturing, wholesale and retail trade, information technology services, and power generation.

In many cases, the experience and assets that SMEs gain through the multiplier effect will prepare them for the moment when the oil and gas wells start to run dry—or the times when revenue streams dwindle because of market fluctuations. That is, these companies stand to gain transferable and scalable skills. Firms that trade oil, gas, or petroleum products such as gasoline can become familiar with world market trends and expand into the wider commodities trading sector. Law firms will be able to offer a wider range of services, helping clients outside the oil and gas sector to achieve regulatory compliance, to navigate licensing and permit procedures, or to consider their options under new legislation. Construction companies can leverage their familiarity with local conditions and their ties to other operators, using them as a basis for bidding on contracts in nearby or neighboring states. Software engineers can team up with local schools to offer training in code writing, web design, and other high-demand skills, and their students will be able to work in any industry that uses computers.

Luck, Location, and Labor

Of course, it will be easier to start local content implementation in the parts of Africa that have oil and gas. Producer states will not only attract FDI but will also generate demand for many additional services, thereby creating openings for local entrepreneurs willing to seize new opportunities.

But there is also room for other African countries to get in on the action. We can see an example of this by looking to the island-state of Singapore.

Even though it produces very little on its own, Singapore plays a key role in global oil and gas trade. It is home to Asia's main energy futures market, the Intercontinental Exchange (ICE; www.theice.com), and is the third-largest physical oil trading hub in the world—as a result, many commodities traders have set up shop there. Singapore is also a major refiner and supplier of petroleum products, and it sports many large oil, LNG, and fuel storage depots.[3]

Additionally, the country has become one of the mainstays of the oilfield service sector. It hosts the local and regional offices of multinational giants such as TechnipFMC, Schlumberger, and Baker Hughes. It has also fostered the development of home-grown players such as SembCorp Marine and Keppel FELS, which are the largest two builders of offshore rigs in the world.

And since it is home to more than 3,000 service providers of all sizes in the area of marine and offshore engineering, Singapore is also a source for countless varieties of equipment, vessels, and services for use at underwater oil and gas fields. This is a profitable business. It currently supports about 10,000 local jobs and pumps billions of dollars into Singapore's economy each year.[4] Presumably, it has also generated more jobs and more revenue through the multiplier effect—but not so much that the national economy is entirely at the mercy of world oil and gas markets.

It is tempting to think that Singapore came to this happy state by virtue of its geography. The former British colony lies at a crucial point along international shipping lanes, putting it in a good position to service vessels moving from the Indian Ocean to the Pacific Ocean and vice versa. (Indeed, it has long occupied the top spot on the list of the world's largest bunkering ports.)

But the island-state's fortunes are not merely a product of good luck and a favorable location. Singapore has worked hard to expand its capabilities, beginning in the 1980s, when local firms first provided services and supplies for vessels involved in oil and gas projects in Malaysia and Indonesia. Over the next two decades, their successes inspired other Singaporean entrepreneurs to branch out into other areas of the marine and offshore engineering sector.

Many of these efforts have flourished. Singaporean investors have combined their own determination with the government's business-friendly policies (as well as the continued growth of the hydrocarbon sector between 2002 and 2014) to establish places for themselves. Many companies have also been hurt by the oil price crash that began in mid-2014, but their troubles have not dislodged the country from its position as the linchpin of Asian petroleum markets.[5]

There is a lesson for Africa here. Singapore, a former colonial subject, found a way to turn itself into an industrial and engineering heavyweight. Despite its own lack of oil and gas reserves, it became a major player in the energy sector. And it did this by maximizing its own advantages—not just its geography and its history of involvement in shipbuilding—but also its people, with their skills, ambition, and knowledge of local conditions. Its government acted deliberately to encourage investment wherever possible, making room for foreign partners while also supporting local investors.

African countries ought to try something similar. Whether or not they produce oil and gas, they too have strong assets—especially human capital. They can draw on a large pool of workers who are eager to find work, gain skills, and exercise their entrepreneurial drive. These ambitious men and women have what it takes to build and launch companies capable of providing oil and gas producers with solutions for their engineering, marine, transportation, industrial, legal, and other dilemmas. They may have to start small, but if they can find their own niches in the market (and count on support from business-friendly governments), they will eventually be able to grow and pursue major projects. They could, for example, work up to building an offshore service and ship repair base off the coast of Nigeria, in a spot that is more convenient for African and foreign companies than, say, Stavanger in Norway. Or they could use South Africa's well-developed financial sector as a springboard for expanding African banks' role in the financing of oil and gas development and service contracts. If they take this path, they will be able to create thousands—perhaps even millions—of new jobs, both directly and through the multiplier effect.

And these jobs will benefit Africa in ways that even I can't imagine yet!

8

A "RECIPE" FOR
ECONOMIC DIVERSIFICATION

Economic experts certainly seem to agree on the following two points: first, that diversification is preferable to the "resource curse," in which natural resource extraction and exports are the most important factor in a country's economic performance; and second, that there is no easy path toward diversification.

The convergence of opinion is strong—and experts use startlingly similar language to describe the challenge.

In a March 2017 blog post, a senior manager at the World Bank wrote: "[There] is no magic recipe for diversification."[1] The United Nations' Framework Convention on Climate Change made a nearly identical statement in a technical paper in October 2016: "It must be clear that there is no miracle recipe for achieving diversification overnight."[2] In September 2013, the U.S. Federal Reserve Bank of St. Louis published an article bearing the title "What Are the 'Ingredients' for Economic Growth?"[3] And finally, in April 2017, BizNis Africa reported that a high-ranking representative of Deloitte's Africa division had tried to list "some of the ingredients for successful economic diversification," even as he cautioned that there was "no simple recipe for success."[4]

But what if the path towards diversification could be reduced to a recipe? Would we see African politicians and businessmen urging their colleagues to combine one set of amendments to local-content regulations with two anti-corruption drives and four draft laws on fiscal reform—with just a dash of management consulting to season the final product?

Would we eventually witness something akin to the U.S. reality show *Chopped*, with African countries competing to determine which combinations of the same ingredients yielded the best results?

This is, of course, a fanciful scenario. Even with all the talk about ingredients and recipes, discussions of Africa's future typically do not play out along the lines of cooking contests. I happen to agree with the experts on this point. I don't believe that there is a single, set formula for economic diversification.

What's more, African oil and gas producers don't have any obvious examples to follow within the continent. Not one of the African countries that depend on resource extraction has completed the process of diversifying its economy.

Botswana, for example, has been hailed for its efforts to take the spotlight off diamond mining so that finance, agriculture, logistics, communications, and the service sector can take the stage.[5] These measures have succeeded in bringing the share of GDP generated by diamonds down from the previous level of 50 percent,[6] so the country certainly deserves praise. Even so, the diversification drive is still a work in progress. As of late 2018, Botswana still depended on diamonds for about 25 percent of its total GDP and 85 percent of its export revenues.[7] Meanwhile, agriculture served as a livelihood for more than 80 percent of the country's population while accounting for less than 2 percent of GDP.

But this doesn't undermine the case for economic diversification. And I do believe that there are logical ways to move towards this goal.

Oil and Gas as the First Step

One way to start the journey toward diversification is by embracing the oil and gas industry—not just for its own sake, but also for its ability to serve as a bridge to other types of economic activity.

Some African countries have started taking steps in this direction by building oil refineries, sometimes with the goal of securing additional investments from foreign investors and sometimes in the hope of being able to produce enough gasoline and diesel fuel to meet their own needs and also to serve export markets.

Nigeria, for example, is now working to overcome the fact that its four major refineries cannot cover domestic demand.[8] The country hopes to shed its dependence on imports within the next few years, after the completion of the massive Dangote refinery in the Lekki Free Zone. This plant, which the Dangote Group aims to complete in 2020, will process crude oil from Nigerian fields. It will eventually have a throughput capacity of 650,000 bbl/d and will turn out enough gasoline, jet fuel, diesel, and petrochemicals to serve the export market while also meeting domestic demand in full.[9]

Projects of this type can help generate revenue that supports diversification, but they only represent one piece of the puzzle.

Moving Down the Chain: Power Generation

To fill in the gaps, I suggest moving even further down the chain and looking at the way hydrocarbons are used after they reach the market. Upon examination, it is clear that oil and gas are not just materials that yield fuel for cars and airplanes; they can also be used to produce electricity. Natural gas is especially important on this front since power plants can burn it more cleanly than petroleum products. As such, power generation offers a path to economic diversification—and monetization of a larger share of African gas production.

There is a great deal of room for growth here. Nigeria, for example, is not just Africa's largest oil producer; it also has more gas than any other African state. With reserves estimated at nearly 5.3 trillion cubic meters, it could easily become a major player in the realm of gas-to-power projects. But it will have to overcome decades of inertia first.

Producers working at Nigerian fields have a long-standing habit of concentrating on oil and treating their gas as a nuisance, suitable only for flaring. The government has tried to change course; it imposes nominal fines on companies that burn their gas away and joined the World Bank's Global Gas Flaring Reduction (GGFR) partnership in 2015. Yet the country is still wasting too much of its potential. Data from the Nigerian National Petroleum Corporation (NNPC) shows that in 2016 alone, Africa's largest oil producer flared nearly 7 bcm of gas worth about $710 million.[10]

But it's not just about the money: These volumes could have been used to support 3,500 MW of power generation capacity, nearly double the current operational capacity.

The extra capacity could have helped the country produce another 750 TWh per year of electricity, more than enough to break the cycle of incessant and incapacitating blackouts. And in turn, these additional electricity supplies could have helped business and residential consumers make greater contributions to the Nigerian economy.[11]

The government does have some understanding of the costs of a lax approach to gas flaring. In 2017, the administration of President Muhammadu Buhari unveiled a new domestic gas utilization initiative, saying it was ready to offer incentives to companies that reduced flaring rates and that arranged to sell their gas to buyers who could use it to generate electricity, to power industrial facilities, or to serve as cooking fuel. The agency designed to implement this plan, the Nigerian Gas Flare Commercialization Programme (NGFCP), has touted it as a "unique and historic opportunity to attract major investment in economically viable gas flare capture projects whilst permanently addressing [a 60-year-old] environmental problem."[12]

So far, though, the Buhari administration has not put its words into action. It has certainly talked about its expectation that NGFCP will create 36,000 new jobs directly and another 200,000 positions indirectly, but it has not yet said when it intends to begin working with producers to make gas available to domestic buyers. Nor has it revealed when gas sales might start.

There are multiple lessons to learn from Nigeria's experience on this front. First, focusing on gas has the potential to pay off handsomely, as it prevents the loss of potential revenues. Second, gas doesn't just offer financial benefits; it can also be put to use outside the oil and gas sector as a fuel for power plants. Third, using gas to generate electricity helps people and businesses by lessening the risk of outages. Fourth, when people and businesses can sustain their activities without fear of a blackout, they make more significant contributions to the economy. Fifth, and finally, public sector programs can help support the expansion of gas utilization—provided that the government's commitment is practical as well as theoretical.

Moving Down the Chain: Fertilizer and Other Possibilities

These lessons are not only applicable to gas-to-power projects. They are also relevant for other economic diversification efforts that use oil and gas as a starting point.

Electricity generation is not the only other use for gas, of course. Producer states that prioritize agriculture, for example, they will have compelling reasons to build fertilizer plants—and to use their gas as raw material for these facilities. In turn, the new factories will make substances that farmers can use to increase crop yields.

The Republic of Congo is probably a prime candidate for such an initiative, as it would benefit greatly from diversification. The country is heavily dependent on oil, which accounted for no less than 65 percent of GDP, 85 percent of all government revenues, and 92 percent of total exports in 2017.[13]

Agriculture, by contrast, contributed only 7.24 percent of GDP in the same year,[14] with 4 percent—more than half of that figure—coming from subsistence agriculture, which occupies around 40 percent of the entire population.[15]

Presumably, these subsistence farmers could do better if they had more access to fertilizer, and what better way to provide that access than to use locally produced gas to make that material? This is the logic behind Brazzaville's support for plans to build a fertilizer plant near the port of Pointe-Noire. Haldor Topsoe A/S of Denmark struck a deal on the $2.5 billion project with MGI Energy, a Congolese company involved in gas production, in 2018. The partners hope to begin work soon and will need about three years to finish construction.

Speaking in September 2018, Congolese Economy Minister of State Gilbert Ondongo said he believed the project would help the country's economy in two ways: by giving a boost to the agricultural sector and by encouraging trade.

"Similar plants have been constructed in Bangladesh, India, and Pakistan, and they helped those countries to become self-sufficient in agriculture," he told the Bloomberg news agency. "The place where the plant will be built will make it easy for its fertilizer to reach local, regional, and international markets."[16]

If this project comes to fruition, it will benefit the Republic of Congo on multiple levels, as outlined above. It will allow the country to monetize its gas reserves and generate momentum in another part of the economy. It will help farmers gain access to supplies of fertilizer, which they can use to increase productivity and output in the agricultural sector. In turn, agriculture will be able to make greater contributions to the Congolese economy as a whole.

Assuming, of course, that the government provides the necessary backing for this development, both in theory and in practice.

The Right Kind of Support

This brings me to another point: the necessity of offering state support for diversification projects not just for the sake of individual projects, but for the sake of the economy as a whole.

In other words, this approach should be a matter of policy and not an ad hoc response to individual investment proposals. African countries should do this to prevent oil- and gas-producing areas from being brought low by fluctuations in energy prices, as has happened in the oil boomtowns of North Dakota.[17] They should do it to create more options for Africans who are ready to work—after all, not everyone wants to work in the resource extraction sector! They should do it so that other sectors of the economy can flourish and create jobs—not just directly, but indirectly, since every new business that opens up will create a need for additional companies that can keep workers, goods, and services moving to the places where they are most needed.

And they should do it in order to build up capacity in industries that will outlast oil and gas. Hydrocarbons are finite resources; every field will eventually run dry. African producers should encourage businesses that give their workers opportunities to develop transferable skills that are useful both inside and outside the oil and gas industry: information technology, communications, logistics, manufacturing, finance, and trade. They should work to build up capacity for the production of cotton, cocoa, and other traditional commodities that are sometimes pushed aside in the rush to develop fuel and energy resources.

Certainly, these state supports ought to build on the links between oil and gas and related sectors of the economy. In other words, they should encourage gas producers to pursue gas-to-power projects, to construct new fertilizer plants, to establish municipal gas distribution networks, and to use locally produced petrochemical feedstocks in the manufacture of high-tech plastics and other goods.

But they can also help to connect other sectors to the value chain.

More specifically, African governments should invest some of the revenues they earn from oil and gas production in economic diversification; they should invest in other promising sectors that have no direct links to energy, such as fishing and tourism. They should also take advantage of the assistance that the Norwegian government and other institutions provide to countries seeking to optimize the management of money earned from resource extraction.

If they take this approach, they are more likely to see local businesses create jobs, both directly (in the sectors in question) and indirectly (in areas that facilitate the movement of goods, services, and workers in those sectors), and make bigger contributions to economic growth. In turn, these new jobs will foster growth in many parts of the economy.

Onward and Upward

What will this growth look like? Unfortunately, I can't cite any long-term success stories specific to Africa yet.

But I *can* point to an example of a country that has the potential to move in this direction, using oil and gas as a starting point and then looking for new opportunities further down the chain. That country is Equatorial Guinea, which reported its first offshore discoveries in the mid-1990s and then rapidly became dependent on oil and gas. In 2015, those commodities accounted for 86 percent of total exports, 80 percent of government revenues, and 60 percent of GDP.[18]

This degree of reliance on hydrocarbons is obviously problematic. It has left the country vulnerable to events such as the oil price shock that began in mid-2014, as well as the peaking of domestic oil and gas output shortly thereafter. It has also raised the question of how to make the most optimal use of human capital and other natural resources.

Notably, though, Equatorial Guinea's government has already started formulating an answer to this question. It is working within the sector, expanding opportunities for the monetization of gas through such projects as the construction of LNG and LPG plants at a processing complex on Bioko Island.[19] It is also working outside the sector, arranging for production from offshore fields to be delivered to the AMPCO methanol plant and the Malabo thermal power plant (TPP).[20] And in May 2018, it said it wanted to expand the Bioko Island gas complex so that it could serve as a regional megahub capable of preparing both domestic and foreign gas for processing into LNG, reloading and delivery to other locations, and producing larger amounts of petrochemicals and electric power.[21]

As a result, gas has already helped generate upward momentum in more than one sector of the Equatoguinean economy.

And there will be room for much more growth as work on the megahub moves forward. The project's success will hinge on trade with other countries—namely, with other gas-producing states seeking access to the facility. As a result, every Equatoguinean citizen who plays a role in discussions with third-party suppliers and buyers will be in a position to gain skills in the area of foreign trade negotiations.

In turn, workers who gain these skills will be able to apply them elsewhere. For example, if they decide to take or create a job in the tourism sector, which the Equatoguinean government identified in 2014 as a potential avenue towards diversification,[22] they will already have experience in persuading foreign customers to choose their country over other options.

So, let's hope that officials in Malabo recognize their potential and strive to maximize it! They have a fighting chance to reach this target if they enact policies that support investment in different industries— and if they use oil and gas revenues to fund such endeavors.

Chile: Not Just Copper Now

Chile is widely recognized as an example of success in economic diversification.

But, over the last 50 years, it has succeeded in reducing the share of copper and related products in total exports down from nearly 80 percent to about 50 percent. And it has done so even as it has pushed production up more than tenfold, going from about 500,000 tons per year in the early 1960s to around 5.5 million tons per year in 2005 and subsequent years.[23] In 2017, the World Bank described it as "an example of a diversified economy, exporting more than 2,800 distinct products to more than 120 different countries."[24]

So how did Chile manage this feat? Through a combination of economic and political reforms carried out over a period of more than 30 years.

The political element is important, given that Chile's efforts to foster economic diversification did not have much success until the early 1970s, after General Augusto Pinochet seized power from Salvador Allende, a socialist, and established an authoritarian government. Pinochet's regime began by working to overturn President Allende's program, which featured price controls, subsidies, high import tariffs, and restrictions on foreign investment. It then proceeded with its own agenda, which emphasized the importance of free markets and free trade.

This approach proved successful enough, despite its origins in political turmoil, that Chile has mostly continued to move in the direction of economic liberalization. Even after the government started to loosen restrictions on civil rights in the 1980s—and even after Pinochet stepped down from the presidency in 1989, the country has pushed forward with market-oriented reforms.[25]

And many of the reforms it has enacted are exactly the sort I'm talking about.

Take the decision to spend public funds on non-extractive industries, for instance. The government gave investors in the forestry sector incentives to plant Monterey pines, which grow more quickly in Chile than in any other region. These trees have become a key source of export revenues, as they can be used to make pulp and sawn wood products that fetch a reasonably high value on the open market. Additionally, it has sought to promote fisheries. As a result, it has become the world's second-largest exporter of salmon.

Of course, it hasn't been simply a matter of telling people to plant trees or go fishing. Chile has also taken steps to bolster the credibility of its sovereign wealth fund, cut tariffs in the hope of hastening integration into the global economy, set up programs to help entrepreneurs launch small and medium-sized enterprises (SMEs), and established public-private partnerships (PPPs).

It has also identified several priority sectors for future investment—global services, specialty tourism, mining, functional foods, and the cultivation of birds and pigs.

Chile's example has important lessons for Africa:

- Political and economic reforms are important in a general sense, as is evident from the fact that the goals of economic diversification and liberalization have remained in place even as governments have come and gone.

- Governments can offer valuable support to market-oriented reform programs, such as the establishment of PPPs.

- Diversification must entail growth in disparate sectors of the economy, including those with no direct connection to extractive industries, such as Chile's emphasis on food production in the agricultural sector.

- Investors should also look for unique opportunities that may not arise anywhere else, such as Chile's Monterey pine projects.

If African countries do these things, they will find themselves in possession of valuable tools that will shorten the journey towards economic diversification.

9

CALLING ALL LEADERS!
MORE ON GOOD GOVERNANCE

"WE NEED LEADERS THAT UNDERSTAND that they are running their country for the benefit of every single individual. Every child in this country is his responsibility; we need people who really believe in that, who cannot go to sleep because some people cannot eat or cannot find medicine."

I couldn't agree more with this beautiful sentiment from Mo Ibrahim, founder of The Mo Ibrahim Foundation, an African foundation established in 2006 to support good governance and leadership across the continent.

And I believe that African leaders are heeding this call.

Bill Gates, arguably one of the most successful businessmen in the world, agrees.

"Although 2016 was a tough year for many African economies, almost every trend on the continent has been moving in the right direction over the last decade. Per capita income, foreign investment, agricultural productivity, mobile banking, entrepreneurship, immunization rates, and school enrollment are all heading upwards. Poverty, armed conflicts, HIV, malaria, and child mortality are all on the decline—steeply so in many places."

Over the past decade, the continent has made astounding gains. The World Bank's "Doing Business in 2005"[1] report ranked Africa in last place in terms of its pace of reform. Yes, about what you'd expect, given the political and socioeconomic climate at the time. Then we began to witness a stirring: The 2007 index positioned the continent in third place among the world's fastest reformers, citing at least one reform in two-thirds of African nations. Today, the momentum of positive reform efforts is noteworthy across the continent. The 2016 report ranked five African countries in the top ten for improving nations and credited sub-Saharan Africa alone for almost a third of all regulatory reforms that simplify doing business.

Ernst & Young's annual (and aptly named) "Africa Attractiveness Survey"[2] of international respondents in 2011 confirmed the positive outlook:

- 68 percent saw Africa as a more attractive investment destination than in 2008.

- 75 percent were optimistic about Africa's prospects for the subsequent 3 years.

- 43 percent were planning African expansion.

As of the 2015 attractiveness survey, Ernst & Young fully expects to see compound annual growth rates in excess of 5 percent through 2030 in 24 sub-Saharan African countries. Successful reform initiatives, supported by both local governments and the private sector, are helping transform the continent's prospects.

Thanks to groups like the Investment Climate Facility for Africa (ICF), reform is coming. The ICF and other independent organizations foster initiatives that make it possible for businesses "to register, pay their taxes, solve commercial disputes, clear goods through customs, and so much more, in a quick, simple and transparent manner. This simplification and efficiency is helping to speed up economic growth, ultimately changing the lives of millions of Africans."

And what about the most recent release of "Doing Business"? Outlooks continue to shine brightly in the south, in particular: As of May 2018, a third of all the regulatory reforms that the report documents were in sub-Saharan Africa.

"Sub-Saharan Africa has been the region with the highest number of reforms each year since 2012. This year, 'Doing Business' captured a record 107 reforms across 40 economies in sub-Saharan Africa, and the region's private sector is feeling the impact of these improvements. The average time and cost to register a business, for example, has declined from 59 days and 192 percent of income per capita in 2006 to 23 days and 40 percent of income per capita today."[3]

Sound Fiscal Policies for Revenue Management

The African continent has seen some serious economic gains over the past two decades. After a period of stagnation, we saw high average growth rates from smaller economies like Ghana, larger economies like Nigeria, and even "fragile states" like Angola.

But Christopher Adam, Oxford Professor of Development Economics, cautions that these past gains might now be in jeopardy.

"Ultimately it is fiscal policy that will play the decisive role in ensuring that Africa's macroeconomic adjustment is successful. It needs to be designed in a way that does not undercut the growth-promoting effects of recent infrastructure investments. It may then preserve the gains in poverty reduction and improved service delivery that materialized in health and education," Adam wrote in an article for The Conversation.[4]

To maintain the forward progress, Adam calls for macroeconomic balance and cautions against excessive taxation or curtailing foreign exchange—strategies he says only embolden the black market and worsen widespread shortages. "Decisive action is needed to navigate the difficult economic waters that lie ahead without undoing the gains of the past two decades," he wrote. "Success will require difficult political choices, especially on taxation and government expenditure."

The International Monetary Fund names the following "Five Keys to Smart Fiscal Policy:"[5]

- Countercyclical (smooths the business cycle).

- Growth-friendly (supports long-term economic growth factors of capital, labor, and productivity).

- Promoting inclusion (ensures that growth is shared among the people, who fully participate in the economy).

- Supported by a strong tax capacity (has a stable source of revenue through taxation).

- Prudent (is cautious and sensible).

And around the continent, we are seeing evidence that leaders are implementing these keys.

Plummeting oil prices on the global market have significantly stifled economic growth in the petrostates, whose economies rely on their energy revenues. Despite this, Nigeria is weathering the economic storm rather well, receiving positive ratings for its top 5 banks—despite the clutches of a recession—for the first time in some 20 years.

Why?

In response to the global financial crisis that hit in 2008, Nigeria introduced capitalization requirements and reforms to bank oversight to enhance transparency and consolidate government finances. And in 2017, an accounting regulation change eliminated the one-year waiting period for banks to fully write off non-performing loans, enabling them to clear up their balance sheets immediately using capital reserves and keeping all five national banks technically solvent.

This is excellent news for Nigeria. But it's also a beacon of hope for the rest of the continent: Yes, Nigeria is blessed with a wealth of oil reserves—but we've seen that, in the past, this nation has let this bounty cloud better judgment. In short, Nigeria was the poster child of the resource curse. If Nigeria can start turning it around, other countries can, too.

And I'm not just talking about oil and gas. A sound fiscal policy helps form the backbone of a solid economic management strategy that will promote growth and prosperity for all. Of course, a country can't decide which natural resources will be discovered within its borders—but the lawmakers of that country do decide which policies to adopt regarding those resources.

And their decisions impact their economy.

As the National Resource Governance Institute reminds us, "When managed prudently, oil, gas, and mining investments and the vast revenues they generate can sustain development efforts and make a lasting positive impact on the life of citizens. However, without proper policies, frameworks, and oversight, these same investments have the potential to destabilize public financial management systems, bring negative environmental and social impacts, and increase the risk of corruption."[6]

Just as Nigeria is hopeful that its new accounting regulations will continue to push them forward in positive strides, Tanzania also introduced new laws for its extractive industries. This eastern African republic is rich in minerals, including gold and other precious metals, and an important element of the new legislation was increasing the taxation in the mining industry. The result: a lofty 74 percent tax rate that gave Tanzania the highest mining taxes anywhere on the planet.[7]

And while this exorbitant rate might have been a good way to pad the government coffers, all it really accomplished was to anger the citizenry and create an unwelcoming business environment. After a year in place, however, Tanzanian President John Magufuli announced the government's plan to reassess the fiscal regime. The concern is that the new tax strategy hasn't struck the right balance between being too low for the government to really capitalize on the resources versus being too high to promote investment. A secondary concern is that higher taxation might actually be causing increased tax evasion—further cutting into the government's revenue stream.

It seems President Magufuli might have read Professor Adam's work! While the legislation might not have been a success, this decision, at the very least, shows the Tanzanian government's understanding of this complex situation and its willingness to continue improving the regulations.

Tanzania might look to the south to see how it can be done.

One example of a government that has developed an effective economic policy is Botswana. The majority of this landlocked nation is covered by the Kalahari Desert, leaving little opportunity for agricultural ventures. Prior to 1970, it was considered one of the poorest countries in the world. . . but that changed with the discovery of diamonds, which brought about dramatic growth in GDP, per capita income, and a balance of payment surplus. But the diamond bonanza did more than lift the nation out of extreme poverty: The government was also forward-thinking enough to institute a policy of continually reinvesting revenue from its diamond industry for the socioeconomic benefit of its people, funding such social services as its transit system, education, and healthcare.

Or Tanzania could consider the successes to the west.

Ghana's innovative Petroleum Revenue Management Act (more on that later) outlines mechanisms for collecting and distributing oil revenue, with clear specifications on percentages used to fund the annual budget, set aside for future generations, and invested back into the industry and the infrastructure. The well-crafted legislation created a fiscal regime that ensures that all oil revenue is openly accounted for, deposited into its appropriate "basket," and then used for its intended purpose.[8] Ghana's legislation offers a well-designed fiscal system that accounts for the nature of the oil industry and the intrinsic uncertainties of its E&P, as well as the government's capacities to promote the industry while generating revenues to support socioeconomic development of the nation.

Combatting Corruption by Just Saying "No"

Of course, we can talk about positive business climates and the importance of well-designed government policies for managing oil and gas revenue until we're blue in the face—but it won't mean a thing if bribes continue to be business-as-usual.

We've talked about the hazards of foreign "aid." But in addition to the potential for countries becoming reliant, here's yet another slant: Financial "help" prevents good governance by promoting distance between a government and its people. Rather than focusing on enhancing citizens' needs like housing, education, healthcare, or access to energy, governments may instead look for opportunities to please the donors.

Writing for *The Spectator*, Harriet Sergeant puts it more bluntly: "When foreign donors cover 40 percent of the operating budgets of countries such as Kenya and Uganda, why would leaders listen to their citizens? Schmoozing foreign donors comes first."[9]

While my outlook might not be as pessimistic, I do agree that the "schmoozing" often amounts to bribery. And bribery, whatever the form, is taking place at all levels. Companies pay bribes to get their proposals approved. Government courts accept bribes to affect the outcome of trials. And even at the individual level, people hand over bribes to get access to better public services—services that should be freely available to all.

This is not a smart business model. I've seen it time and time again: Once the payments start, they never stop. Businesses that push themselves into the market through bribes pay to get in, then keep paying to stay in, and then face hefty fines that they pay to get out.

When it comes to bribery, my advice is simple: Just don't pay.

And, yes, it really can be that simple—but we all have to refuse. It's up to every one of us to stand up and speak out. We must be a combined and cohesive voice for ethics, morality, and fairness to push Africa out of this rut of corruption once and for all. When we walk into communities where we see corruption or witness a government not treating people with respect, we must firmly state that we cannot play a role there.

Oil and gas companies should lead this charge. It only makes sense: Their influence is mighty, and they are the trailblazers in many aspects already.

Industry is already doing that, thanks to initiatives like the U.K. Bribery Act, the U.S. Foreign Corrupt Practices Act (FCPA), and the Canadian Corruption of Foreign Public Officials Act (CFPOA). These acts outline how countries respond to offenses such as offering, giving, or accepting a bribe, and they carry stiff penalties for violation. Penalties for failing to comply can include being barred from tendering for government contracts, significant fines, and even criminal convictions. In addition, many anti-corruption organizations have sprung up to back up governments in their campaign toward universal fair practice.

"Enforcement of U.S. extraterritorial bribery legislation has dramatically escalated in the past decade and shows little sign of abating," Reagan Demas, a partner at Baker & McKenzie LLP in Washington,

D.C., told Financier Worldwide in 2012. "Other countries have passed similar legislation and are beginning to enforce those new laws. In the wake of criminal settlements with companies operating in Africa in the oil and gas, mining, telecommunications, freight forwarding and other industries, businesses are recognizing the importance of a well-developed compliance program when operating in these higher-risk/higher-reward jurisdictions."[10]

The Push for Transparency

The Extractive Industries Transparency Initiative (EITI; www.eiti .org) sets a global standard for transparency in oil, gas, and mining. EITI promotes a more transparent business environment by shedding light on what companies do with the oil, gas, and minerals they produce, where their revenue goes, and what jobs were created. At the same time, EITI requires governments to report the revenues they receive from the extractive industries. EITI compliance creates a level playing field for companies, and the resulting transparency contributes to improved political stability and reputation for the countries. And that, in turn, improves the compliant country's investment climate.

Meanwhile, Publish What You Pay (www.publishwhatyoupay.org) is a global civil society coalition that helps citizens of resource-rich developing countries hold their governments accountable for the management of revenues from the oil, gas, and mining industries.

Other more broad-based groups expand their reach beyond the energy sector. The UN Global Compact (www.unglobalcompact.org) asks companies to embrace, within their sphere of influence, a set of core values in the areas of human rights, labor standards, the environment, and anti-corruption. Likewise, the Global Corporate Governance Forum supports regional and local initiatives to improve corporate governance in middle- and low-income countries, and Transparency International is a global civil society organization battling corruption.

And on the continent itself, Africa has its share of groups fighting for just practices:

- The Africa Governance, Monitoring and Advocacy Project (AfriMAP) aims to monitor and promote compliance by African states with the requirements of good governance, democracy, human rights, and the rule of law.

- The African Parliamentarians Network Against Corruption (APNAC; www.apnacafrica.org) is working to strengthen parliamentary capacity to fight corruption and promote good governance.

- The African Peer Review Mechanism (APRM; aprm-au.org) is a system introduced by the African Union to help countries improve their governance.

- The Business Coalition Against Corruption (BCAC) of Cameroon, originally established to equip member companies to address corruption, expanded to represent British, Canadian, French, Italian, and U.S. companies operating there.

- Business Ethics Network of Africa (BEN-Africa; www.benafrica.org) facilitates interaction between academics and practitioners who share an interest in business ethics.

- Eastern, Central and Southern Africa Federation of Accountants (ECSAFA; www.ecsafa.org) strives to build and promote the accountancy profession in the eastern, central and southern regions of Africa.

- Information Portal on Corruption and Governance in Africa (IPOC; www.ipocafrica.org) is an online resource portal that can act as a primary reference point for those interested in combating corruption and promoting democratic governance in Africa.

- Open Society Initiative for Southern Africa (www.osisa.org) collaborates on human rights, education, democracy building, economic development, the media, and access to technology and information.

- Southern Africa Forum Against Corruption (SAFAC) aims to build the capacity of anti-corruption agencies in the Southern African Development Community (SADC) region to develop effective anti-corruption strategies and to create synergies with other anti-corruption stakeholders.

Anti-corruption organizations aren't the only ones striving to eradicate corruption in Africa. Many African governments are taking steps to eradicate it as well. Transparency International recently added these nations to their "least corrupt" list:

- Cape Verde
- Lesotho
- Mauritius
- Namibia
- Rwanda
- South Africa
- Senegal
- Seychelles

But Africa's anti-corruption "superstar" might be Botswana, which has consistently topped Transparency International's list of Africa's least corrupt countries. Botswana's federal government created the Directorate on Corruption and Economic Crime (DCEC) in 1994, in response to a string of corruption scandals. The directorate battles corruption through investigation, prevention, and education efforts. Since its launch, it has earned international praise for its innovative programs, which include outreach to youth and rural communities.

Today, the government can punish corruption with prison sentences up to 10 years, a fine of 500,000 Pula ($64,000), or both. The U.S. State Department reports that the Botswana government obtains 16 to 20 convictions a year for corruption-related crimes and has not shied away from prosecuting high-level officials.

Botswana shows us that one of the resource curse's most damaging effects, corruption, can be defeated. The nation embraced its natural resources and created a positive culture in which to manage its diamond market, which is now the envy of the world. By turning away from the ills of the past, cutting red tape and graft, and investing their revenues into human resources, the country has achieved improved business rankings, increased incomes, and enhanced lives of the Botswanan people.

Transparency Initiatives: Seeing It All Clearly

A vital piece of the anti-corruption puzzle is absolute transparency. And when it comes to transparency, we can learn a thing or two from Ghana.

The country is new to the oil and gas industry, very new. Their major find, the Jubilee Field, was only discovered in 2007. At that point, the country had zero experience in extractive technologies.

Perhaps because of this complete lack of experience, because the country had to work diligently to get up to speed quickly, Ghana took deliberate and calculated steps to ensure that its bounty of natural resources would be nurtured into something beneficial. Most importantly, the country set forth provisions to ensure the sustainability of the sector and safeguard the interests of future generations.

The Ghanaian government worked tirelessly to create the Petroleum Revenue Management Act (PRMA). When it was finally introduced in 2011, it established a comprehensive regulatory structure of reliability and accountability that includes some unprecedented transparency mechanisms:

- Industry news and developments are published every month in national newspapers and on the internet.

- There is a clear division between the state budget and oil revenue and a limit on how the government can use its part of its budget.

- The Annual Budget Funding Amount controls the government's share of oil and gas income; each quarter, up to 70 percent of the capital must be paid into the fund for strategic development.

- The Petroleum Holding Fund, part of the Bank of Ghana, regulates the allocation of oil and gas revenue—and all revenue details are available to the public.

- The people are encouraged to weigh in and debate whether spending conforms to development priorities.

- A Public Interest Accountability Committee (PIAC) monitors compliance and provides independent assessment on revenue management.

- The Petroleum Commission took over the supervisory role from the state-owned Ghana National Petroleum Company (GNPC), which was revamped to enable it to focus on upstream development.

How did this inexperienced government come up with what I consider the most effective and most transparent legislation for managing hydrocarbon resources on the entire continent?

It all started with education.

Instead of blindly jumping at the money, Ghana learned as much as possible about its new energy endeavor. The country reached out for advice from successful international partners. By applying the best practices of those who had succeeded before, and steering clear of their missteps, they avoided the need to reinvent the proverbial wheel.

In addition, the country focused on advancing its domestic training capabilities. For example, in 2015, the Kwame Nkrumah University of Science and Technology introduced its brand-new Petroleum Building and Laboratories Complex.

And last but certainly not least, the leaders of Ghana understood the importance of public approval. Ghana was already EITI-compliant with its mining industry requirements and qualified easily for its oil industry before the start of oil production in 2010. Over the course of that year, groups from various sectors held open forums to gauge the public's understanding of the industry and to maintain the highest degree of public involvement and process transparency possible. These meetings brought together community members of all walks of life, from business people to farmers to schoolchildren, to really get a feel for what Ghanaians had to say about oil development in their homeland.

"In a small way, a social contract between citizens and government emerged," wrote Joe Amoako-Tuffour, who served as a technical advisor on tax policy to Ghana's Ministry of Finance and Economic Planning.[11]

I dare say that this was, on the contrary, no *small* thing but a very great and impactful step. Through unprecedented transparency, the government was proving its dedication to the people.

Firm and Fair Local Content Policies Strike a Balance

I see too much to talk about local content, but the results and focus on results must be a priority. Sometimes with local content, you have the feeling of an overcrowded field of preachers feverishly contending for the attention of the same choir. Too many people talk about local content with little knowledge of how the oil industry works or understanding that we need to find the right balance.

Local content policies are derived from a simple philosophy: A nation's natural resources belong to the people, so the people should benefit from their development. Although the exact definition remains a bit elusive and fluid, fair opportunities for local communities remains the crux of the issue for many African countries.

The goal is to get more locals employed in the energy sector and to make more local companies suppliers to the industry. But just what does "local" mean? And just how local are we talking? Are we also including regional content from neighboring and nearby states (or from more distant African countries)? Furthermore, how can we all ensure that local and regional content becomes part of a country's—or a region's—everyday approach to doing business?

These questions highlight how complex the issue is. Take Nigeria's Niger Delta, for example. Oil and gas operators are feeling the growing pressure to hire their workers and buy all products specifically from Rivers State. Or look at Tanzania, where researchers have found that, while residents appreciate local content efforts, they remain suspicious of the motives and the ultimate outcomes. This distrust stems from the government's failure to consult with locals during the policy development process.

A further complication could be the perception of inaction. By that, I mean that local content policies do not—*cannot*—bring about immediate change. As with any new policy, it takes time to draft, implement, and notice. All stakeholders need to recognize that local content regulations are based on the principle of long-term improvement; the lack of an immediate increase in local hiring, for example, does not signal that reform is stalled.

Local content policy for the energy industry—or, really, any natural resource industry—must be dynamic. The oil and gas market fluctuates dramatically, and regulations must be able to accommodate this. Policies need to be designed to handle such change.

Plus, the extractive technologies change rapidly, and the training and education needed can easily surpass local capabilities. It's just not realistic, for instance, to require that 100 percent of the labor will come from indigenous workers. That will simply serve to scare away potential investors. We can't have our lawmakers establishing requirements so burdensome that companies don't want to come to Africa. In short, we want companies to bring in the finances.

We want them to bring in the technology. We want them to bring in the job opportunities.

To a large extent, however, indigenous workers and supply industries have not historically reaped the kinds of economic and social rewards one would expect, and that's the case even in African countries with bountiful stores of oil and natural gas.

Big companies—maybe oil and gas companies in particular—still have a lot of ground to make up to overcome the mistrust that has cultivated over the years, borne of the locals' past experiences with less-than-honorable businesspeople. The best and most ethical approach to maintaining trust is by establishing open communication from the beginning and respecting the needs of the community as much as possible.

Yes, all businesses think about profits. But there's so much more to be gained by helping the local environment in progress and development. Setting local people up for success will ultimately contribute to a company's growth and profitability.

Do not underestimate the knowledge and determination of the locals. Overlooking the qualified local people is a missed opportunity. In fact, hiring expatriates might be one of the biggest mistakes that companies make in Africa. It's an unnecessary expense, costly in terms of both paychecks and the wider repercussions on the community.

Let's start with the presumption of national staffing. Make hiring locally, whenever possible, the standard rather than the exception. Let's get into the position of nurturing future leaders who can put their considerable understanding of the area to work for the good of a country and for the good of the continent.

Two shining examples of local-content-done-right are in Angola and Nigeria.

I encourage African leaders to study the socioeconomic impact of Angola LNG in Soyo, a joint venture between Sonangol, Chevron, BP, Eni, and Total. Angola LNG has committed to providing social benefits to the community—like renovating the Soyo municipal hospital, refurbishing and expanding the Bairro da Marinha School, improving city roads, developing a new road and bridge connecting Kwanda Island to the Soyo Industrial Zone, and constructing a gas-fired power plant for the community.

The Angola Ministry of Public Administration, Employment and Social Security (MAPESS), meanwhile, has been providing vocational training that enhances the plant's ability to benefit the community. The MAPESS Vocational Training Center in Soyo was built with the LNG plant in mind by the Angolan government with support from the Norwegian vocational education foundation RKK and the Norwegian government.

Also worth studying is Nigeria LNG Limited (NLNG). Incorporated as a limited liability company in 1989 to produce LNG and Natural Gas Liquids (NGLs) for export, the company is owned by the Federal Government of Nigeria, represented by Nigerian National Petroleum Corporation; Shell; Total LNG Nigeria Ltd.; and Eni.

NLNG estimates that it created more than 2,000 jobs every time one of its 6 trains were constructed, and it could create as many as 18,000 additional jobs for its proposed 7-train expansion. The company has also provided training opportunities for Nigerians and created 400 new jobs (captains, engineers, seamen, and ancillary workers) when it acquired six new vessels in 2015.

I must note that it is important to distinguish between local content and corporate social responsibility. People do not need handouts. They need to be appreciated for their contribution.

Effective Enforcement

Of course, there's more to local content policy than the drafting of it.

Local governments must share in the vision and have practical mechanisms for ensuring compliance. Without oversight, local content regulations can be easily "forgotten." Just as detrimental are the drafts of local content legislation that are so loose that compliance is either practically guaranteed or downright impossible.

Case in point: Tanzania's Production Sharing Agreement requires operators to "maximize their utilization of goods, services, and materials from Tanzania" without suggesting requisite levels of utilization or the mechanisms to accomplish this. Angolan legislation, on the other hand, is clearly outlined but sets forth different laws for different regions and lacks a single supervisory institution. Meanwhile, the

Petroleum Law in Mozambique states that all oil and gas companies must be registered on the Mozambique Stock Exchange—but it fails to define "oil and gas companies." It also stipulates that only foreign companies registered on the Mozambique Stock Exchange can carry out petroleum operations without clearly outlining what constitutes "petroleum operations."

On the other hand, those with highly prescriptive policies are faring much better in terms of the kinds of successes they've achieved. The regional evidence paper "Local Content Frameworks in the African Oil and Gas Sector: Lessons from Angola and Chad" for ACODE, a Ugandan public policy research and advocacy think tank, determined that the more tightly woven the local content framework, the better.

No local content policies can be effective without the establishment of a fully empowered government regulatory agency to lead public enlightenment, communication, and education—and to take firm actions against defaulters.

And enforcement is, of course, essential to this success.

Nigeria is widely considered an example for sub-Saharan Africa. Nigerian local content laws, for example, are clearly spelled out: Milestones, percentages, and timelines are etched in stone.

Nigeria's National Content Development and Monitoring Board (NCDMB) is a great example of a successful monitoring approach. In fact, the NCDMB has shown its teeth: It hasn't shied away from ensuring compliance with the national local content policies. It made an example of Hyundai Heavy Industries by banning its participation in Nigeria's petroleum industry until it proved its compliance with the requirements of local employment.

	Before Local Content	**After Local Content**
Average Industry Spend	USD* billion	USD 20 billion (USD 4 billion locally)
Contribution to National Revenue	71%	80%
Contribution to Export Earnings	90%	97%
Contribution to GDP	12%	25%
Local Value Added	10-15%	40%
Use of Workforce	More Expatriates	More Nigerians

Source: Energy Synergy Partners, 2015
Best Practice for Local Content Development Strategy: The Nigerian Experience[12]

Realistic goals are also important in shaping policies and promoting success. Obviously, local content policies that are unfair or unreasonable will hold no water—and may, in fact, simply serve to inhibit the progress of the industry across the continent.

The strength of the local content policies in Equatorial Guinea, for example, is its balance: While its government understands that the sustainability of the country and the industry coincides with indigenous success, it also recognizes that the oil and gas industry is a highly technical segment that demands both highly trained staff and companies that adhere to the strictest guidelines for health, safety, and environmental protection.

The government enacted requirements for international companies to hire Equatoguineans, contribute to training programs, and work with local subcontractors. They were careful to balance the need to boost local industry, however, with the limitations of the *current* local industry. They understood how unrealistic it was to require 100 percent local content until more training, education, and local capacity in that field is created.

Building local content takes time, and until they have successfully created local capacity in the many sub-sectors it takes to service the oil and gas industry, there is a need for international firms. Equatorial Guinea struck this balance, such that international companies can trust the services provided by Equatoguinean companies, and indigenous companies have the ability to grow.

Continued Nurturing Needed

Successful reform initiatives, supported by both local governments and the private sector, are helping transform the continent's prospects. But as Ernst & Young cautions, "Africa's continued rapid growth is not inevitable, and will not simply take care of itself . . . We should not take belief in Africa's rise for granted."

Or consider the advice of Tanzania's former President Benjamin Mkapa: "We have shown that it is possible. Now it is up to African countries to follow the example set by ICF and to pursue greater investment climate reforms that will spur Africa's development and unleash the entrepreneurial spirit of its people."

In other words, we can't sit back, reveling at our early successes.

Natural resources only become a curse when poorly managed and when their extraction is done without proper supervision. Governance is the only deciding factor when it comes to a country's natural resources becoming a curse or a blessing.

10

INDUSTRIALIZATION: LINKING PROMISE TO PROSPERITY

EVERY NOVEMBER 20 SINCE 1990, the United Nations has observed Africa Industrialization Day. The UN hopes that this annual reminder will help raise awareness and motivate the continent toward economic diversification and reduce its exposure to external shocks, not the least of which is the volatility of the oil and gas market.

The ultimate goal, of course, is to eradicate poverty through employment and wealth creation.

But in the nearly 30 years since the tradition started, not much has changed.

Consider this: Africa's manufacturing value added (MVA) as a share of GDP is the lowest in the world.[1] Sub-Saharan Africa's average, a mere 11 percent, is about what it was in the 1970s. You only have to compare that figure to Europe and Central Asia (16 percent), South Asia (16 percent), and Latin America and the Caribbean (14 percent) to see how far Africa lags behind. Granted, MVA as a share of GDP has been declining worldwide for more than two decades, corresponding to the rise in the service economy. But in Africa's case, there's no such seesaw effect. Africa's MVA hasn't lost ground to gains elsewhere. In most regions of the continent, it has just never been very good.

What if we look at the figures a different way? Will the yardstick of MVA per capita improve our perspective? Sadly, that only makes things seem grimmer: In 2015, MVA per person was just $144 in sub-Saharan Africa compared to $3,114 per person in Europe and Central Asia, and $1,123 in Latin America and the Caribbean.[2]

True, some sub-Saharan African countries are doing better than others. For example, MVA per capita reached $2,124 in Equatorial Guinea in 2015; Mauritius and Swaziland weren't terribly far behind at $1,209 and $1,188, respectively, putting them in the same class as Latin America and the Caribbean.

But why haven't we seen more progress? After all, well before the UN made it official, the international community was already focused on the industrialization of Africa. More to the point, how can Africa use its energy resources to industrialize itself, and what parts do government and business play?

A Path for Overcoming Old Patterns

With all of its rich agricultural and extractive resources, Africa should be enjoying resource-based industrialization and the wealth that comes with it. But there are two intertwined factors getting in the way. For one, the continent exports raw materials rather than using them at home. And it does that not so much because it wants to, but because it has no choice: The lack of infrastructure makes production in Africa too expensive.

Of course, I'm not the first person to bring this up. In 2014, when South Africa's then-minister of mines Susan Shabangu spoke at the Mining Indaba conference, she said Africa needs to "shift from exporting of largely raw material to ensuring that minerals serve as a catalyst for accelerated industrialization through mineral value-addition."

I find her assertion no less true today than it was then, and it certainly applies to the extraction of oil and gas. Instead of being used for transportation and to light communities out of darkness, Africa exports much of its hydrocarbon bounty. In fact, of all the commodities Africa exports, crude oil is fourth on the list, behind only palm oil, gold, and diamonds.

To make matters worse, petroleum-based finished goods such as agricultural fertilizers and electronics are being imported back to Africa, with premium prices attached!

Sadly, this pattern of trade is nothing new—the extractive model of exporting primary commodities for value addition along global value chains dates back to colonialism. And it affects a wide swath of industries, not just oil and gas.

A UN Economic Report on Africa illustrates a similar scenario with cotton. In 2012, for example, countries including Benin, Burkina Faso, and Mali accounted for about 16 percent of global cotton exports. Yet just 1 percent of Africa's total share, representing about $400 million, had been processed into fabric on the continent itself. Instead, Africa spent $4 billion importing cotton fabrics,[3] meaning the revenue Africa generates from cotton production is just a fraction of what it spends on manufactured goods.

We can't blame historical paradigms for everything; however, we have to get beyond old ways of looking at things and move forward. And while we're taking responsibility for the continent's issues, we can't deny the harm our infrastructure deficit does to our progress.

Just take a look at the cocoa fields of Ghana and Côte d'Ivoire. Together, those countries produce 60 percent of the world's cocoa. But do they reap 60 percent of the world's revenues from chocolate bars and bonbons? Hardly. Historically, they have made less than

$5 billion on exports even though the global supply chain is worth more than $100 billion. With an infusion of cash, Côte d'Ivoire was able to increase its cocoa processing capacity. However, it is still second behind the Netherlands in processing volume, and the Dutch don't grow a single cocoa bean. Because of infrastructure limitations, Côte d'Ivoire can only go so far in the value chain: It turns its harvest into industrial cocoa that is then sent to Europe, Asia, or the United States for manufacturing.

The problem isn't simple or inexpensive to fix: There's no waving a magic wand to turn oil into fertilizer, cotton into clothing, or cocoa into candy. But it's not impossible. Some African countries have broken through the barriers of infrastructure and are reaping the rewards of resource-based industrialization.

One of the best examples of this is Botswana.

As the Brookings Institution reports, where Namibian diamonds were once sent in uncut, unpolished form to diamond trader DeBeers in London, they are now transported to Botswana, where they are processed before entering the global value chain. This is a powerful example of intra-African trade, something sorely missing on the continent.

Even better, after Botswana renegotiated its contract with DeBeers, the company moved many of its operations to the capital city of Gaborone. This arrangement has expanded jobs, income, and services; in other words, the country has utilized its resource wealth to the benefit of all. That's just one reason Botswana is among the world's leaders in personal economic freedom and why its people have access to free education and improved medical care.

Unfortunately, though, Botswana is something of a rarity, and it should surprise no one when Ivorian cocoa or Malian cotton is sent abroad rather than being processed here.

We simply lack the logistics and power to keep things moving, both literally and figuratively, which adds considerably to the cons of doing business in Africa. World Bank studies show that poor road, rail, and harbor infrastructure adds 30 to 40 percent to the costs of goods traded among African countries. In sub-Saharan Africa, the lack of electricity, water, roads, and information and communications technology (ICT) cut business productivity by as much as 40 percent.

Unless we can build roads and railways and turn fossil fuels into that fundamental element called electricity—a situation World Bank Group President Jim Yong Kim described as "energy apartheid"[4]—industrialization will remain at a standstill.

Adopting New Paradigms

However well-intentioned, campaigns like the UN's Africa Industrialization Day can't overcome the infrastructure deficits that keep the continent from achieving its potential. Real change, if it is to occur at all, must be accomplished by Africans in Africa, and by the companies working here and benefiting from African resource wealth.

New oil and gas discoveries are adding potential to Africa's economy. And the recent rebound in global commodity prices has translated into renewed optimism and investment across the continent's energy value chain.

But think back to the last time commodity prices were high, roughly from 2000 to 2011. Oxfam, a confederation of charitable organizations, says that despite Africa's remarkable economic growth then, much of the wealth never made it to the general population. Instead, it was siphoned off by political elites "through shell companies established to own or do business with oil, gas, and mining operations." In fact, Oxfam suggests that around 56 percent of all illicit financial flows leaving Africa between 2000 and 2010 came out of the oil, metals, ores, and precious minerals sectors.

Corruption of this magnitude only adds to the chasm between rich and poor on a continent that nearly leads the world in the unequal distribution of wealth.

Where the money went, we can't be exactly sure, although it probably speaks to the undeniable advantages of offshore bank accounts, tax avoidance, and other shelters. Policymakers are working to prevent this kind of thing from happening again. As an example, we can look to the framework called the African Mining Vision (AMV).

Formulated by African nations and adopted in 2009 by the African Union, the AMV's aim is to move the continent from its historic status as an exporter of cheap raw materials to manufacturer and supplier of knowledge-based services.

At its essence, the AMV seeks to be the catalyst for resource-based development and industrialization. Its playbook includes a compact between governments and the business community to derive maximum value from mineral extraction, while ensuring all parties are accountable, share responsibility for outcomes, and honor their reciprocal obligations.

At its most basic level, the AMV calls for a number of government actions, including the development of human capital and improving the quality of the business environment—both commendable goals.

More specifically, the AMV charges governments with providing supporting infrastructure including roads, rail ports, energy and water, and telecom, and establishing an industrial base through backward, forward, and sidestream linkages—that is, relationships with suppliers, distributors, and business services, among others.[5]

For Nigeria, a Shift in the Right Direction

Although AMV is the first pan-African initiative of its type, individual nations have undertaken similar systematic strategies, with varying degrees of success.

In Nigeria, for example, industrialization has been a goal since the 1960s, when large oil and natural gas finds began shifting the economy away from its agricultural base. Unfortunately, the history of their efforts is fraught with setbacks.

The First National Development Plan intended to replace the country's heavy reliance on imports with industrial growth. During this period, 1962–1968, the construction of the Kainji dam across the Niger River gave credence to the promise of hydroelectric power—but so far, that dream has not been realized. In 2017, the dam generated just 500 MW of electricity, which is hardly enough to keep the lights on in a country of 170 million people.[6] Now, nearly 50 years after it was built, the dam is finally getting an upgrade that should increase its capacity to 922 MW, but only time will tell if it can make good on that prediction.

The Second Plan, in effect from 1970 to 1974, was built upon the economic jolt that came with the discovery of vast hydrocarbon reserves, which quickly propelled Nigeria to the rank of major oil and gas producer. The government used its newfound revenues to kickstart a variety of projects that spanned a number of industries, from iron to sugar to pulp and paper. However, because the country lacked the technological prowess to get this industrial surge up to speed, most are either gone now or operating at low capacity.

This brings us, of course, to the Third Plan, which coincided with the oil boom of the late 1970s and foresaw public sector investment in heavy industry. Unfortunately, the private sector had a different vision and preferred to invest in consumer industries that required imported machinery and imported raw materials.

As the Brookings Institution noted, "This had a debilitating effect on real industrial growth."[7]

It's fair to say Nigeria has made little progress in the way of industrialization since, although its dependence on imported machinery is just as great as it was 40 years ago.

However, the tide may be turning with the development of the Lagos Free Trade Zone (LFTZ). Designed to serve as a trade and logistical hub for all of West Africa, with active road, rail, and sea links, the LFTZ focuses on specific sectors: petroleum refining, petrochemicals, and agroprocessing. For an investment of at least $1 million, companies become capital shareholders with access to exemptions from taxes and import/export licensing requirements. Located on more than 800 hectares, 65 kilometers from Lagos, the development includes internal roads and drainage, utilities, street lighting, commercial buildings, and a housing complex for workers.

The format seems to be effective. The first tenant was an oil company, although not one associated with hydrocarbons: Palm oil refiner Raffles Oil has invested $30 million in the LFTZ since 2012.[8] Additional tenants, including manufacturers of vegetable oil, cereal packaging, and milk, have brought the total investment above $150 million.[9] So far, however, there is no petroleum investor among the lot.

Creating Enabling Environments in Kenya

While Nigeria is finally beginning to make strides toward industrialization, it's possible that energy upstart Kenya may leapfrog it, thanks to a federal plan that encourages industrialization by planning for infrastructure.

It is estimated that Kenya holds about 10 bbo, about 766 million of them proven—not a trivial amount but nothing to compare with Nigeria's proven reserves of 40 billion bbl and 5 tcm of natural gas.

Currently, Kenya is producing only about 2,000 bbl/d, although, at full capacity, that number could reach 80,000 bbl/d.

Despite being significantly smaller than Nigeria by those measures, Kenya is equally eager to leverage its resource riches into greater industrial wealth. Like many other African nations, Kenya has been going through a period of de-industrialization: Although its manufacturing base is considered quite sophisticated, especially compared to its East African neighbors, it has been growing at a slower rate than the economy, which expanded by 5.6 percent in 2015.[10]

To turn things around, the government of President Uhuru Kenyatta has developed an industrialization plan that borrows a page from the industrial cities of Saudi Arabia, the Lagos endeavor, and the AMV template.

To create an enabling environment for manufacturing, business, and trade, the plan proposes establishing Special Economic Zones (SEZ) in eight strategically located towns across the country, most likely Mombasa, Kisumu, Athi River, Nakuru, Narok, Isiolo, Lamu, and Machakos. The program will launch sector-specific flagship projects—including appropriate infrastructure and utilities—in agroprocessing, textiles, leather, construction services and materials, oil and gas and mining services, and IT.[11]

The fact that Kenya includes infrastructure in its SEZ planning seems like a good indication of future success, with ramifications beyond attracting new business and building an industrial base. After all, when you incorporate water supply, sanitation, sewage disposal, electricity, and other sustainable services into a development, you also provide access to those things to people living nearby, improving their quality of life.

Setting the Future Course Today

I'm very hopeful that these policies, plans, and actions will yield profitable results. At the same time, there's no question that if Africa is to take full advantage of its resources, sufficient infrastructure is required. The amount is staggering: Preliminary and partial estimates by the African Development Bank suggest that Africa's annual infrastructure investment needs amount to at least $100 billion.

We have a chance to make the right moves right now.

To take advantage of the projected economic growth from recent natural gas discoveries, Africa will need storage facilities, pipelines, and distribution networks—opportunities for engineering as well as manufacturing. To keep gas and associated product moving between African countries—rather than to other parts of the world—will require better transportation networks.

Africa is a land of opportunity with more than enough natural resources necessary to reduce poverty and link promise to prosperity through industrialization.

As President of the African Development Bank Group, Akinwumi Adesina said, "Africa must quit being at the bottom of the global value chains and move to rapidly industrialize, with value addition to everything that it produces. Africa must work for itself, its people, not exporting wealth to others."[12]

Port of Point Lisas

For the developing world, there's perhaps no better example of how natural resources can fuel industrialization than Trinidad and Tobago's Port of Point Lisas Industrial Estate, located midway between Port of Spain and San Fernando.

The product of government, business, and visionaries, Port of Point Lisas is a world-class petrochemical and heavy industrial complex built around deepwater port facilities—and created around the idea that the island's natural gas resources could be the source of steady revenue.

For decades, Trinidad's ample natural gas reserves had been considered nothing more than a cheap way to keep its oil production and refining facilities humming along; in the 1950s, its use expanded to power generation.

By the 1960s, though, people began to see the abundant resource less for what it was and more for what it could be: the basis for an industrial revolution that would change Trinidad's fortunes.

They wondered: What if we could attract natural gas users who would consume large amounts while producing feedstocks for both export and downstream industries? Wouldn't that add considerable jobs and inject cash into the national economy?

To fulfill that dream would require port facilities capable of accommodating large vessels, but that was just the start. Businesses located at the estate would also need utilities, which would require the development of infrastructure. And the site would have to be a free trade zone.

When I spoke with Eric Williams, a geologist who served as Minister of Energy and Energy Industries in the early 2000s, he explained the thinking at the time the estate was being conceived: If Trinidad and Tobago were to develop its own natural gas downstream sector, it would need the capacity to provide widespread, reliable electricity and water services.

As the main entity to foster and promote the industrial estate, the Point Lisas Industrial Port Development Company Limited (PLIPDECO) began selling shares to individuals and institutional investors to finance those efforts; the government, which had originally wanted to sit more or less on the sidelines, took over PLIPDECO soon after and began mobilizing capital to assist with infrastructure and provide leverage for international negotiations. It also invested in and began running the pipeline that would feed the estate with offshore natural gas.

Early projects included an ammonia plant, steel mill, cement plant, and a facility that made furfural—a solvent produced from sugar cane, which was a nod to the industrial site's original function as a sugar plantation. Today, the estate houses than 103 tenants, including 7 methanol plants, 9 ammonia plants, 1 urea plant, 3 steel plants, a power plant, and smaller light manufacturing and service companies.

Although the Point Lisas estate succeeded in diversifying Trinidad's economy, PLIPDECO isn't resting on its laurels.

In an interview with the Oxford Business Group, PLIPDECO President Ashley Taylor said they are working to position the estate as a logistics center for the consolidating, repacking, and relabeling of cargo. Land space for the warehouse systems has already been identified.[13]

11

TECHNOLOGICAL SOLUTIONS FOR OIL AND GAS

THE LONG-STANDING STEREOTYPE of Africa as a technological back-water is dissolving, and rightfully so. In fact, I have an old friend who says, "If you want to create an app, go to Africa."

He's on solid ground when he says this. African consumers have embraced mobile telecommunications, smartphones, and wireless internet, and this enthusiasm has generated momentum in all sorts of places. It's not unusual now to come across an older African woman, a grandmother who grew up in a farming community without learning to read or write, who has two cellphones and uses the internet to sell her produce.

Local innovators are going a step further, using these new resources to roll out solutions that meet local needs. For example, Africa has led the way in developing mobile money apps, which help consumers who have limited access to banking services. These technologies were born in East Africa and are now spreading rapidly across West Africa.[1] The first big player was M-Pesa, launched by the Kenyan mobile network operator Safaricom in 2007. M-Pesa paved the way for the debut of competitors such as M-kopa and Sportpesa in Kenya and has now set up shop outside Africa, serving countries such as Afghanistan and India.[2]

And foreign investors have noticed. They now see Africa as a crucial target market, with a billion people eager to buy high-tech goods and services—computers, smart devices, telecommunications equipment, streaming media, and mobile applications. As Erik Hersman, the founder of iHub in Nairobi, said in 2013, "[Big] tech companies [are] viewing Africa as the last blue ocean of consumer demand for technology."[3]

Overlooking Oil and Gas

Hersman's comment is revealing. It takes note of Africa's embrace of the Third and Fourth Industrial Revolutions, but it does not reveal the whole scope of the continent's potential. Instead, it highlights a problem.

It is a reminder that African tech innovators have mostly drawn attention for their contributions to mobile money, retail trade, entertainment, healthcare, and telecommunications—and not to oil and gas. They haven't made as much progress with respect to the energy industry, so oil and gas producers and service companies working in Africa have continued to rely on technology imported at significant cost from Europe and the United States.

For example, it was U.S.-based Baker Hughes that developed and deployed a deep-learning artificial intelligence (AI) solution for offshore platforms in African waters. Meanwhile, local service companies such as Nigeria's Lagos Deep Offshore Logistics Ltd. (LADOL) have not achieved anything comparable yet. Nor have they taken the steps needed to launch cybersecurity initiatives that can ensure the safe operation of these new technologies. If they want to do so, they will have to work harder to develop their own capabilities.

This is unfortunate. Oil and gas already play a crucial role in many African economies, and with a boost from new technologies, they could become an even larger source of revenue and good jobs. Innovations such as the development of new ways to drill wells and handle equipment, the design of new seismic data collection programs, the management of petroleum data systems, and the monitoring and protection of internet-connected equipment have the potential to redefine how business is done in this sector. They may also help oil and gas operators attract talented young workers who are looking for ways to use their high-tech skills on the job.

If these investors could economize by turning to local or regional suppliers, they surely would—and Africa would benefit if they did, since the money in question would remain within the continent.

But to reach this destination, African enterprises should not wait around, hoping to catch the attention of a sympathetic foreign partner. Nor should they expect government agencies to pave the way by adopting local-content regulations. Instead, they must find their own niches, look for new ways to meet investors' needs, and show that they can actually perform at a high level. They also should take pre-emptive action to identify the potential security risks of existing information technology systems.

What's more, they should work actively to negotiate alliances with foreign investors that already have tried and true technologies, as well as the capability to deliver them. Outside investors of this type can be good partners, provided that they are willing to commit to transferring advanced technologies to Africa and training local workers in their use.

So far, though, African companies have not often pursued such partnerships, nor have they built up their capabilities on their own. Instead, foreign companies have continued to take center stage.

The Benefits of Technology

African companies that set their sights on the oil and gas sector have the opportunity to make a real difference. Better equipment and more sophisticated software will benefit African fields much more than their counterparts in the West—say, offshore fields in the North Sea or onshore deposits in the Permian Basin. African tech innovators can—and should—do more to exploit these gaps, especially in areas where foreign companies have not been active.

According to C. Derek Campbell, the CEO of Energy & Natural Resource Security, Inc., African companies should take concrete actions that demonstrate their readiness to guard against cybersecurity breaches in their newest and most sophisticated systems. "African producers need to first understand the threats that exist in the cyber domain, determine which of those threats post the most danger to their operations, and establish the identity of their potential 'enemies' who would use those threats against them," he told me. "Having this understanding can enhance the selection of robust risk mitigation solutions that can prevent a catastrophic cybersecurity breach."

African companies aren't the only ones poised to benefit from being proactive on this front: Advanced technologies such as artificial intelligence (AI), advanced analytics, and robotics can go a long way towards making oil and gas projects around the globe more profitable, which will benefit the energy sector as a whole.

As McKinsey & Company has noted, oil and gas firms that use advanced analytics to direct their predictive maintenance programs can reduce maintenance expenses by as much as 13 percent. (They can also secure lower prices for new equipment.) Similarly, geospatial analytics can trim the cost of keeping a supply network up and running by 10 percent. Even more impressively, adding a 4D component to a 3D seismic survey can improve recovery rates from hydrocarbon reservoirs by up to 40 percent.[4]

Oil and gas companies, particularly those in Africa, also should look for new ways to make use of hydrocarbons, such as supporting gas-to-power projects. On the production side, they can develop equipment and software to optimize output levels at natural gas fields and conserve associated petroleum gas that might otherwise be flared. They can use 3D printers to turn out small replacement parts, eliminating the need to wait for a delivery from abroad. In the transportation arena, they can focus on security and monitoring systems for pipeline, rail, and road networks. When infrastructure is inadequate, they can use drones to deliver equipment or parts to remote locations. As for electricity production, they can provide power stations and transmission grids with advanced controls, meters, and monitoring technologies to ensure steady, reliable, and secure deliveries.

They should also design new and improved versions of existing facilities, as South Africa's MOGS Oil & Gas Services has done for tank farms by setting up a 50:50 joint venture with Hamburg-based Oiltanking GmbH. This venture, known as Oiltanking MOGS Saldanha (OTMS), is building a huge new storage depot for crude oil in Saldanha Bay, at the southern tip of the continent.[5] The facility will eventually have 12 interconnected tanks capable of holding no less than 13.2 million bbl, enough to cover domestic demand for about 3 weeks. It will be similar in design to a nearby tank farm that South Africa's government built in the 1970s with the aim of ensuring that the country never ran out of fuel, no matter how many suppliers proved reluctant to violate UN sanctions on doing business with the apartheid regime. But it will have far more advanced features than the existing depot. For example, it will be outfitted with sophisticated safety equipment and monitoring systems and will use design materials that help minimize evaporation loss.[6] Additionally, it will include a network of pipes that link all the tanks together so that the depot can combine different varieties of oil, ranging from heavy sour crudes to light sweets, into custom blends.

This system will put OTMS in a position to provide customers with precisely the type of crude they need. It will also allow the venture to take nearly instant advantage of fluctuations in the price of different varieties of oil, without the need to wait for slow-moving marine tankers to bring in new cargoes.

If African innovators join MOGS in thinking up new ways to serve oil and gas operators, they will add enormous value to their home countries' economies. They will create many new jobs and generate billions of dollars in revenues, all of which will go to local or regional market. They will make the energy industry more efficient, more reliable, and more profitable. They will also put African companies in a position to start offering their services around the world.

We are already seeing some steps in the right direction. I'm excited about the Federal University of Petroleum Resources, Effurun (FUPRE), a hub for petroleum training and research in Nigeria.

Since its establishment in 2007, FUPRE has drawn accolades for its innovations and technological accomplishments, such as drafting low-cost plans for mini-oil refineries and petrochemical plants and creating a pneumatic power generator powered by compressed air. A FUPRE team recently visited Equatorial Guinea's Ministry of Mines and Hydrocarbons to discuss a partnership. If the two countries move forward with this initiative, they will be able to set up a much-needed international petroleum innovation center for Africa.

Meanwhile, FUPRE has also worked with corporations to play a role in collaborative projects such as the design and construction of a 20-seat marine vessel, the re-manufacturing of new automotive components from end-of-life parts, and exploratory work on a technology that would create electrical power by water current. The latter project "will make possible the powering of ocean vessels by wave power without the need for diesel fuel," FUPRE's Vice-Chancellor, Akaehomen

Okonigbon Akii Ibhadode, told *The Guardian* in April 2019. "It is currently being tested at Mudi Beach Resort on [the] River Ethiope [in] Abraka to light up areas of the resort."[7]

Indigenous companies also should look to the example of Friburge Oil & Gas, a pan-African oil and gas and mining services provider headquartered in Angola that has been partnering with international technology providers to drive efficiency and environmentally friendly production methods. Those efforts include a partnership with a Norwegian waste treatment company to provide slop and sludge treatment services in central and western Africa.

"They are very willing to teach us and are open about skill transfer," Business Development Manager Dalila Iddrissu told OrientEnergy Review in 2017. "Our plan includes the outright purchase of all listed equipment and machinery for the operations, and these would be operated by Angolans."[8]

We need to see considerably more examples like these.

And to get there, we must start addressing the challenges African oil and gas companies face on the technological front.

Technology, Infrastructure, and Education

Some of the most obvious difficulties facing indigenous companies are the long-standing focus on the export of raw materials, the underdeveloped nature of the industrial and manufacturing sector, the inadequacy of infrastructure, and the disparities in access to educational opportunities.

Going forward, investment in infrastructure will be crucial. Africa needs to develop networks that can support technological innovation, especially fiber-optic networks that offer the most up-to-date options for connectivity and internet access. Investors are already working to build these systems around the continent, but they ought to work faster. They should also improve power transmission grids to ensure reliable electricity supplies to facilities such as servers and wireless networks, while upgrading traditional infrastructure such as roads and utility service as well.

Of course, while infrastructure is important, I believe that education should be an even higher priority. The more Africa invests in education, the more prepared it will be for the future. The continent does not have time to wait for a third party or a government agency to do this. Instead, it must embrace the challenge—and accept that education is not a quick fix. Students everywhere have to spend years learning before they're ready to use their skills, so Africans must do the same and commit to putting in the time.

But what kind of education will Africans need to move the oil and gas sector to a higher technological level? Should private-sector investors develop programs that focus specifically on skills that can be used in the oil and gas industry?

The answer: No. Instead, they should work to improve education all around.

I'm speaking from personal experience here. One of the best things that ever happened to me was getting an American education. If I had studied in Europe or one of many African countries, I might have taken the traditional route of specializing in one subject without taking time to develop any other skills. But, in the U.S., I had to look beyond my own narrow interests. I took courses in music, social sciences, and liberal arts, while also learning about science, mathematics, and computers. By the time I graduated, I was a more well-rounded person. I had developed the ability to use my God-given skills, but I had also gained the ability to communicate my ideas and interact in the workplace.

So, I'm in favor of giving African students the opportunity to get a broad-based education. Private-sector investors and schools should seek to develop programs that have technology at the center but do not neglect liberal arts and social sciences. After all, how much will the continent benefit if its brightest and most ambitious people turn out to be the best app developers or the best code writers, but they lack the ability to make a presentation to the people who can fund their projects?

At the same time, keeping technology front and center will ensure that our students have in-demand skills they can use in any sector of the economy—in oil and gas, but also in power generation, industrial processes, manufacturing, finance, communications, and trade. These skills will still be relevant in the long term after the oil and gas fields run dry—especially for members of the millennial and centennial generations, who will spend all of their working years in a world dominated by technology.

What Can the Government Do?

It's hardly a bad thing if African governments pay attention to education and try to support and fund new programs. But the private sector must take action and make things happen, rather than counting on the authorities to take the lead.

An excellent example of private-sector initiative is India, a country that has gone from being poor and underdeveloped to becoming a hub of technological innovation. India is home to many thousands of people who are now working with major Western tech companies to develop software, as well as other products and services. This happened because Indian investors saw the subcontinent's technological gaps as an opportunity. They went looking for young people who had skills, and they devoted time, energy, and a lot of money to build up the workforce they needed to exploit that opportunity. Their gamble paid off, and now these workers are attracting investment—and earning more money to build up the Indian economy.

Africa may not be able to replicate these results exactly. It does not have the same economic and political resources as India, and it is divided into many countries, which means that investors must navigate more borders and negotiate with multiple governments. But we can learn something important from India's example: Countries eager to push ahead on the technological front don't need to wait for the government to make the first move.

This is not to say that African governments don't have an important role: Indeed, they will bear a heavy load of responsibility. They must develop, adopt, and abide by policies that build confidence for domestic and foreign investors. They must uphold the rule of law, protect property rights, discourage and punish corruption, and ensure transparency and accountability in both the public and private sectors. They must take action to encourage the introduction and development of new technologies.

And they must work to prevent state agencies from duplicating their efforts or working at cross-purposes.

Governments must also protect the best interests of their constituents, especially local entrepreneurs and workers. They can do this by offering subsidies or tax breaks when appropriate and by investing in education at all levels. Additionally, they can establish public-private partnerships (PPPs) to promote education and entrepreneurship and expand ties with other African states. They can also look further abroad, turning to institutions such as Norway's sovereign wealth fund for advice on the development of workable standards or joining international bodies such as the Extractive Industries Transparency Initiative (EITI).

But the changes must go beyond reforms and rhetorical statements in favor of good governance. They must include a change in outlook. African governments are not running short on policy—quite the opposite! They're awash in legislative and regulatory programs drawn up by the World Bank, the U.S. Agency for International Development (USAID), and other agencies. But they aren't implementing any of the plans drawn up by the well-meaning, well-educated specialists from these institutions. This is not a problem that can be solved by consulting even more PhDs. Africa doesn't need more PhDs. It needs Ph-Dos: people who are willing to take action. Getting caught up in the paralysis of analysis is not going to get the continent where it needs to go. We have to make it happen!

African governments should also take great care not to politicize technology or treat it as an enemy of progress or an impediment to security. In Cameroon, for example, the government began shutting down the internet in the English-speaking regions of the country in early 2017. It kept these two regions, known as the Southwest and Northwest provinces, offline for a total of 230 days between January 1, 2017, and March 31, 2018, and artificially restricted data speeds on other days during the same period.[9]

The internet shutdown was a purely political phenomenon. It happened because the Cameroonian government, which is dominated by officials from the country's French-speaking regions, hoped to stifle political demonstrations in the Anglophone Southwest and Northwest provinces. But the crackdown severely disrupted business activity in Buea, a city in the Southwest province known as Silicon Mountain. Buea had been Cameroon's main technology hub before the shutdown. Today, many of the innovators, designers, app developers, and entrepreneurs who set up shop there have fled the country.[10]

This is the *wrong* way to go. African governments should tread carefully and avoid taking action that might drain the local talent pools—especially if they are home to large numbers of young, savvy workers who are already accustomed to using technology to maximize convenience and generate profits.

African Technology Success Stories

Taking all these steps to introduce and deploy new technologies could prove to be an uphill climb, given the obstacles that Africa faces. But the continent has one major advantage: human capital. Many of its people are ambitious, intelligent, and eager to start their own businesses, and there are real-life examples that show just how high African entrepreneurs can rise.

For instance, I'm impressed with Cameroonian Rebecca Enonchong, the founder and CEO of AppsTech and the I/O Spaces incubator for members of the African diaspora in the United States. She is also the chair of ActivSpaces (the African Center for Technology Innovation and Ventures), and she supports the development of African technology through her service as the board chair of AfriLabs, a network organization of more than 80 innovation centers across 27 African countries, and is a founding member of the African Business Angel Network.[11]

In 2017, Enonchong was included in the 100 Most Influential Africans in Science, Tech & Innovation by the *New African* magazine, and *Jeune Afrique*'s 50 Most Influential Africans.

In a 2018 interview with Africa.com, Enonchong said her love for computers began while she was providing finance and accounting services for a hotel. "I happened to have one of the powerful computers because I had to do a lot of financial analysis and modelling. As soon as I touched a computer, not to simply play with or write a paper, but to actually deliver something, I thought, 'This is so powerful.'"

Enonchong said she eventually started working at a computer store part-time, but she quickly realized that she wasn't going to make any money: "I would spend it all buying stuff from the store," she said. "I would take my computer apart and put it back together. I was one of those people who would be in line when a new version of software came out. That's really how it started. And I've never stopped loving technology. I adore it."

Enonchong learned more about technology as a freelance writer, blogger, and aggregator of African tech news on Twitter. In fact, she learned practically everything from scratch, beginning in 1999, when she launched her own company, AppsTech, to provide enterprise software solutions. "I started with literally no money and despite my best efforts, never raised any funding," she wrote in a blog post about her career. "I was a *woman* tech founder. I was a Black woman tech founder. I was a Black *African* woman tech founder."

In the beginning, however, Enonchong didn't think about obstacles. "Because I was not conscious of how difficult this was, I could be bold. And bold I was," she said. "With very little savings and no financial backing, I set out to build a global multi-million-dollar business."

After writing her business plan, she created a company website in English and French. "I spent days studying the web sites of companies like Arthur Andersen, PwC [PriceWaterhouseCoopers] and Capgemini and mimicked [their] look and feel. The site wasn't very nice but in those days, neither were my competitors' [sites]. I couldn't yet afford an office, but I did get a virtual business address I could use on the web site and on a business card. I didn't include a title on the card. I wanted the flexibility of being the CEO when I wanted or just one of the engineers if the situation warranted. I might have been a one-person business but I presented myself as a global corporation."

Enonchong landed her first client at an industry conference and invested the revenue from that job into her business. "I rented an actual office [and] hired a part-time assistant. I never used any of those funds to pay myself. In fact, I was homeless and couch-surfed for two years before I finally got my own place."

One of her strategies, from the beginning, was to seek out the best minds in her industry. "As often as possible, I tried to find the brightest [people] in the African community. Congo, Nigeria, Côte d'Ivoire, Central African Republic, Sudan, Cameroon, and more were all represented at AppsTech. This in addition to China, Korea, India, France and the United Kingdom. Most of them were much smarter than I was. Although some were obviously intelligent, they didn't necessarily have specific industry experience."

Every decision and purchase was based on the idea that the company was a global operation. And because Enonchong despises red tape, she made the simplification and streamlining of processes one of her top priorities.

Within four years, AppsTech had established seven offices across three continents and was serving customers in more than fifty countries. "We had generated tens of millions of dollars in revenue," Enonchong wrote. "By the time our model caught on, we already had established ourselves as the market leader. We had weathered the tech bubble and had seen many of our competitors, even some a hundred times our size, disappear."[12]

You could say that Enonchong and I have something in common: We're both passionate about transforming Africa. She sees technology playing a leading role. "It's one of the easiest and simplest ways to build our economy—through digital innovation," she told world-bank.org. "I really believe that it's one of the areas that can have the most impact that requires the least investment."

Another entrepreneurial star in Africa is Njeri Rionge of Kenya. This tireless businesswoman, now in her early 50s, got her start at the age of 20, selling yogurt to high-school students from the back of a friend's car while also working as a hairdresser. She then moved on to trade in luxury goods, taking economy-fare flights from Nairobi to London and Dubai so that she could bring coveted items back to Kenya for resale.[13] After launching several more business ventures, she moved into the technology sector, using $500,000 of starter capital to launch an internet service provider (ISP) in Kenya.[14] She did this in 1999, when projects like hers entailed significant risks. At that time, internet access was seen in Africa as a luxury, a fashionable accessory for the continent's most affluent and influential figures.

Rionge wasn't just trying to dispel the popular conception of the internet as a plaything for movers and shakers, something out of reach for average consumers. She also had to contend with active resistance from the authorities, as government officials, regulatory agencies in Nairobi, and the state telecommunications operator all raised objections to her plans. But she persevered, and her ISP, known as Wananchi Online, became Kenya's first mass-market provider of internet connectivity. The company helped bring Kenyans of all back-grounds online for the first time ever and has now expanded into other countries, becoming the largest ISP in East Africa.

Since engineering Wananchi Online's success, Rionge has moved on to other projects. Within the last 15 years, she has continued to act on her passion for start-ups, setting up Ignite Consulting, a business consultancy; Ignite Lifestyle, a healthcare consultancy; Insite, one of Kenya's most popular digital marketing outfits; and Business Lounge, Kenya's leading incubator of emerging enterprises.

These examples show that Africans have the skills and the drive to succeed—and, perhaps more importantly, the ability to discern and address unmet needs in a way that creates a whole new market, virtu-ally from scratch. But they also demonstrate that African innovators who target a specific niche within the wider economy can eventually have a big impact in multiple sectors. And that can include oil and gas.

African countries that support these innovators can create a new cohort of entrepreneurs. This group will have skills that will not just be in demand among oil and gas producers. They will also be able to write software, design equipment, and create new solutions for many other companies working in local and regional markets: oilfield service providers, marine and onshore transportation operators, logistics companies, robotics specialists, delivery services, construction firms, surveyors, job recruiters, bankers, securities and commodities traders, and financial consultancies.

If innovators can meet these needs, they will build up every link of the oil and gas industry's value chain—and the money they earn will remain within Africa, benefitting local economies and strengthening trade ties between neighboring and nearby countries. In the long term, they will also be able to apply their experience elsewhere, perhaps by expanding into foreign markets and hopefully by adding value to other sectors of the economy, such as agriculture or manufacturing.

This is not a pipedream. Enonchong and Rionge have already shown that it can be done. They identified openings in the market, exploited them, grew their companies, and moved on to apply the lessons they'd learned to other sectors. I can't wait to meet the people who will follow their examples and find new ways to support the oil and gas industry with technology.

12

OIL AND GAS COMPANIES CAN HELP RESHAPE AFRICAN ECONOMIES

U NTIL FAIRLY RECENTLY, IOCs were all about offering "gifts" to appease African host companies.

Fortunately, that's changing. IOCs are realizing that African communities are much more interested in corporate social responsibility (CSR) efforts that help them build better futures for themselves than they are in handouts with negligible or short-term benefits.

As a result, we're seeing an uptick in community projects with the potential to bring meaningful improvements to everyday Africans' lives. Examples include the specialized oil and gas industry training Aker Solutions of Norway is providing in Angola, the capacity-building and infrastructure programs multinational Tullow Oil operates in Ghana, and Chevron's extensive investment in public schools in Nigeria's Delta State.

Those are just a start. There are oil and gas companies putting real thought and effort into supporting local communities—perhaps they just need to do a better job in publicizing their activities.

The industry is also prioritizing higher transparency more than ever, having finally fallen into step with existing international regulations and initiatives to champion anti-corruption policies (see Chapter 9).

So, it's not a question of *if* the collective partners of the oil and gas industry will play a significant role in helping African countries, economies, and people. In fact, they already do.

The real wait-and-see is *what* they will do to make the most positive impact.

Will this positive impact be in the form of the African governments creating an enabling environment for IOCs? Or indigenous oil and gas industry companies seeking business relationships and knowledge transfers from IOCs? Or independent and national oil companies following IOCs' positive examples?

For the sake of Africa's future, I hope it's all three.

Africans Helping Africans: Sharing Opportunities and Knowledge

While companies can make significant changes through CSR projects, from capacity-building to environmental protection, they shouldn't overlook the importance of supporting local business communities, whether that involves partnering and buying from indigenous SMEs or sharing knowledge and technology. All of these efforts go a long way toward bolstering sustainable economic activity and growth.

I'd like to see more concerted efforts to support indigenous businesses, especially from African companies who've already established themselves. Don't get me wrong; we need foreign companies. But local companies—companies with a deep understanding of the culture, challenges, and dynamics within their communities—have tremendous power to make a positive impact.

It can be done.

Dovewell Oilfield Services is a strong example. After establishing a partnership with Peerless Pump Company in the American state of Indiana to manufacture and supply pumps in Nigeria, Dovewell made it a priority to find local engineers to help them install, engage, and maintain those pumps. They also established a valve maintenance company, which has allowed the company to employ and share technology with significant numbers of indigenous people and companies.

"Dovewell Oilfield Services Limited aims to be a force and a significant player across the entire value chain of the oil and gas industry in Nigeria specifically, and West Africa in general," Tunde Ajala, the company's executive director, said in early 2019.[1]

Of course, other indigenous companies—and business leaders—are strengthening the communities where they do business, too.

Take Atlas Petroleum International and Oranto Petroleum, founded by Prince Arthur Eze in 1991 and 1993, respectively. (Eze is usually referred to as Prince Arthur Eze because he is descended from tribal royalty.) The Abuja, Nigeria-based companies, which comprise Nigeria's largest privately held, Africa-focused E&P group, operate in multiple countries throughout the continent.

Both companies have pursued aggressive exploration in frontier areas, capitalizing on the high rewards of frontier exploration. The diversity of the companies—with Oranto focusing on exploration and Atlas focusing on production—is a strategic investment strategy that Eze conceptualized and implemented.

His business model reverses the pattern of large exploration blocks going to multinationals, leaving local players with what's left. Eze, who serves as executive chairman of Oranto Petroleum, has made it a priority to grab up valuable oil acreage and sell pieces of it to IOCs as the value increases.

Eze also is known for his commitment to philanthropy, from his $12 million donation to help fund the construction of an Anglican Church Youth Development Center in Otuoke, Nigeria, to his $6.3 million donation to Nigerian flood relief efforts several years ago.[2]

His businesses are making a positive difference, as well. After South Sudan's Ministry of Petroleum awarded an exploration and production sharing agreement for Block B3 to Oranto Petroleum in 2017, the company began constructing two primary schools in central South Sudan.

"The construction of these two schools is a reflection of Oranto's engagement to invest in social infrastructure in all areas where we operate in Africa," Eze said. "Oil has to benefit all citizens, and education is key to development."[3]

Oranto also is financing an education program, in conjunction with South Sudan's Ministry of Petroleum, to train 25 teachers in the most underprivileged parts of the country.[4]

Then there is Sahara Group, a Nigerian energy and infrastructure conglomerate co-founded by Tope Shonubi and Tonye Cole that has demonstrated a commitment to empowering communities where it works. Through the Sahara Foundation, the company supports health, education and capacity building, environmental, and sustainable development initiatives.

A sampling of the company's outreach efforts includes:

- Food Africa, a collaborative initiative between Sahara Group, the United Nations Sustainable Development Goals Fund (SDG-F), Roca Brothers (SDG-F Goodwill ambassadors and Spanish chefs), and the Kaduna State Government to alleviate poverty by providing opportunities for indigent farmers to access loans and grants through established farmer cooperatives.[5]

- The recent renovation of the University of Juba Computer Center in South Sudan.

- The company's new #LookToTheBook initiative, which strives to foster a reading culture among African youth. Sahara volunteers will host reading events in host communities and work to provide less-privileged children with easier access to books.

Sahara Group also has demonstrated a commitment to supporting the economies of its host communities. In addition to hiring local workers and partnering with local companies and suppliers, the company is developing infrastructure projects in oil and gas, utility concessions, industrial and business parks, real estate, hospitality, agriculture, health care, and specialty government-backed projects.[6]

Also making a difference for good is Shoreline Power Company Limited, a Nigeria-based power solution company that operates throughout sub-Saharan Africa under the leadership of CEO Kola Karim.

During the last 20 years, Karim has grown the business into an integrated energy company with upstream, midstream, and downstream operations. Karim, by the way, is a success story, too: The 2008 Young Global Leader Award winner serves on the Africa Advisory board of the London Stock Exchange and the Global Agenda Council on Emerging Multinationals of the World Economic Forum. He is a polo player and a patron of African art, and he co-manages Project HALO, which stands for Help and Aid for Less Opportuned and is the charity he and his wife, Funke, founded to help underprivileged children in Nigeria and the United Kingdom.[7]

Another African oil and gas leader making a positive difference is Nigerian-born Kase Lawal, chairman of Houston-based energy company, CAMAC (Cameroon-American), which operates in Africa and South America.[8] At one time, CAMAC was the only energy company on the New Stock Exchange that was controlled by African Americans.

Today, CAMAC is one of the largest Black-owned businesses in the U.S., generating more than $2 billion a year.[9]

From the time it was founded, CAMAC has supported scholarships, endowments, internships, arts education programming, and other educational programs in the U.S., Nigeria, and South Africa. The company's charitable arm, the CAMAC Foundation, promotes health, education, and cultural arts initiatives in the communities where CAMAC operates.

We also can look to the example of Tradex, a subsidiary of Cameroon's national oil and gas company, which specializes in the trading, storage, and distribution of petroleum products. In a prime example of African companies supporting one another, Tradex has been storing products at Luba Oil Terminal Equatorial Guinea (LOTEG) for the past several years.[10] In December 2018, the company received authorization to distribute petroleum products and derivatives in Equatorial Guinea. Leaders in both countries praise this step as an opportunity for further economic growth and job creation.

From CSR initiatives to the creation of local job and business opportunities, these kinds of efforts are critically important. I believe that a key element in creating an enabling business environment is increasing the participation of Africans in the oil and gas sector. We need to open more doors in the industry to ensure that Africans are part of the complete value chain by creating business opportunities across all segments, oilfield services, upstream, midstream, and downstream.

Indigenous Businesses and the Battle Against Corruption

As I've said many times before, regulations play a big role in establishing cooperation and information-sharing among all stakeholders.

We need to have the right kind of policies, and that comes from the top. Africa's leadership needs to demonstrate—through words *and* actions—that the "old way" of doing business is no longer appropriate.

And we can't forget about the role individual companies should play in curtailing corruption. Aside from the obvious reason—that corruption is wrong—it is bad for business. It hampers economic growth, impedes worker productivity, discourages investment and financing, and reduces much-needed government investments in education and training. Companies need to have a strong compliance department that ensures they are consistently and honestly publishing what they pay. No question about it, this is critical information.

Sometimes it might not just be leadership that runs afoul. Remember this: The people represent the company—and their missteps can cost dearly. What I see is that most government employees in Africa are poorly paid. So, it's no surprise that a public servant living hand to mouth will readily accept a bribe from the businessman who offers him four month's pay to "help him out." When his job isn't paying him enough to afford a decent life, it's hard for him to turn that down.

Offering a living wage should be the first line of defense against unethical behavior.

After that, writing employment contracts that include anti-bribery clauses helps ensure that all business relationships are conducted equally, fairly, and properly—as long as the same strong policies exist and are enforced in every region where the company operates.

Businesses can also fight dishonest conduct through internal policies and training. That kind of effort might include extensive corruption risk assessments and educating staff, subcontractors, consultants, and partners on how to handle requests for bribes, along with the establishment of clear-cut consequences for giving in to such requests.

Companies must establish their own anti-corruption manual that details their corporate policies and provides staff training. It is imperative that all personnel are well-trained in anti-corruption measures and that constant checks are in place to ensure compliance. This serves a two-fold purpose: It keeps all staff on the same page, and it shows authorities a dedication to curbing corruption. In the event of an investigation, an established (and well-taught) corporate policy is the best defense and carries much more weight than merely claiming, "We're not doing anything wrong."

The good news? We're facing a global shift against corruption.

It helps that most organizations (not just the oil and gas sector) are joining anti-bribery groups and implementing the best practices, thereby helping to level the playing field. Individual companies are increasingly refusing to be part of it, creating a network of ethical role models for others to emulate.

I've seen a lot of companies that have refused to pay and have done business well. Sure, in the beginning, it's hard. . . but the fortitude earns them the respect of both the local authorities and the other companies in their industry.

The Role of National Oil Companies: Do They Owe the Community?

We also should be able to count on NOCs and national gas companies to support indigenous SMEs. In fact, I believe that should be one of their primary responsibilities.

Just think of all the aspects of running a large oil or gas operation. You need to have vehicles and office supplies and food services—and a whole range of other things. National companies can play a significant part in ensuring that legitimate local service providers are given preference. Rather than, for example, importing all of the food for sale in their employee cafeterias from Europe or America, it needs to become standard practice to work with local service providers to buy produce grown in the community. This simple step of buying into the local agricultural base empowers everybody, and everybody benefits from it.

But the potential of NOCs to benefit African countries doesn't stop there. One Ernst & Young analyst described NOCs as "custodians of a nation's resource development and energy security."[11] I like that. NOCs play a vital role in providing revenue for their countries—revenue that, ideally, is used strategically to provide much-needed infrastructure and to promote stability, sustainable employment opportunities, and diversification. To do that, NOCs need to be strategic themselves so they can adapt to market volatility, technological advances, and the challenges posed by competitors.

In Africa, NOCs can play a significant role in supporting a vibrant oil and gas economy—but the extent of the help varies from country to country. The impact of the NOC depends on its ability to mobilize resources, whether on its own or through strategic joint ventures with partners of its own choosing.

Unfortunately, having a strong central government has not helped us very much in this aspect. But isn't strong government good for stability? Doesn't a strong government enable strong business? Well, the sad reality is that this strength has actually held back development, especially in creating value and building infrastructure at the local level.

Sure, I understand that being government-owned can be a challenge.

For one, government sees NOCs as part of their major revenue stream into the country. That makes it difficult for these companies to retain their own cash resources to do some of the things that are needed to stay competitive and contribute to strong national economies. Another challenge NOCs face is keeping costs down. In the global economy, extremely sophisticated multinational supply chains can put NOCs at a disadvantage. The multinational players are able to call in financial and logistic resources that NOCs don't have because they're restricted to the national environment.

But successful NOCs find ways to overcome such restrictions.

Economic clustering, which brings together groups of companies with ties to a particular industry, is a strong strategy in many industries and in many parts of the world. National companies that work with their governments to encourage this clustering do a better job stimulating all aspects of the economy. Think, for example, of the tourism industry: A beautiful new upscale hotel won't draw many guests if there aren't appetizing restaurants with ready sources of food, easy transportation options with agents available to facilitate arrangements, shopping opportunities with sufficient staff, or even medical facilities to assist the unfortunate traveler. African oil and gas countries would benefit from the same type of approach.

Another avenue for enhancing profitability and competitiveness is partnering with IOCs, which helps NOCs gain specialized skills, expertise, technologies, and access to infrastructure—and share risks with their partners. The IOCs, meanwhile, get access to the NOC's petroleum reserves.

Victor Eromosele, a former general manager of finance of Nigeria LNG and now chairman of the Centre for Petroleum Information, said in 2012 that NOC-IOC partnerships make sense where there is a common agenda and mutual respect.

"IOCs bring technology and finance to the table. NOCs have the hydrocarbon reserves . . . If history is anything to go by, the push-pull relationship between NOCs and IOCs will continue into the foreseeable future."[12]

I'm hoping that the recently announced partnership between the National Oil Corporation of Kenya (NOCK) and global oil and gas services company Schlumberger will be a strong example of the kind of cooperation and respect that Eromosele described. NOCK engaged

Schlumberger in April 2018 to support national capacity building in field development planning and production optimization.

Even more exciting is that the companies' agreement includes a comprehensive skills transfer exercise—a project-based learning opportunity—for 25 young staff members from NOCK and Kenya's Ministry of Petroleum and Mining. In addition to classroom and field-based learning, the project includes one-on-one mentoring with National Oil staff members and Schlumberger subject matter experts.

Another promising new NOC-IOC partnership, an agreement between Angola's state-owned Sonangol and French multinational Total, will focus on fuel distribution and lubricant sales in Angola. If that goes well, Total says, it would like to expand the partnership to petroleum product logistics and supply, including imports and primary storage of refined products. Of course, this is hardly the first agreement between Sonangol and Total; instead, it's the result of a long, successful history of partnerships on upstream activities.[13] Hopefully, the end result of this new deal will be sustainable job and business opportunities for Angolans.

African NOCs also can look to other parts of the world where state-owned oil and gas companies have matured quite successfully into viable competitors on the global energy market. With their growing strength, those companies have started boosting their domestic markets by hiring more home-grown operators, contracting with more local suppliers, and nurturing entrepreneurship. Not only that, but they've also begun influencing efforts abroad.

In this regard, we see impressive action out of Brazil, Malaysia, and Norway. The NOCs in these three nations have raised the bar.

- Petrobras, Brazil's largest company, is one of the largest energy companies in the world. It has developed breakthrough technologies for exploration, development, and production in ultra-deepwater pre-salt oil fields that operators from other countries are trying desperately to emulate.

- Despite declining production, the Norwegian NOC Statoil has risen to a globally competitive level thanks to its partnerships with universities and research institutes. In fact, companies that partnered more heavily with Norwegian researchers in Norwegian institutions received preferential access to new concession blocks and increased investments from Statoil to improve their R&D capabilities.

- Malaysia's PETRONAS has expanded well past its original intent of managing and regulating the domestic upstream oil sector. Instead, it learned from partnering with ExxonMobil and Shell how to expand its capabilities beyond its borders and now operates in more than 30 countries.

There's no reason why African NOCs can't follow their examples.

Equatorial Guinea's Minister of Mines and Hydrocarbons, Gabriel Mbaga Obiang Lima, recently agreed to participate in a short interview with me about NOCs.

Lima said he hopes NOCs in Africa will not follow the path of those in Asia and Middle Eastern nations that have become more like national energy companies (NECs).

"NECs are a mistake because NOCs' role is oil and gas, not wind or solar or other energy sources," he said. "African NOCs have missed that part that they should concentrate on. My view is that they were supposed to be the ones bringing a solution regarding the management of our resources, and they haven't done it. Their ministries have had to go to IOCs themselves and negotiate new deals and try to keep things moving. The problem has been that those NOCs ended up working more like ministries and civil servants with secure jobs. Whatever happens, they will not be blamed, and they will still receive their paychecks. Meanwhile, ministers are being blamed for everything that has happened. Ministries are not responsible for trading or getting into assets, but have been wasting their resources on this regardless because NOCs were not fulfilling their operational responsibilities."

Lima also commented on the secrets to his country's success—and the importance of African countries supporting one another.

"Equatorial Guinea has been talking to all African producers, listening to ideas of Nigeria and Ghana on structuring industry and doing local content, and then implementing them back home. We are not strict on planning, because industry changes every year. Industry is transforming quick and fast. African nations (and NOCs) need to learn to talk to each other and share lessons, and then implement them."

13

FOLLOWING NIGERIA'S LEAD
ON MARGINAL FIELDS

Most of the news about Africa's oil and gas sector focuses on big, dramatic events: the start of production at Angola's ultra-deepwater offshore oilfields, Royal Dutch Shell's announcement of stoppages at the Bonny export terminal following civil unrest in the Niger River Delta, Tanzania's plan to invest $30 billion in a huge new LNG plant, and protests against plans for hydraulic fracturing in South Africa's Karoo shale basin.

This is unfortunate. It reinforces the journalistic habit of putting the spotlight on the most spectacular topics and ignoring smaller-scale success stories.

In this chapter, I'm going to narrow the focus so I can tell you about one of those smaller success stories: the Nigerian government's deliberate effort to develop marginal oil and gas fields.

First, a bit of background: Nigeria began looking into marginal field development in the 1990s, after a number of international majors declined to develop some of the sites they had been awarded, saying that the reserves in question were too small to warrant their attention. In 1996, the government amended existing legislation to identify these sites as marginal fields and encourage their development by Nigerian companies. It spent the next few years developing guidelines for licensing and then launched the first round of bidding for 24 fields in 2003. Since then, it has handed a few more sites over to local investors, bringing the total number of marginal fields under development up to 30.[1]

The program has drawn some criticism, partly because it has played out painfully slowly. As of late 2018, less than half of the sites awarded to investors had started production, and Nigeria's government was still not saying when it might hold the second round of bidding, originally scheduled for 2013.[2] The first-round awards have raised questions about corruption since many of the awardees appear to have been chosen for their ties to powerful government officials and not for their ability to get the job done.[3] They also played a role in the risk management and corporate governance crisis that led the Central Bank of Nigeria to take over Skye Bank, one of the country's largest commercial banks.[4]

In this context, the new Marginal Fields Bidding Round launched in 2020 has seen the Department of Petroleum Resources (DPR) put a highlight on the transparency of the process while raising hopes to see a new wave of local content development across Nigeria's upstream industry.

Even so, Nigeria's marginal field initiative ought to be counted as a success. It has given more than 30 locally based companies the opportunity to establish themselves and develop their capacities as upstream operators. Also, it has allowed them to do so without assuming the risks (or the costs) of exploration, since all of the fields designated as marginal were confirmed discoveries, surveyed and tested by foreign companies, and known beyond a shadow of a doubt to contain hydrocarbons.

Stepping Stones

Marginal oil fields can serve as a foundation for bigger things. They can help African companies establish their reputations and gain enough standing to earn consideration for larger projects and work with more prominent partners, especially if they find ways to demonstrate that they can use modern technologies to make marginal sites profitable.

This has not always been easy to do. In fact, some of the Nigerian companies that won rights to marginal fields in the first bidding round stumbled at first because they didn't have enough technical expertise to get the job done properly. But others succeeded because they hired ambitious young people with useful skills, such as Nigerians who had already gained experience by working on high-tech projects for foreign majors such as Royal Dutch Shell. They also leaned on Nigerian entrepreneurs who were able to use local networks to optimize their access to goods and services.

In some cases, this included financial services from Nigerian banks. Of course, the ill-fated Skye Bank was one of these, but it was not the only local lender to help fund development work at marginal oil and gas fields. For example, Intercontinental Bank lent $6 million to Niger Delta Petroleum to cover the cost of drilling a workover well, Ogbele-1, which brought the Ogbele field into production. Meanwhile, Union Bank lent a total of $50 million to Britannia-U for work at Ajapa, starting with the $23 million credit that allowed it to achieve first oil.[5]

In other cases, these connections facilitated partnerships with Nigerian companies that were in a better position to bankroll upstream operations. Platform Petroleum, for example, teamed up with a more cash-rich partner, Newcross, to cover its costs at the Asuokpu/Umutu fields. This alliance allowed Platform to become the first to begin production at a marginal license area.

Imitation Is the Best Form of Flattery

Nigeria's successes on this front have been substantial enough to have inspired other African states to promote the development of marginal sites as part of a wider effort to reform the oil and gas sector. In June 2018, for example, Thierry Moungalla, the communications minister of the Republic of Congo, said he hoped the country's decision to join OPEC would lead to progress on this front.

Participation in OPEC "will help us to better liberalize the sector and bring in new players willing to invest even in marginal fields," he told the Bloomberg news agency.[6]

Marginal fields have also drawn attention in Angola, one of the stars of the African oil and gas sector. As of late 2018, the country had retained its position as the second-largest crude producer in sub-Saharan Africa and was also working to boost natural gas yields. But it was also desperate to make up for the losses it had suffered in recent years. Angola's oil output fell by about 20 percent between 2014 and 2018, not least because lower crude prices made its deepwater and ultra-deepwater fields off the coast of the Cabinda province less profitable.[7] In turn, this decline caused the economy to take a hit—no surprise, given that oil and gas and related activities account for about 50 percent of Angola's GDP and more than 90 percent of its exports.[8]

President João Lourenço, who replaced Angola's long-time leader José Eduardo dos Santos in early 2017, hopes reforms will help turn the tide. One of his main targets is Sonangol, the national oil and gas operator. Lourenço's government wants to restructure the company and dislodge it from its position at the pinnacle of the industry, partly by assigning its regulatory and licensing powers to a new state agency and partly by limiting its right to claim hydrocarbon deposits.

But the president is not just thinking in terms of country-wide institutions. In May 2018, he signed a decree that slashed production and income tax rates for marginal fields in half.[9] His government has also said it intends to offer up a number of marginal fields in the Congo, Cunene, and Namibe Basins, during an upcoming licensing round in 2019.

Guillaume Doane, the CEO of Africa Oil & Power, praised this plan, saying in December 2018 that marginal fields might be the best avenue for bringing new and local players into the country's hydrocarbon sector. "There is an antiquated perception that Angola as an oil and gas market is only for the big boys," he told APO Group. "Through marginal fields, Angola is attracting a greater diversity of E&P players that can operate smaller onshore and shallow water resource plays. In the next decade, Angola can achieve historic developments through marginal fields, similar to what Nigeria [has] accomplished in recent years."[10]

A Hole Waiting to Be Filled

Doane's remarks about the opportunities that await smaller companies in Angola highlight the real potential of marginal fields. As Nigeria's example shows, these are the projects that can promote the development of local partnerships, business networks, and other arrangements that can pave the path to success for African companies.

If the Republic of Congo, Angola, and other African countries move forward with these upstream development programs, they will not just be creating opportunities for local companies that are willing to work at small sites. They will also be creating openings for local service providers. Oil companies rarely operate alone; they typically team up with contractors to farm out specific types of work, such as drilling, well servicing, repair and maintenance of equipment, rig transportation, marine services, and subsurface mapping.

In other words, local investors will need partners that can help them get the job done. They will need to establish relationships with companies that can deliver, operate, and move the type of rigs that are best suited for drilling in small fields. If they take on complex projects, they will need to find drilling contractors that have the specific skills and technologies required for directional drilling at unconventional fields or secondary recovery operations at mature sites. If they agree to develop offshore deposits, they will need to work with companies that specialize in marine services.

Historically, most of the companies that have provided services of this type have not been African. They have come from elsewhere and mostly worked for large multinational firms such as ExxonMobil—not for local investors focusing on smaller assets.

This means there is a hole in the market waiting to be filled. Local companies will need partners that can provide services on a scale suited to marginal fields. Angola, for example, will need marine service companies that can supply vessels and equipment for use at offshore fields that are several orders of magnitude smaller than, say, Block 0, where a Chevron-led consortium saw output peak at more than 400,000 bbl/d.[11] Under these conditions, African entrepreneurs who can meet these needs are likely to be much in demand.

They will also have the opportunity to build their reputations—to become known as reliable partners capable of scaling upwards and taking on progressively larger projects. This, in turn, will allow them to expand their capabilities even further over time. It will put them in a better position to bid for marginal fields in neighboring and nearby countries and give them an incentive to invest in research and development programs that focus on African solutions for African challenges. It will also give them extra leverage in negotiations with foreign enterprises, which could provide access to new technologies that have enhanced upstream development in other regions.

Even better, increased activity in the oilfield services industry will create jobs and serve as an impetus for growth in other sectors of the local economy. It will stimulate the construction industry and retail trade since workers will need housing, food, and clothing. It will give a boost to local manufacturers and 3D printing services capable of turning out equipment and parts for use at oil and gas fields. It will support demand for banking, financial, and legal services since everyone involved will need ways to manage money and ensure compliance with local regulations and requirements. It will encourage commodities trading within Africa since local operators will need to find ways to move their product to market, finance transactions, and establish a platform for communication with third parties. Additionally, it will heighten the appeal of technology, creating opportunities for skilled workers who can operate the computers, software, and smart devices that offer the most cost-effective and reliable solutions for handling finances, commodity trades, record-keeping, design, and logistics.

In short, marginal field development programs are nothing short of a golden opportunity for Africa. They lay the groundwork for a rising tide that can lift many boats in the long term, with governments offering local investors the chance to gain a foothold in upstream hydrocarbon development, investors giving more business to local service providers, service providers creating demand in related sectors of industry, and workers in related sectors gaining skills in technology, trading, finance, and the like that will remain useful even after the oil and gas fields run dry.

Government Must Set the Stage

Governments have a crucial role to play in promoting the development of marginal oil and gas fields—and not just in exercising their prerogatives as the source of official policies governing licensing, taxation, operations, and the like. African governments should also work to create an environment that supports entrepreneurs and discourages corruption.

So far, Nigeria has moved the furthest in this direction. To date, it has done more to promote the development of marginal fields than any other African country. Its track record is hardly perfect, but it is the most extensive. It has also generated some genuine success stories.

Take the example of Sahara Group—this Nigerian company has used its participation in the marginal field development program as a springboard for further development. It came into existence as a trader of petroleum products in 1996 and spent the next few years building up its business. In 2003, it built and launched one of the first independently owned fuel storage depots in Nigeria. Then, in 2004, it seized the chance to expand its operations and took part in the first licensing round for marginal fields. It won the right to develop OML 148, also known as the Oki-Oziengbe field, and brought it online in 2014.

But Sahara Group has done more than establish itself as a small-scale upstream operator. During the years when it was preparing OML 148 for development, it also developed other links in the value chain. More specifically, it struck deals for the supply of jet fuel to Nigerian and international airlines; established its own fuel distribution, storage, and marketing affiliates to handle downstream operations in nearly 30 African countries; provided bespoke marine solutions for offshore LNG projects; commissioned two LPG tankers; became a shareholder in several refineries and power plants, and accumulated an extensive portfolio of commercial real estate. Moreover, it greatly expanded its trading operations inside and outside Africa, setting up subsidiaries in Dar es Salaam and Conakry as well as Singapore and Dubai.[12]

Sahara Group is hardly in a position to compete with Shell or the other international majors that have led oil and gas development in Nigeria. Nevertheless, it has succeeded in growing far beyond its original scope. It now earns revenues of more than $10 billion per year and is capable of producing as much as 10,000 bbl/d of oil. It has expanded its upstream portfolio to include another 8 fields across Africa and hopes eventually to see its output rise to 100,000 bbl/d.[13]

Nigeria's marginal field development initiative appears to have been the impetus for all these advances. Sahara Group got its start as a relatively small-scale fuel trader, and it only began to expand far beyond its origins after the acquisition of OML 148. Over the last 15 years, it has become a diversified and vertically integrated company, active in the upstream, midstream, and downstream sectors—and also in the service and power-generation sectors. It has created more than 1,400 permanent jobs in at least 38 countries.[14]

Sahara Group's expansion and advances are a win for Nigeria. They show that government-sponsored programs can give a boost to local businesses that are eager to gain a higher profile. They show that marginal fields are worth developing—not just because of the oil and gas they yield, but also because they contribute to growth in other industries. They also demonstrate that African entrepreneurs are ready, willing, and able to make the most of the resources at hand.

Of course, Nigeria's marginal field initiative has its flaws, as demonstrated by rumors of corruption in the first licensing round and local oil executives' complaints about the ongoing postponement of the second licensing round.

Overall, though, it is a good model for other African countries to follow, and I look forward to seeing Angolan and Congolese companies follow Sahara Group's example.

14

THE CRITICAL ART
OF DEAL-MAKING:
IT'S TIME TO NEGOTIATE
FOR A BETTER FUTURE

LONG BEFORE I BEGAN my legal career, I understood that many of Africa's problems could be tied to the waste of our petroleum resources. Even more apparent was the fact that Africans were not part of any kind of deal-making structure: When negotiations involving foreign investors' oil and gas exploration, production, and revenue-sharing took place, Africans were not at the table—or even in the room.

I asked myself—why aren't Africans part of this economic empowerment? Why are Africa's deals being driven by Westerners?

Those concerns eventually led me to go into energy law and work to change the dynamics I had observed. From the beginning, I was influenced by the lessons of my parents, who taught me not to stand by idly in the face of injustice. Later, I was fortunate enough to be mentored by the late Ron Walters, who was Jesse Jackson's deputy campaign manager. Dr. Walters emphasized the teachings of Charles

Hamilton Houston, the Black American lawyer who helped dismantle U.S. Jim Crow laws. Houston used to say that a lawyer is either a social engineer or a parasite on society. I am determined to be the former: My experiences since law school have been an evolving expression of my deepest held beliefs and my desire to see a better Africa.

Building a legal career in Africa, and later, my own firm, required a great deal of hard work, tenacity, and a Teflon-like exterior to criticisms. Here I was, a kid under 30 with a business plan, guts, and a laptop who believed he could play with the big boys. The big firms and the industry players were not going to make way for a rookie, even though I was qualified with the hunger to succeed. Why would a general counsel or a CEO of an oil company take a chance on me with no track record of winning anything in Africa?

As God is always good to me, I was eventually given more and more business from companies such as Schlumberger, Kosmos, Heritage, Chevron, Lukoil, Afex Global, Vanco (now PanAtlantic), Gazprom, DHL, Suncor, Gunvor, IFD Kapital, and many African petroleum companies and ministries. I did well because I was on the ground and focused on getting results and winning for these clients that trusted me. I took every call, stayed up late at night, cut out crazy friends and negative people, and used the best of my legal education to make Africa work for me.

As the CEO of Centurion Law Group, we went on to represent both the business and government side of oil and gas deal negotiations across Africa. Around the time I was starting this book, we advised Nigeria-based Oranto Petroleum in the landmark acquisition of four strategic oil blocks in the Republic of Niger, and South Africa's state-owned Strategic Fuel Fund in the acquisition of one of Africa's most sought after oil assets, Block B2 in South Sudan.

My experiences have shown, time and time again, that without good deal-making, oil and gas resources lose much of their power to create a better future for Africans. Good deal-making is vitally important. Not only do governments need to negotiate deals that result in long-term benefits for their people, but African companies also need to negotiate deals that keep them on an equal playing field with their competition and empower them to grow, create and sustain jobs, and support the communities they're based in.

For Africa to truly realize all of the benefits oil and gas operations have to offer, we need to see good deal-making across the board.

I can help. While my advice can't replace solid training and experience in deal-making, I can share some helpful principles and, hopefully, help others avoid some of the mistakes I've observed.

Negotiating Fundamentals

First of all, no matter what side of the table you're on, prepare, prepare, and prepare some more. Too many times, I have found myself in negotiations where the other side has not even read the contract or looked at the asset we're trying to discuss! And yet, there they sit with power to make very big, difficult decisions. Basically, they're courting disaster. At best, they're squandering economic opportunities. But they also could be opening the door to agreements with the potential to harm their company or country, not to mention the environment or even local stability.

You've probably heard the phrase, "You get what you pay for." That truth applies to the time and effort we invest in negotiating good deals. There's a reason big companies hire 20 to 30 lawyers, an accountant, a negotiation expert, and more to represent them at the negotiation table. They want to get the best deal possible for themselves. Even if your company or government can't afford a "dream team" to represent your interests, you must do everything humanly possible to make your negotiations fruitful. That means we do the work of gathering information, educating ourselves about the resource to be discussed and the interests of those coming to the table, and making sure we have key decision-makers backing up our terms.

What's more, when trustworthy, practical help is accessible, we should take it, whether that comes in the form of legal representation, guidance from NGOs, negotiation training programs, or volunteer consultants. The New Partnership for Africa's Development (NEPAD), for example, an agency of the African Union, provides technical assistance to help countries make good deals and has offered regional training programs on contract negotiation.[1] Another resource is the Natural Resource Governance Institute, based in Washington, D.C. In 2017, the institute released the Natural Resource Charter Benchmarking Framework, which provides 170 questions that African governments should ask investors about natural resource governance.[2]

It is also vital to consider the perspectives of both parties. As a negotiator, especially on the private side of deal-making, you need to do your best to make sure everyone at the table feels the resulting deal is in their interests; that it's a win-win situation. That's how you sustain healthy, long-term relationships and the give-and-take that truly results in fair deals, both now and in the future. I have a very long-term approach: I want to ensure I'll be able to work with these people for a long time. And if they don't see themselves winning, if they don't see themselves having something that is reflective of what their expectations are, then we have lost as a whole.

As Richard Harroch, managing director and global head of mergers and acquisitions for San Francisco-based VantagePoint Capital Partners, says, never underestimate the value of being a good listener.

"Some of the worst negotiators I have seen are the ones who do all the talking, seeming to want to control the conversation and expound endlessly on the merits of their position," Harroch wrote for *Forbes* in 2016. "The best negotiators tend to be the ones who truly listen to the other side, understand their key issues and hot buttons, and then formulate an appropriate response. Try to gain an understanding of what is important to the other side, what limitations they may have, and where they may have flexibility."[3]

And what's important to the parties in an African oil and gas deal? At the big-picture level, foreign oil companies tend to focus on seeing a fair return on their investments, while governments are more concerned with oil and gas activities' impact on them and their country.

Governments want to develop their countries. They want to create jobs. They want to generate a tax base.

If I'm representing a company, for example, I make sure I've reviewed the national development agenda of the government that the company wants to make a deal with. I need to know if the government has made environmental protection a priority or if their focus is on local empowerment. Say the government is concerned with local content, I want to be ready to show data on short- and long-term job creation, along with the company's commitment to training and hiring local people and partnering with local suppliers.

Another key factor: When you're negotiating, ask yourself what happens after the deal. Are the terms the parties are agreeing to realistic? What has been done to make sure everything being agreed upon actually happens—in a reasonable amount of time? Have we addressed potential obstacles? Have we laid out consequences for a failure to act? What good is a deal, even one with great terms for your company or country, if it can't realistically be executed? I always address how a deal will be implemented and its long-term viability.

In his 2004 article for *Harvard Business Review*, "Getting Past Yes: Negotiating as if Implementation Mattered,"[4] veteran negotiator

Danny Ertel cited the example of the 1998 joint venture between AT&T and BT to bring global interconnectivity to multinational customers. Concert, the resulting $10 billion start-up, was expected to bring in $1 billion in profits from day one. Instead, Concert floundered and went out of business three years later.

"To be sure, the weak market played a role in Concert's demise, but the way the deal was put together certainly hammered a few nails into the coffin," Ertel wrote. "AT&T's deal makers scored what they probably considered a valuable win when they negotiated a way for AT&T Solutions to retain key multinational customers for itself. As a result, AT&T and BT ended up in direct competition for business—exactly what the Concert venture was supposed to help prevent. For its part, BT seemingly out-negotiated AT&T by refusing to contribute to AT&T's purchase of the IBM Global Network. That move saved BT money, but it muddied Concert's strategy, leaving the start-up to contend with overlapping products."

Negotiating with implementation in mind is a lot of work—and requires greater collaboration and communication among the parties at the table—but it also increases the likelihood of shared successes.

A few things to consider:

- Keep all of the parties in the loop: Try tackling fact gathering and analysis together—*before* negotiations get underway. Don't surprise the others with last-minute information or decisions. If you become aware of issues that could interfere with the success of the proposed project, raise them early, and encourage joint efforts to resolve them or develop alternative approaches.

- Ask the tough questions: Test the practicality of the commitments both parties are making. Can everyone deliver? How? Work together to develop early-warning systems and contingency plans.

- Involve key stakeholders: Make sure you know whose approval is needed for the terms outlined in your proposal. Identify who might interfere with implementation and what you will do if that happens.

Governments: You Have to Demand More

Governments have a great deal to lose—and gain—from the success of their negotiating. Not only do the deals they make impact their political futures, but they also impact the lives of millions of people.

One of the most important things governments can do, long before there's any talk of negotiation talks, is to limit themselves to the right kinds of investors. I'd like to see governments go John F. Kennedy on prospective investors to ask, "What can you do for our country?" Will the investor support the country's economic goals? Are they all about profit, or are they willing to consider the country's needs as well?

Think about it, government leaders: There is no reason to accept an LNG project that would take 100 percent of the product created with your country's resources to Europe or Asia or America, especially when you need LNG to power your own country. Your priority should always be using your country's natural resources strategically to better its future.

At the same time, African governments need to be realistic about the challenges they face. There are a slew of issues that complicate dealings with African governments: burdensome tax policies, excessive red tape, unrealistic local content requirements, lack of judiciary protection for contracts, lack of transparency—the list goes on.

Foreign investors are willing to overlook quite a bit for a chance to profit from Africa's considerable oil and gas resources, but it's harder to ask a foreign investor to launch a major capacity building initiative, for example, when a country's policies already make operating there expensive or inefficient. Companies need to see a serious, ongoing effort on the part of government to protect their interests and allow them to make a reasonable profit. I know resolving these policy issues can be time-consuming, but addressing them must be priorities for governments that are serious about reaping the full benefits of their natural resources.

Of course, there's no reason for African governments to roll over and submit entirely to foreign investors' wishes. In fact, I would like to see those negotiating on behalf of African governments to be much more assertive with foreign investors. For example, I have seen too many lawyers passively accept model contracts handed to them by foreign companies. Attorneys, you can politely decline. Don't give the other party undue control.

It's like when you go out jogging or walking with somebody—you don't think about it, but in most cases, one of you adjusts your pace to match the other. Once you accept the other side's contract, you are walking on their time. I think African countries should be the ones setting the pace. They should be driving the terms of agreements and engaging the negotiations from a position of strength. They should be embedding initiatives that allow them to create jobs and training opportunities, to develop infrastructure, and monetize their resources into contracts they draft. (See Chapter 6 for more about monetizing natural resources.)

I'm not calling for unreasonable demands. Again, it's important to consider the needs of both sides. Governments must give investors a chance to generate income from the resources they're interested in and recoup their investments. At the same time, governments need to look at creating value for their country and its people. It's a balancing act. It's challenging, but it's doable.

Promise for Africa

If you have any questions about the power of good deal-making, look at Mauritania and Senegal.

Since Kosmos Energy discovered massive stores of natural gas, as much as 50 tcf, off the coasts of these countries in 2015, one exciting announcement has followed another, as Kosmos—followed by its partner, BP—started investing in local businesses and communities. Petroleum industry training programs were launched. Young people started taking free English classes. Some areas even got electricity for the first time, giving them access to things many of us take for granted.

It's exciting stuff—especially to people living in Mauritania and Senegal. It's also encouraging to anyone interested in the future of African oil and gas. Stories like this are proof positive that oil and gas development can bring opportunity, hope, and prosperity to countries that have historically been at a disadvantage.

Here are just a few examples of how Kosmos and BP have been bringing positive changes to the communities where they work and do business:

- Since its discovery, Kosmos has invested in workplace health and safety training programs for local oil and gas industry suppliers in Mauritania. The multinational also has provided English classes for young people in Nouakchott.[5]

- Kosmos entered a multi-year partnership with the Gérer les Impacts des Activités Extractives (GAED) international master's program, a joint master's degree program on managing impacts from the extractive sector, held at the University of Nouakchott and the Gaston Berger University of Saint-Louis, Senegal. Kosmos is supporting the GAED master's program by providing employees as guest lecturers, hosting field trips and internships, and contributing financial support. GAED students have also joined Kosmos' teams in the field for seismic and drilling Environmental and Social Impact Assessments (ESIAs) in both Mauritania and Senegal.

- Kosmos has also made it a priority to support the Ndiago region, which is directly onshore from the company's license areas near the border with Senegal. For example, community authorities suggested that the local economy could benefit from electrification projects, so Kosmos developed a rural electrification project that now provides power to more than 2,100 people.

- In Senegal, Kosmos consulted with more than 1,000 coastal community residents before completing an ESIA of deepwater exploration activities in the region. Hence, community members' concerns are on record—and hopefully will impact exploration activities. Kosmos also facilitated oil and gas workshops for civil society organizations in Dakar.

- BP, which has partnered with Kosmos Energy to initiate multi-well exploration programs in Mauritania and Senegal, unveiled plans for a long-distance learning center in Nouakchott for oil and gas sector training. The center will be designed in close partnership with Mauritania's Ministry of Petroleum, Energy and Mines.

- In a cooperative agreement with Mauritania's Ministry of Petroleum, Energy and Mines, BP is providing engineering institute École Supérieure Polytechnique in Nouakchott with specialized laboratory equipment and postgraduate scholarship funding.

- In Senegal, BP invested millions to support the new National Institute of Oil and Gas (INPG), created with the goal of building national capacity for Senegal's oil and gas industry. The company has also sponsored thousands of hours of professional English lessons for government employees and have been offering "LNG 101" workshops to enhance Senegal residents' technical and commercial understanding.[6]

- In 2018, BP announced that they would be developing a floating LNG plant offshore Mauritania and Senegal. The facility is designed to provide roughly 2.5 million tonnes of LNG per year. The project will make gas available for domestic use in both countries; this means that Mauritania and Senegal will be better positioned to provide their people much-needed access to electricity, which is key to economic growth and stability there.[7]

It would be accurate to say this activity was made possible by Mauritania's and Senegal's huge natural gas reserves. And the generous commitments of foreign investors.

But, don't be fooled—there's more to the story. I'm certain that behind the scenes, the governments of Mauritania and Senegal played a critical role in making these positive developments possible. They did that through the deals they negotiated with BP and Kosmos, not to mention the inter-governmental cooperation agreement (ICA) they negotiated and signed in early 2018 to make the development of a cross-border natural field possible.

Clearly, good deal-making has far-reaching implications for African people, communities, and businesses.

Another deal that stands out as a model is the landmark 2018 agreement between Noble Energy and Equatorial Guinea's Ministry of Mines and Hydrocarbons that I describe in Chapter 6. I am very thankful to have played a role in the negotiations. The agreement, which also involved state-owned GEPetrol and some third parties, allows Noble to pump 600 bscf of natural gas from the offshore Alen field to the Punta Europa integrated gas complex near the capital city of Malabo.[8]

Before the deal, Equatorial Guinea's only LNG facility received natural gas feed from the aging Alba Field, where production is expected to go into decline within the next two or three years. Under the agreement, a 65-kilometer pipeline will be built to connect Noble's operations to Punta Europa. The pipeline will be designed with the capacity to receive not only Alen's output, but that from surrounding fields, too. This answers not just the need for further feedstock, but also limits the country's dependence on a single downstream project.

Also exciting, at the same time this agreement was signed, Gabriel Mbaga Obiang Lima, Equatorial Guinea's Minister of Mines and Hydrocarbons, announced plans to build a natural gas megahub at Punta Europa. The megahub will aggregate the production of any existing gas and a new natural gas discovery in Equatorial Guinea. It is not exaggerating to say that the country is in the early stages of a gas revolution that will provide opportunities for economic diversification, creation of local content and jobs, and a path for state-owned gas company, Sonagas, to take a leading role in the development and marketing of LNG.[9]

Another encouraging example of good deal-making is the April 2018 project framework agreement that the Ugandan government, through the Ministry of Energy and Mineral Development and state-owned Uganda National Oil Company, made with the Albertine Graben Refinery Consortium (AGRC). The agreement paved the way for the consortium to develop, design, finance, build, operate, and maintain a $4 billion refinery in Kabaale.[10]

This deal didn't come easily, but it does represent a win for Uganda. Because the AGRC is providing project financing, Uganda will gain vital, value-adding infrastructure without incurring more debt.[11]

Life Happens

If negotiation were a science, deals would be arranged like molecules, all neat and tidy and yielding the same result, over and over. Just like putting two hydrogens and an oxygen together always produces water, having the right parties and terms in place would generate success every time.

But negotiation isn't a science. At best, it's a messy art, more like finger painting than photorealism. You simply can't predict with 100 percent certainty what the future will look like. Sometimes, you lose an oxygen molecule, and instead of water, you have poison. And sometimes, something happens halfway around the world that sours your deal. This means finding a way to safeguard your interests under a variety of circumstances is critically important. I always go into deal-making with this thinking.

Unfortunately, there was no way Equatorial Guinea could have anticipated the U.S. shale revolution when it penned its 2004 agreement to sell LNG—some 3.4 million tonnes of it a year—to BG Group. And in fairness, neither could BG or anyone else, for that matter.

The deal called for BG to buy gas from Equatorial Guinea for 17 years, from 2007 to 2024, and send it to the U.S. for processing and domestic sales. The product was priced at a discount to Henry Hub—the gas futures benchmark—which is commonplace. That meant the African nation was getting about $6 per million British thermal units (MMBtu) in 2004 and an even better $15 MMBtu the following year.[12] Not bad at all.

Then, the bottom fell out of the global gas market. With an influx of American shale coming onto the scene, prices fell below $4 MMBtu, eroding Equatorial Guinea's profit.

That's bad enough. But because BG had negotiated terms that allowed it to sell the LNG it purchased from Equatorial Guinea anywhere in the world, the product previously destined for American shores was diverted to Asia, instead—where an overheated market had pushed prices as high as $15 MMBtu. That meant BG was making huge profits off of LNG it bought for hardly more than a song.

Obviously, Equatorial Guinea was upset: You would be, too. But it was hamstrung by the fact that it had failed to negotiate a profit-sharing agreement with BG for any gas sold to non-U.S. buyers. The country also lacked a renegotiation clause.

After a new set of negotiations—a process that I was fortunate to be part of—BG agreed to give the government the larger of 12.5 percent of Asian profits or $20 million per quarter.

BG also agreed to social programs supporting maternal and child health, malaria prevention, and sanitation projects.

Since then, BG Group was sold to Royal Dutch Shell, which inherited the 12.5 percent deal.

Fortunately, with the now-Shell deal wrapping up in a few years, Minister of Mines and Hydrocarbons Gabriel Mbaga Obiang Lima has a chance to return to the negotiating table. He told *Reuters* he wants more royalties and shorter terms—50 percent for three to five years beginning in 2020.[13] And while he still doesn't have a crystal ball into the future, at least that shows better vision.

This LNG offtake deal was the sexiest deal in Africa ever for a trader, and it continues to be presented as an example of how not to do a deal in oil and gas training courses.

Fair enough. But I would suggest there's another takeaway to consider: You can always fix bad deals while respecting the sanctity of contracts. While the end result still wasn't perfect, Equatorial Guinea was able to recover significant revenue from BG.

We have every reason to believe Africa will be seeing more landmark O&G deals; deals with the potential to significantly impact African businesses, communities, and people.

More and more Africans are being educated. And more and more Africans want, and expect, to help the continent.

Whether they align themselves with African companies, governments, or civil society, I'm confident this new generation will be playing a role in negotiating contracts that are good for everyday Africans.

A Few Thoughts for This Generation

I have a few words of advice for this generation, for Africa's young attorneys and deal-makers: Never lose sight of the significance of your work. By negotiating effectively for African businesses and governments, you can play a huge role in transforming the lives of hundreds of thousands of Africans. Few things in life are more satisfying. I'm proud of the law group I've built, but I consider the work I've done to get justice for and empower African individuals, businesses, and communities among my greatest successes.

I am the first to advise many young people to avoid feeling entitled to anything. No one owes us anything. We have to earn it. Our approach and success in oil and gas negotiations stem from our deep preparation and mindset.

I have stated many times: You succeed when you look for mentors and let them mentor you. It's important to have someone who's promoting you when you're not in the room. Next, be stubbornly loyal. Don't try to pull a fast one because you know more than others! Further, embrace your trials and shortcomings: They teach you to be a better person and lawyer.

I have seen too many young lawyers who, when they get a chance to be on a podium, tend to spend more time being celebrities than being around colleagues or supervisors. You have not yet earned and completed a deal, so it's best to avoid having a big head. It is crucial to have a strong focus on building your skills because clients really want you to be good at what you do. Your writing, critical thinking, and in-depth industry skills can't hurt you. Most clients want to know who is working on their deals, but they don't care about your race or nationality. They want to know you are qualified and can get the job done.

Commit to work. Cut out a lot of BS. Pay your dues, as your time to shine will come. Always ask yourself, "Am I adding value to the firm or the company?" Don't think you are in the firm to be the labor union representative or the head of diversity.

Don't walk around the firm or negotiate with arrogance, and don't give off a sense that you are entitled, or your opinion matters on every subject. You are not owed anything. It is important to not cry discrimination on every issue, whether it is sexism, racism, or xenophobia. You beat them with excellence and success. I see it every day. I simply work hard, and success follows.

You must understand that building a successful practice calls for something not taught in law school: the ability to hustle and deliver on deals. I have always had run-ins with young lawyers because I can be a tough, goal-oriented taskmaster. I have a fierce sense of urgency that many others don't share. Working for Centurion is not for the naïve or the fainthearted—I don't tolerate young lawyers viewing Centurion as merely a job. Everyone has to give their maximum effort all the time. The truth is, I am harder on myself. I am never satisfied, and I just believe I can win bigger and do the deal better. The most important outcome for me is to have people around me achieve more than they ever thought they could.

The wisdom and advice Ron Walters shared with me holds true for you today: Each one of us has a mandate to use our education to impact communities and to promote economic growth and empowerment.

So, yes, seek career success and prosperity. But, in the end, choose to do good: Use your skills to make sure that everyday Africans receive their fair share of the benefits the continent's natural resources can provide.

15

THE CONNECTION BETWEEN ENERGY SECURITY AND SOCIAL SECURITY

Picture, if you will, the following scenario: Battle rages in a dusty city, once a bustling seaport. Workers scatter in all directions, seeking cover from the eruptions of automatic weapons fire. On one side stands an armed brigade of angry men under the command of powerful outlaw commanders seeking to stake out their turf in a restive province. On the other side stands a phalanx of stern-faced soldiers, grimly working to restore central control over this crucial site. In the background, the sound of fighter jets is still faintly audible over the roar of the fire now consuming the storage facilities that once held valuable goods destined for the export market.

Sounds like an action sequence from a Hollywood movie, doesn't it?

It's not. Instead, it's a slightly melodramatic description of something that actually happened at Ras Lanuf, one of Libya's biggest crude oil export terminals. In mid-June 2018, the facility was rocked by fighting between rebel forces alleged to be under the command of Ibrahim Jadhran, the leader of a militia group that helped oust the country's former leader Muammar Gaddafi, and members of the Libyan National Army (LNA) under the command of Field Marshal Khalifa Haftar, who controls most of eastern Libya. The episode left Ras Lanuf, already reeling from previous battles, in shambles.

The consequences of this event went beyond the damage inflicted upon the battlefield. The fighting led Libya's National Oil Corporation (NOC) to declare force majeure on loadings from Ras Lanuf and Es Sider, another terminal on the country's eastern coast. NOC Chairman Mustafa Sanalla told reporters on June 19, 2018, that the rebels had set fire to several large oil storage tanks and then stalled NOC's efforts to extinguish the blaze. This caused "catastrophic damage" to the terminal and effectively cut Libya's petroleum output by 400,000 bbl/d, he stated.[1]

Meanwhile, other observers were even more pessimistic than Sanalla. One source told *Reuters* that the clashes in Ras Lanuf and Es Sider had reduced Libya's production capacity by 425,000 bbl/d, and another put the figure closer to 450,000 bbl/d. These are not small numbers, especially since Libya was producing a bit more than 1 million bbl/d at the time.[2]

True, the LNA did retake the ports relatively quickly. It also moved swiftly to bring the terminal facilities back online so that Libyan crude output could move back up to its former level.[3] But it lost a substantial sum of money during the week or so when loadings were suspended and oil could not be sold at the usual rate. It also lost a certain amount of credibility, since the attacks raised questions about its capacity to retain control of infrastructure that plays a crucial role in Libyan oil exports. It also drew attention to its own peculiar position, namely, that of retaining control over the majority of Libyan territory without ever gaining international recognition.

And this brings me to the point of this chapter: security. I strongly believe that if Africans want to make the most of this continent's natural resources, they will have to make stability and safety a high priority.

I can't emphasize this point enough: African countries simply must do more to address political and civil discontent in areas where oil and gas producers are active. If they don't, they will run the risk of alienating investors and losing access to funds. They may have to postpone or cancel work on vital infrastructure such as pipelines and cross-sector initiatives such as gas-to-power projects. Even worse, they could stymie efforts to develop the capacity of local actors, including Africa-based companies involved in oil and gas extraction, field services, trading, transportation, construction, and other related industries.

I know these concerns are valid because I've seen things like this happen again and again. So has C. Derek Campbell, the CEO of Energy & Natural Resource Security, Inc., a U.S.-based company that offers security solutions for oil and gas operators. When I told Mr. Campbell about my plan to write this book, he had quite a bit to say about the necessity of preparing for a crisis.

"Government- and commercially-owned energy systems are quickly becoming principal targets for terrorists, rogue organizations and hostile states, all while being exposed to natural disasters," he wrote in a March 2019 email to me. "Protecting and improving the resilience of energy systems mandates vigilance, contingency planning, and training—ultimately requiring energy stakeholders to be actively engaged in the protection of their critical energy infrastructure and natural resource assets."

Campbell also stressed that African oil and gas producers could not isolate themselves from the impact of civil unrest or conflicts, especially since future security issues are likely to intersect with efforts to expand the use of new technologies in the industry.

"Security threats, physical and cyber, pose an immense threat to all major sectors of the oil and gas value chain. This is largely due to the fact that the sectors are not independent verticals. They overlap and are interdependent. A physical or cyber-attack on an upstream asset can cause operational challenges [in the] midstream [sector] that can cause financial catastrophes at the downstream end," he wrote. "The same is true in reverse: A downstream physical or cyber-attack can disrupt midstream operations and bring upstream activity to a halt for a producer. The same scenario can be applied to power assets—generation, transmission, and distribution."

Campbell was speaking in general terms, but I'd like to take a closer look at the security challenges we're seeing across the continent—and start looking at ways to address them.

The War on Oil and Gas Assets—
and on Quality of Life

For Bubaraye Dakolo, coughing fits are part of life in the Niger River Delta. That's what he told DW in 2017 when he described the impact of gas flaring near his small village near Yenagoa in the Niger Delta, which accounts for the biggest share of Nigeria's crude oil output. "Suddenly everything smells like gas," said Dakolo, head of the Ekpetiama clan. Sometimes he and his neighbors can barely breathe, he added.[4]

Gas flaring, which can cause flames to shoot as high as 10-story buildings, is a regular practice at oil fields in the Delta region. Producers do it because it's easy—and because they'd rather not bother with the gas they find in their wells. But flaring has sometimes made it difficult, or impossible, for local farmers to grow crops. And it has clearly impacted residents' quality of life and health.[5]

Government leaders have repeatedly promised to address the problem. Nevertheless, flaring continues. This is one of the many reasons that some residents of oil-producing areas have come to feel that they have no options—and have been stealing crude (a practice known as "bunkering") and damaging oil-industry assets such as pipelines. This theft has far-reaching consequences. In 2017, Maikanti Baru, the group managing director of Nigeria National Petroleum Corporation (NNPC), said that the vandalism of the country's pipelines had reduced the amount of oil flowing to market by 700,000 bbl/d in the previous year.[6] In turn, these incidents have fostered widespread corruption and theft throughout the industry.[7]

But it's not just about thievery and the loss of output. After all, oil stealing is not unique to Nigeria; it also has been a problem in Ghana, Uganda, Morocco, Thailand, Russia, and Mexico, among other countries. It's sometimes a matter of life and death. On occasion, outraged Delta residents have resorted to more violent actions against oil industry personnel. A few militant groups have even kidnapped and killed oil company employees.[8]

Desperate acts such as these arise from the frustration that wells up in places when a select few elites benefit from oil revenue while individuals and communities are left to deal with the damage that comes along with oil production.

And flaring isn't the only type of environmental assault that has generated anger in the Niger River Delta area. There were more than 12,000 spills in the region between 1976 and 2014. These incidents devastated the area's fishing industry and posed additional health and quality of life concerns.

Yamaabana Legborsi, 32, recently told CNN how the spills affected his childhood in the Gokana community. "We could not play in the sand like other children [because we were] covered in black crude. My mother was especially worried it was not safe, [and] so were other parents. We could not also eat the fishes that washed away from the river. You would see crude all around the water," he said.[9]

I am not for a second saying that theft, vandalism, and violence are acceptable responses to the difficulties facing the people of the Delta. In fact, in some cases, these acts have worsened the situation. While more than half of the spills reported between 1976 and 2014 were caused by pipeline corrosion and tanker accidents, the rest were a result of mechanical error and sabotage, the Journal of Health and Pollution reported last year.[10]

Africa Needs Local Solutions

How can we begin to turn this situation around? Like most complex problems, it will require a complex, multi-pronged solution. Part of that solution should include economic diversification efforts.

Nigeria's Minister of State for Petroleum Resources, Dr. Emmanuel Ibe Kachikwu, recently said that the Ministry of Petroleum Resources intended to develop a policy that would encourage people living in oil-producing areas to form cooperatives, which would then be able to set up and own modular refineries.[11] That's a start, but the people of the Delta have heard the government make promises before. It will take real action, as well as programs with the potential to impact large portions of the population, to make a difference.

Africans will also need to combine efforts to create job opportunities and economic growth with practical steps to prevent and mitigate environmental damage in the Delta. That's why I'm excited about the work of Eucharia Oluchi Nwaichi, who is looking for sustainable ways to undo the damage created by oil spills. In March 2019, Chemistry World noted that Nwaichi, an environmental biochemist at the University of Port Harcourt, was conducting research on phytoremediation, a method that uses plants and microbes to break down and eliminate environmental contaminants.

Chemistry World also reported that she and her students were working to establish close relationships with residents of the Delta communities that have borne the brunt of the environmental assaults on the region. Without this effort, she said, researchers and government officials cannot count on building up local support for interventions, even if the new methods hold out the promise of restoring the land for agriculture.[12]

We also can follow the creative example of Sustainability International (SI), a U.S. nonprofit organization that is working with the village of K-Dere in Ogoniland to clean up an oil spill at a fish farm and using cryptocurrencies to pay workers. In 2017, the NGO hired local women, as well as former members of militant groups, to clean up an oil spill at a fish farm in the Gulf of Guinea. The venture-funded project was successful, and not just because it achieved its aim of cleaning the fish farm, but also because it trained workers in the use of the technologies needed to gather operational data.[13]

Chinyere Nnadi, the co-founder and CEO of SI, told *The Huffington Post* in 2017 that the cleanup was designed to make participants feel empowered and in control of their economic lives. "Community members previously had no way to break the cycle of government and corporate corruption that has imprisoned their citizens in their polluted tribal lands," he explained. "With SI, we give each citizen the choice to put down their guns and pick up their cell phones, giving up bullets and picking up Bitcoin. This transforms each person from economic prisoner into an entrepreneur who earns a living by doing good for their community and their local environment."[14]

Of course, we can't—and shouldn't—expect NGOs to carry the whole load. Oil companies, other businesses, and local authorities must play a large role in mitigating environmental damage and addressing the other factors contributing to oil theft and vandalism.

And there has been some action on this front. I was happy to learn in March 2019 that Henry Seriake Dickson, the governor of Bayelsa, had founded a commission to conduct an inquiry into oil spills in the Niger Delta. John Sentamu, the Archbishop of York, has promised that the probe will look into the "environmental and human damage" affecting oil-producing areas.[15]

We also need to see national governments help each other address theft, and fortunately, there are some examples of positive cooperation. For example, when the Panamanian oil tanker MT *Maximus* was hijacked by Nigerian nationals off the coast of Côte d'Ivoire in February 2016, the navies of Ghana, Togo, and Nigeria, together with the U.S. and France, tracked the vessel to the waters of São Tomé e Príncipe and intercepted it.

"With the blessing of the São Toméan government, Nigerian Navy special forces performed an opposed boarding of the *Maximus*. The pirates were arrested (though one was shot and killed), the *Maximus* crew were freed, and the cargo recovered," states the Atlantic Council report.[16]

Don't Forget Technology

Technology should be part of the solution, as well. As I mentioned, there are innovative technologies with the potential to address environmental concerns.

Technology also can be used to discourage theft. We're already seeing that in Ghana's Petroleum Product Marking Scheme. This program mandates the use of identifying markers in refined fuels as a means of combatting theft, which had become a wide-ranging problem.

In 2017, a representative of the country's National Petroleum Authority described the scheme:

"The most promising means of combating fuel theft and diversions . . . is fuel 'marking.' Fuel marking has been around in one form or another for some time, but in recent years, covert molecular fuel markers have been developed that are virtually impossible for thieves to detect. Such markers allow stolen or diverted fuel to be identified and recovered, and perhaps more importantly, used as admissible scientific evidence to prosecute fuel thieves and smugglers in courts of law. One of the most successful programs to date is Ghana's Petroleum Product Marking Scheme, instituted by the country's National Petroleum Authority in 2013. The program allows inspectors to determine if the gasoline or diesel sold at filling is legal and offenders are subject to being fined or jailed."[17]

We also need to encourage locals to be part of the solution in areas where oil thefts and vandalism take place. One promising example is NNPC's plan for commercialization of associated gas that might otherwise be flared from Niger River Delta wells. The company's group managing director, Maikanti Baru, said in April 2019 that NNPC intends to set up partnerships that would allow local communities to benefit from the use of gas for economic development projects.

"For us as operators, we will continue to dialogue with the bodies so as to create [an] enabling operating environment for the [oil companies] and for the communities," he said at a ceremony marking the start of his position as the national leader of Host Communities of Nigeria (HOSTCOM).[18]

Groups, Gangs, and Violence

African leaders got a tragic reminder of the need to pay attention to security issues in January 2010, when Angolan gunmen opened fire on a visiting football team from Togo. Several days later, a plane brought the living and dead back to their home country. A group of women, loved ones of the victims, threw themselves on the ground in anguish. They were not the only ones to feel the pain and devastation that separatist groups have sown in Angola.

"Our boys went to Angola to celebrate the best in African football, but they came back with dead bodies and bullet wounds," Togbe Aklassou, a traditional ruler from Togo's capital, Lomé, said shortly after the attack.[19]

This was one of many troubling examples of violence to take place in Angola since 2000, and just one of many acts by separatist groups seeking independence for Cabinda, an oil-rich province separated from the rest of Angola by a thin strip of territory belonging to the Democratic Republic of Congo.

More recently, in May 2016, five men claiming membership in the Front for the Liberation of the Enclave of Cabinda (FLEC) reportedly climbed aboard an offshore gas platform operated by Chevron and demanded that foreign workers leave or face the consequences.[20] No further raids on the platform were reported, but separatist groups did intensify their efforts against the Angolan armed forces in subsequent months.[21]

Events of this type are a thorn in the side of Angola's government. So far, its strategy for limiting rebel activity has involved maintaining tight control over Cabinda while placing few constraints on the activity of investors in offshore oil and gas reserves.[22] The province of Cabinda also restricts access to visitors by requiring special permits, and it tasks soldiers with protecting construction sites along the coast and the fenced-in compounds where foreign oil company employees live. This strategy has helped keep conflict at relatively low levels, but it has also strained the capacity of the armed forces.

Meanwhile, Angola is not the only African state that has had to decide how to respond when violence threatens oil and gas production.

Look at Mozambique, for example. Several years after the discovery of massive gas reserves in the Rovuma Basin off the coast of the northern Cabo Delgado province in 2010, the country saw an uptick in civil conflict. By late 2017, a militant Islamist group known as Al Sunnah wa Jama'ah had begun staging assaults on villages near the installations and campsites occupied by men working for Anadarko, the U.S. company that was the first to invest in the Rovuma Basin, and its contractors.[23]

In June 2018, Anadarko responded to worsening conditions by imposing a lockdown on workers at the site of a gas liquefaction plant in Palma. Attacks have continued since then, and an employee of Anadarko, Gabriel Couto, was reportedly beheaded in March 2019.[24]

The Mozambican government has responded to such incidents by taking a harsh approach to Al Sunnah wa Jama'ah. In mid-2018, the commander of one military unit said his soldiers were ready to kill suspected militants on sight. Meanwhile, Anadarko and other investors, such as Italy's Eni, beefed up security measures for their personnel. In fact, Anadarko indicated in a 2019 advertisement that it was looking to buy armored vehicles capable of withstanding hits from AK-47 automatic rifles. Of course, now that Chevron has purchased Anadarko, it has inherited the opportunities and challenges in Mozambique.[25]

Then there's Nigeria. In addition to the ongoing pattern of oil resource theft and vandalism mentioned above, the country is home to what has been described as the world's deadliest militant group: Boko Haram. The group has launched an insurgency that has, according to United Nations estimates, led to the internal displacement of 1.7 million people and the killing of more than 15,200 people since 2011.[26]

Nigerians also live with the constant danger of killings and kidnappings by bands of thieves such as the Zamfara bandits. This group often targets and kidnaps poor land farmers—and then murders them when their relatives cannot afford the ransom. In April 2019, security experts reported this group had killed 200 people in a period of just a few weeks.[27]

I realize that the battle against violent groups and gangs is likely to continue for some time. But Africans will have a much better chance of success if they seek to address the problems that make them vulnerable to these groups in the first place. Governments must work harder to address the issues that help violent groups recruit new members because. After all, these are the reasons people feel hopeless and disenfranchised. They also need to take an honest look at the gap between the wealth that their petroleum resources have generated and the impoverished populations of the regions where oil and gas are produced.

Civil War and Instability

In 2017, my company, Centurion Law Group, successfully negotiated one of the biggest and most difficult deals in African oil and gas to date. It concerned a project in South Sudan, where we were working with that country's government and Nigeria's Oranto Petroleum to open the door for exploration work at Block B3.

The exploration and production-sharing agreement (EPSA) that resulted from those negotiations allowed Oranto to begin comprehensive exploration and long-term development. This was a significant development, not only because the EPSA was the first to be signed in South Sudan since 2012, but also because it signaled a renewal of hope. The idea was this: If we can succeed here, we can succeed anywhere on the continent.

You will recall that at that point, South Sudan had already experienced years of civil conflict. Tensions began building long before the country achieved independence from Sudan. They dated back to the 1970s, when vast oil reserves were discovered in the southern part of Sudan. All of the oil extracted there went to the pipelines and refineries that Khartoum built in the north, perhaps in an attempt to prevent secession.[28] The northern and southern regions of the country could not agree on how to share oil revenues, and this led to fighting. Eventually, in 2011, Sudan split into two separate nations.

The southern part, now known as South Sudan, remains one of Africa's least-developed countries.[29] But in 2017, the new country's government renewed its commitment to economic revival through investments in utilities and infrastructure, particularly in the oil and gas sector.

Since that time, I've continued to support South Sudan as executive chairman of the African Energy Chamber. In early 2019, the chamber entered into a technical assistance cooperation agreement with the South Sudanese Ministry of Petroleum with the aim of strengthening the country's capacity to manage its hydrocarbons sector and wealth. And later in 2019, the chamber launched a global investment drive for South Sudan, expressing its confidence that the country could achieve lasting peace.[30]

Even so, I understand there is still a lot of work to be done to build long-lasting stability in South Sudan.

When this young country gained independence in mid-2011, it had high hopes of turning the oil deposits that had previously filled the coffers of Khartoum into a reliable source of income. So far, though, it has not been able to sustain peace. As a result, the hydrocarbon sector has not reached its full potential. Conflict has caused a number of oil fields to stop producing, reduced the volume of petroleum available for export via pipeline, stemmed the largest stream of money flowing into the state treasury, and complicated negotiations over the building of new infrastructure.[31] It has also discouraged new investors from signing on to efforts to stabilize crude production[32] and has slowed the process of developing and implementing a new legal framework covering subsurface resources.[33]

There have been signs of hope since the signing of a peace deal between President Salva Kiir and rebel warlord Riek Machar in

September 2018. This development has led serious investors to take a new look at the country, which does possess the third-largest oil reserves in sub-Saharan Africa. In December 2018, Juba secured pledges for more than $2 billion worth of investment, with Malaysia's Petronas and Nigeria's Oranto Petroleum (the same company I mentioned above) teaming up with a local player, Trinity Energy, to spend $1.15 billion on an oil block and the government-backed Strategic Fuel Fund of South Africa offering $1 billion for the construction of a new refinery and pipelines.

Despite these positive signs, the road ahead is likely to be long and bumpy. South Sudan's current legal regime has been in place since 2013 and may need to be tweaked in order to ensure the safety, transparency, and stability of oil industry operations under the new government. At the same time, the country is still heavily dependent on investment from China National Petroleum Corporation (CNPC), whose management team in Beijing may balk at reforms that do not uphold the company's interests.[34]

Meanwhile, the new government's stabilization efforts will have to address the fact that a significant portion of the country's oil infrastructure sustained damage during the civil war. These losses have not only compromised the safety and security of the civilian population in crude-producing areas but have also given rise to many spills, leaks, and other environmental hazards. The Ministry of Petroleum has made these stabilization efforts a key priority.[35]

And as bad as that is, I'm even more dismayed to hear about the human rights violations that have been reported in South Sudan, including acts of murder and rape.[36]

While putting an end to atrocities like these will take a concerted effort by government and military leaders, I do believe that economic stability must be front and center of the peace and recovery efforts of South Sudan. That's why I want to see South Sudan's leadership open up new blocks to exploration, especially to African investors. It's time to build refineries, pipelines, urea, ammonia and fertilizer plants, power plants, and large agricultural fields. It's also time to set up technology hubs!

In the end, it is business that creates jobs and hope. South Sudan and other African countries don't need aid; they need economic revival and enterprise. Our leaders need to understand this. We cannot afford to think small in our drive for peace, investment, and stability when what we really need are big, pragmatic, common-sense solutions.

I truly believe that revenues from petroleum and related industries could make a valuable contribution toward economic revival in many of the African countries struggling with instability.

This could be true for Sudan, too. As I wrote this book, the future of the country remained very much in doubt. The uncertainty stems from events in April 2019, when President Omar al-Bashir was removed from power, and the Transitional Military Council took control. Mass protests followed as Sudan's people demanded a civilian government.

Because of this upheaval, the Sudanese petroleum industry is likely to have difficulty attracting much in the way of foreign investment any time soon, at least until the instability in the country is resolved. This is a problem, given that Khartoum is still reeling from the loss of oil fields to South Sudan in 2011.

Ideally, Bashir's removal will lead to the establishment of a permanent government. Once a new and stable regime is in place, Sudan will hopefully be able to use its natural resources to contribute to long-term peace and economic growth.

Looking Forward

I wish I could offer a formula for eliminating the different forms of violence plaguing African nations with petroleum resources. Obviously, there are no one-size-fits-all solutions.

But, on a general level, I'm convinced that solutions must combine multiple factors: better governance and law enforcement, greater accountability for oil and gas companies, outside-the-box technological innovation, economic development—and above all, meaningful responses to the grievances that leave people feeling overlooked and hopeless.

Giving people more control over a share of the massive revenues that oil and gas generate would go a long way in that regard. We must ensure that people realize significant benefits from the oil and gas industry, not just experience the downsides of production.

16

MANAGING
OIL AND GAS REVENUE

In Shreveport, Louisiana, Laura FitzGerald is known as the "Belle of the Wells."[1]

After learning how the land and oil rights industry works, FitzGerald, a former oil company employee, struck out on her own. She founded Illios Resources in 2004 and began amassing oil rights and selling them to oil companies. She has since accumulated more than 18,000 acres of mineral rights and made millions of dollars.[2]

She later wrote about her successes, particularly outstanding for a woman in this field, for a company blog:

"Growing up, my older brother always told me I could do anything a guy could do. I think that had an effect on me. I believe it to this day, and I believe it's true for any woman who puts her mind to a task. The simple fact of the matter is that this is America. Financial independence is the birthright of every American. If we relentlessly execute our vision, course correct when necessary, and push through the resistance, we will win."

What a statement. FitzGerald's attempt to encourage other female entrepreneurs was predicated on the idea that if you live in the U.S., you already have a leg up when it comes to achieving your financial goals.

I don't know if that's true across the board, but as FitzGerald's story demonstrates, being in the U.S. certainly opens the door to opportunity when it comes to oil and gas resources. Even landowners who never work in the petroleum industry have a very real chance of profiting from the sale of their property's mineral rights. Around 2012, states paid out more than $54 billion in royalties to landowners whose property was the site of oil and gas fracking, according to data from the National Association of Royalty Owners (NARO). "There are millionaires being made every day from North Dakota to Pennsylvania," Jerry Simmons, director of the NARO, told Business Insider at the time.[3]

During the oil boom in 2012, some North Dakota towns seemed to be packed with people who'd made big money selling mineral rights to their property, *Reuters* wrote. "Average income in Mountrail County, the hub of the North Dakota oil production boom, roughly doubled in five years to $52,027 per person in 2010, ranking it in the richest 100 U.S. counties on that basis, including New York City, and Marin, California. The boom could be creating up to 2,000 millionaires a year in North Dakota."[4]

Granted, North Dakota oil towns saw their share of troubles a few years later, when the oil boom fizzled out. But the point is, the lives of everyday people there were changed because of natural resources on their property.

Imagine the transformation in African lives and communities if women here could pursue their goals the way that FitzGerald did. Or if property owners in, say, Cameroon or Nigeria could benefit from the discovery of oil on their property.

Unfortunately, that's not how things work in today's Africa. If you discover oil on your property, it's a non-event—you have nothing. Whether natural resources are found on private property or community property, they belong to the state. Period.

To make matters worse, Africans often feel left out when the state decides how to spend the money those natural resources generate. Those feelings of being disregarded are major drivers behind the violence we're seeing in the continent. People feel the not-so-pleasant impacts of oil and gas operations, from oil spills that impact the environment to declining income opportunities in other sectors. And they see little to none of the myriad benefits that petroleum revenue could and should be delivering, from financial and economic benefits to infrastructure, education, and healthcare programs. Instead, oil revenues are supporting large, unwieldy central governments and lining the pockets of a select few.

It's the resource curse in a nutshell.

We shouldn't be waiting for foreign governments or aid organizations to come in to fix this. It's our obligation to find ways to start changing this dynamic. We should be looking at the examples of countries that do manage oil resources effectively. We should be considering the creation of trusts that manage and protect resources specifically for communities. We need to find a way to ensure that more stories about oil and gas changing everyday people's lives take place in Africa.

Unfair and Unbalanced

For the people in the Niger Delta, day-to-day life can be harrowing at best, with violence, kidnappings, and extreme poverty all too common. The root causes of the turmoil there are complex: from long-standing religious and ethno-regional tensions to conflicts over land use to ongoing attacks by militant groups, which manage to draw support from disaffected locals living in poverty. But without a doubt, mismanagement of oil revenue—and failure to use it to improve the lives of the indigenous population—is fueling the fire. Locals have lost patience with foreign oil corporations reaping the rewards of oil production, while their standard of living remains unimproved and unacceptable. Frequent oil spills in the region, more than 7,000 between 1970 and 2000, have only incensed people there further and led to the formation of militant groups that have attacked both oil workers and pipelines.[5]

More than a decade ago, Sebastian Spio-Garbrah, an African analyst for the Eurasia Group, reported that billions of dollars in oil revenue generated in the Delta were simply disappearing. "The Niger Delta receives more money per capita than anywhere else in Nigeria," he told PBS. "The problem is that this money has then been mostly siphoned off, misspent and abused."[6]

Nigeria's 1999 Constitution attempted to address this. According to the constitution, at least 13 percent of all revenue made through contracts with foreign oil producers must go back to the oil-producing states. The states, in turn, are expected to spend that revenue on things that would benefit the states' population.

Clearly, that hasn't been the reality. In Nigeria, the World Bank has estimated that as a result of corruption, 80 percent of energy revenues in the country only benefit 1 percent of the population. As Nigerian Folabi Olagbaju of Amnesty International said in 2007, "Oil exploration has not led to social and economic development for the peoples in the oil-producing states. It has benefited the Nigerian ruling class."

More than a decade later, little has been done to improve the situation. And unfortunately, Nigeria is not an outlier among African nations with petroleum reserves.

Cameroon, for example, also has had a case of "disappearing" oil revenue. Since oil was discovered in Cameroon in 1977, approximately $20 billion has been paid in oil rents—but only 54 percent of the money appeared in the government budget.[7]

And how has Cameroon's resource wealth played out for Cameroonians? There has been some good news on the economic front: During the last decade, the country's gross domestic product per capita has grown by 4 percent annually, above the global average of 2.6 percent.[8]

Other figures, however, show oil revenue failing to impact the lives of the people who need help most: 48 percent of the population continues to live below the poverty line. Healthcare is sparse, and Cameroon's life expectancy is only 57 years for males and 59 years for females.

Some might argue that local poverty and disenfranchisement, particularly in the South-West region of Cameroon, have contributed to the Anglophone crisis taking place. Since late 2017, it has resulted in violent clashes, the deaths of scores of people, and the displacement of tens of thousands.

The crisis has its roots in African Colonialism and the German colony of "Kamerun" being divided between France and England by the League of Nations following Germany's defeat in World War I. In 1960, when Cameroon gained its independence, English-speaking residents were given the option of joining the French-speaking portion of Cameroon or becoming citizens of neighboring Nigeria. They voted to stay, but since that time, have described unfair treatment, with education, roads, and healthcare in their western region of the country being neglected—despite the production of tens of thousands of barrels of oil per day in the South West, an English-speaking region.[9]

Some English-speakers want their grievances addressed, while others are calling for a more extreme solution: the creation of an independent state which they refer to as "Ambazonia." English-speakers have complained about the unbalanced distribution of revenue from natural resources.

Their concerns resonate strongly with me: I am from the Manyu division in the South-West region. These grievances are valid. We aren't producing jobs at the rate we should, and the private sector is suffering from high taxes, corruption, and red tape. Millions of young Cameroonians don't have healthcare. Children and teenagers are senselessly being killed. I believe the only way out is a conversation that includes all of the people involved, all of the stakeholders. All of the country's residents should be treated with dignity, justice, and equity.

Another troubling case is the worsening situation in Libya. It would be fair to say that the country has been in a state of turmoil since the uprising of 2011 put an end to the 42-year rule of Muammar Gaddafi, and various forces started battling for control of the country's oil reserves.

Mustafa Sanalla, chairman of Libya's National Oil Corporation (NOC), has struggled to keep the crude flowing while militias have fought over oil facilities. His staff members have been killed and kidnapped. He was nearly killed when the NOC headquarters were attacked by ISIS. At one point, the Petroleum Facilities Guard, an armed force charged with protecting Libya's oil facilities, had to shut down the country's largest oil field. Interruptions in oil production have cost the country $100 billion in lost revenues in the last 5 years, Sanalla estimated in early 2019.

The production cuts are a major problem in Libya, which relies heavily on its oil revenue. There has been a collapse in public services, healthcare in particular.[10] About a third of the population is living in poverty, without access to clean drinking water or sewage systems.[11]

While these examples are extremely troubling, I still believe it is possible to learn from them and put an end to resource revenue mismanagement. And that process should begin with a serious examination of those who manage their revenue well.

Looking to Norway

In the 1960s, Stavanger was a small Norwegian fishing town with a declining economy and dwindling population. These days, Stavanger is Norway's fourth-largest city and a popular tourist destination. It is home to a university, a concert hall, several museums—including the popular Norwegian Petroleum Museum. Huge ships travel daily from the town's harbor to oil platforms offshore. And Stavanger is not unique in Norway; it's a picture of the transformations that occurred nationwide after oil and natural gas reserves were discovered in 1969.

The petroleum reserves were key to the change, but what really made the difference was Norway's strategy for managing the massive revenues it has generated. As a result of that approach, Norway has been able to use its $40 billion in annual revenues to spread prosperity around the country.

That's not to say there weren't a few missteps along the way. Almost immediately after the country started exporting oil and gas, revenues poured directly into the government budget. Within a few years, however, Norway's booming oil and gas exports started putting the country at risk of moving from a diverse economy to one that depended heavily on petroleum.

"Norway had four years of Dutch disease, where wages went up, factories lost their top people to the oil industry, and foreigners coming in to invest in the oil boom drove up the value of the currency so high that customers in other countries could no longer afford Norway's other export products," said Farouk al-Kasim, who was with Norway's Oil Ministry at the time. "Initially, the government reacted by handing out subsidies, and we went deeper into the mire."[12]

Fearful for Norway's economy, the government searched for a solution. In the mid-1970s, upon al-Kasim's recommendation, Norway started investing profits from state-owned oil companies into technological research that not only enhanced the country's extraction abilities, but also helped other Norwegian industries—including construction, transportation, manufacturing, even hospitality—develop and grow.

And in 1995, Norway took a more dramatic step: It started limiting government expenditures of oil revenue to 4 percent. That money was to be used for infrastructure and public projects, along with investment in foreign financial markets. The remaining revenue was put into a sovereign wealth fund that, as of 2014, had grown to $890 billion.

Norway has remained highly committed to transparent fund management. The public has access to every investment made, as well as risk exposure and performance. Fund managers meet regularly with lawmakers and journalists.

Norway's prime minister Jens Stoltenberg summed up his country's approach to resource revenue in a 2013 speech at the Kennedy School of Government at Harvard University. Norway became one of the wealthiest nations in the world, he said, by refusing to spend its massive revenues, placing them in a fund, and only using its annual returns. "That way the fund lasts forever. The problem in Europe with the deficits and the debt crisis is that many European countries have spent money they don't have. The problem in Norway is that we don't spend money we do have. That requires a kind of political courage," he said.[13]

It would be fair to say that many African countries have been guilty of spending oil money they don't have yet. Others are guilty of misspending the money they do have, money that could pave the way for a brighter future.

While Norway's model may not be a perfect fit for African countries, there are elements of it that would work. They include:

- Using only a percentage of oil revenue for capital expenditures. That percentage does not necessarily need to be as low as 4 percent: African countries need investments in infrastructure, education, healthcare, and other human services to improve the quality of life for everyday people and grow the economy.

- Spending on capital projects prudently, with the understanding that oil and gas prices are volatile, and revenues will ebb and flow.

- Channeling revenue into projects and initiatives that not only benefit the petroleum sector, but can spill over into other industries and foster economic diversification.

- Setting aside large portions of revenue. Save it. Invest it. Earmark it for citizens and communities.

It may not be long before a variation of Norway's sovereign wealth fund is in place in Africa. In February 2019, Kenya's government released a draft law for creating one.[14] If the law goes into effect, petroleum and mineral revenues would be channeled into one of three directions: savings, a budget stabilization fund, or a fund for domestic spending and investment. Kenya does not rely on petroleum money, it only represents a small percentage of fiscal revenue, but a fund like this is a promising step forward in terms of transparently managing natural resource revenue. The law includes fund objectives, clear deposit rules, public disclosure requirements, and competitive, transparent selection of external managers.

The Natural Resource Governance Institute (NRGI) has pointed out, however, that the law would introduce risks to public money as well. For one thing, board members would be nominated by the president's office, which also would be the sole oversight actor. The NRGI recommends taking steps to ensure that at least three board members are nominated by parties other than the president and that parliament, the parliamentary budget office, and an independent external auditor review the fund's performance regularly. I strongly agree.

Increasing Local Control

In their paper, "Petroleum to the People, Africa's Coming Resource Curse—And How to Avoid It," Larry Diamond and Jack Mosbacher made a radical suggestion: that African countries need to hand new revenues directly to people as taxable income. "By taking control of these revenues out of the hands of the political elite and restoring the link between citizens and their public officials, this 'oil to cash' strategy offers the best hope for tomorrow's oil-rich African nations to avoid the fate that has befallen so many of yesterday's," they wrote.[15]

If an African country adopted their proposal, it would commit to depositing a predetermined percentage of its oil revenues directly into citizens' bank accounts, much like U.S. governments do with Social Security payments. And just like Social Security, these payments would be taxed—at a rate poor families could manage, Diamond and Mosbacher noted.

They believe the taxation part is critical because it would restore the accountability that exists when governments rely on their people for revenue. This "oil-to-cash" approach has already been laid out by scholars at the Center for Global Development. They argue that by paying taxes on the money they received, citizens would shift from passivity to active engagement with their governments.

Diamond and Mosbacher aren't the only ones to make a case for channeling petroleum revenue directly to citizens. Shanta Devarajan, senior director, development economics, with the World Bank, has made similar arguments.

"If, instead of making [unaccountable] public-spending decisions with their oil revenues, governments were to distribute these revenues directly to citizens [in equal amounts to all citizens], and then tax them to finance public goods, there would be at least two effects. First, citizens would have a better idea of how much revenues there were. Second, since expenditures were being financed from their tax payments, citizens may have greater incentive to scrutinize these expenditures," he wrote in 2017. "Even without the additional scrutiny, simply the lump-sum transfer of just 20 percent of oil revenues is sufficient to eliminate extreme poverty in Angola, Republic of Congo, Equatorial Guinea, Gabon, and Nigeria."[16]

To be honest, I'm on the fence about this strategy. I agree with the benefits of citizens supporting governments with taxes, but the direct deposits would rely heavily on a level of federal government transparency and cooperation that we rarely see. What would prevent governments from "shaving off" some of the revenue they receive before sharing citizens' percentages?

I do like a number of the points raised by Diamond and Mosbacher, beginning with the idea that Africans don't need their governments deciding what's best for them when it comes to spending revenue.

"The argument that poor people don't understand their best interests as well as bureaucrats and public servants do is a paternalist myth," they wrote. Excellent point, gentlemen.

Instead of depositing revenue directly into individual accounts, or channeling nearly all of the revenue into a sovereign wealth fund like Norway does, I think there is real potential for the idea of natural resource revenues going into trust funds that would be established for—and managed by—African communities.

An agreed-upon percentage of revenue would be added to the fund regularly. Deposits wouldn't be made by federal governments but by oil and gas companies. Community members would serve on a board of trustees to manage the fund and invest deposits, joined by trustees or advisors outside of the country who could provide impartial technical guidance on trust management. Income generated by the trust fund would be used for the benefit of the local population, and community members would have the power to decide how that money is used. Money transferred in and out of the account would be made public, possibly on a website. Of course, establishing this kind of system would require legislation or policies, and making that happen would require cooperation at the federal level.

In a 2004 article about community-based trust funds for the North Carolina Journal of International Law and Commercial Regulation, Emeka Duruigbo pointed out that trust funds are far from a foreign concept in sub-Saharan Africa:

"In Amodu Tjani v. Secretary of Southern Nigeria, Viscount Haldane stated: 'The notion of individual ownership is quite foreign to native ideas," Duruigbo wrote. "Land belongs to the community, the village or the family, never to the individual. All the members of the community, village, or family have an equal right to the land, but in every case the Chief or Headman of the community or village, or head of the family, has charge of the land, and in loose mode of speech is sometimes called the owner. He is to some extent in the position of a trustee and as such holds the land for the use of the community or family."[17]

The paper cites the example of the Alaska Permanent Fund (APF), created by an amendment to the Alaska Constitution in 1976. Today, 25 to 50 percent of mineral revenues paid to the state are deposited into the fund for current and future Alaskans. The fund is managed by the Alaska Permanent Fund Corporation, which receives guidance from an independent board of trustees. Alaska has set up additional oversight by giving its legislative branch final approval of fund investments. And the public is involved in oversight, too, because removal of board members is effective only when accompanied by a statement disclosed to the public containing the reasons for removal. Citizens also have access to information about how much the fund earns and how the revenues are distributed.

In 1982, the fund started making annual dividend payments to residents. Between then and 2015, the fund has issued a total of $22.4 billion to eligible citizens in amounts ranging from $330 to $2,000 per person. Note the fund distributes dividends; it doesn't involve a government transferring a portion of their oil revenues directly to citizens.

Alaska's approach would be a good fit for Africa, writes Landry Signé, a David M. Rubenstein Fellow in the Global Economy and Development Program with the Brookings Institute. "The success of such a fund is not just the redistribution of natural resource profits, but also the transparency that such a distribution will require, and the improvement of the associated governance processes. In fact, reducing the discretionary power of leaders in allocating the revenue from natural resources will reduce unaccountable governance, rent-seeking practices, and corruption," he wrote.[18]

Africans also should take a look at the Nunavut Trust of Canada, a community-managed fund established as part of the Nunavut Land Claims agreement in 1999. The agreement led to the creation of Nunavut territory and called for the indigenous Nunavut people to receive $1.2 billion in compensation money over a 14-year period. The money was channeled through the Nunavut Trust, which was charged with protecting and enhancing the funds for the benefit of the people.

In her report, "Caspian Oil Windfalls: Who Will Benefit," Caspian Revenue Watch Director Svetlana Tsalik described the fund as a promising example for other underdeveloped oil-producing nations. "Unlike government-run oil funds, the Nunavut Trust is a community-managed fund. It has earned strong returns while maintaining accountability to its constituents. The Trust also demonstrates how these communities can be compensated for the negative external consequences of oil development, and how they can turn such compensation into an enduring source of income."[19]

I am confident that establishing trust funds for communities would help us overcome a multitude of oil revenue mismanagement problems.

- Instead of watching an elite few put petroleum revenue in their pockets while they deal with the consequences of extraction, everyday Africans would see tangible benefits in their own communities.

- Individuals would finally have a say on how oil revenues are invested and how returns are spent. Their voices and insights would be valued and capitalized upon.

- Communities would not have to rely on governments to be "middlemen." Companies would make the payments directly into the fund.

- Communities could invest fund returns into programs that translate into improved quality of life and job opportunities. As a result, disenfranchisement, desperation, and violence would decrease.

- Communities, if they chose to, could invest in projects that help protect their environments, which might reduce instances of militant groups attempting to shut down E&P activities.

Lessons Learned:
The Chad-Cameroon Pipeline Project

On its face, the revenue management program proposed for the Chad-Cameroon Pipeline had everything going for it: stakeholder buy-in, oversight mechanisms, and the potential to change Africans' lives for the better. Once it was put into practice, however, it simply didn't work.

A little history: In 1988, more than a decade after oil was discovered in Chad, the governments of Chad and Cameroon and a consortium of foreign oil companies agreed to build 300 oil wells and a 1,070-kilometer pipeline that would span from the Cameroon coastline northeast to the Doba oil fields in southern Chad.[20]

Because Chad was a low-income country with a long history of civil war, commercial banks and consortium members insisted that a multilateral development agency be brought in as a partner to help mitigate risk. The World Bank agreed to fill that role and serve as the project's key guarantor. What's more, they decided to use the project as an opportunity to bring about positive changes in Chad. The World Bank convinced Chad's president, Idriss Déby, to earmark 85 percent of Chad's oilfield revenue for socioeconomic programs such as education, healthcare, and rural development. They also pressed the Parliament of Chad to pass a law on revenue management that called for consistent monitoring and the creation of an oversight committee with four representatives from civil society.

In 2003, the pipeline was completed, and Chad began exporting oil. By the end of 2006, more than $440 million was transferred into a London escrow account for the Chad government.[21]

Unfortunately, problems started emerging as soon as 2004, when the Chad government failed to fully comply with certain aspects of the arrangement. In 2005, Déby announced plans to seek re-election, sparking a rebellion by possible successors. Toward the end of that year, Chad's parliament approved reforms to the arrangement that had been proposed by Déby. The government now had greater access to the oil revenues for discretionary use, and security was now listed as a priority, opening the door for increased military spending. The World Bank suspended all payments and froze the oil revenue account.

After a rebel attack in 2006 nearly removed Déby from office, and a collapse of state seemed likely, the World Bank relented and agreed to most of the government's changes to the revenue management program. But by 2008, after another rebel attack, the World Bank determined that the model it had in mind for revenue management simply wasn't going to happen and ended its involvement.[22]

What can we learn from this? For one thing, Chad's production and export activities came online too quickly, before Chad had time to build up the kind of institutional capacities it would need to take in, manage, and distribute large volumes of oil money.

But the program's greatest weakness was that it was created and managed by an outside organization. I've said it before: It's up to Africans to address the challenges of Africa. The World Bank was well-intentioned, but the program they put in place didn't align with the realities on the ground in Chad.

Ultimately, the World Bank's idea of pulling oil revenues into a fund that would help Chad's people was a sound one. Now, we just need to see African shareholders launch an initiative of their own.

17

AMERICAN INGENUITY AND AFRICA OIL AND GAS POTENTIAL

SHAWN SIMMONS WAS a middle school student in Houston, Texas, the first time someone encouraged her to consider a career in engineering.

"Our amazing teacher, Ms. Moore, suggested I look into engineering during one of our frequent talks outside classroom instruction," Simmons wrote in a 2016 article about mentoring for *STEAM* magazine. "Since I admired and respected Ms. Moore, I listened intently to what she had to say and then and there decided to apply to Booker T. Washington High School for the Engineering Professions, a Houston high school specializing in engineering."[1]

Fast forward a couple of decades, and Simmons found herself living and working in Lagos, Nigeria, in her capacity as an environmental and regulatory supervisor for ExxonMobil Development Company.

"I was fortunate enough to be part of the team that launched a woman's network and its inaugural 'Introduce a Girl to Engineering and Science Day' in Nigeria," wrote Simmons, a petroleum and environmental engineer with a doctorate in environmental toxicology.

These days, Simmons is back in the Houston area, where she continues to encourage girls and mentor women. She returns to Nigeria three or four times a year, however, in her current role as environmental and permitting manager for ExxonMobil's Gulf Coast Growth Ventures. One of her many responsibilities is to help ExxonMobil remain compliant within Nigeria's environmental regulations.[2]

"I'm enjoying Africa and the projects there," Simmons recently told Diversity/Careers in Engineering & Information Technology. "It's all so big and exciting, and I like that."[3]

You could say Simmons is an ambassador of sorts: For the Nigerians she's encountered, she's provided a glimpse of American culture and perspectives while making a positive impact in community members' lives. At the same time, she has been playing an important role in helping a major oil and gas multinational operate successfully in Nigeria.

That dynamic is a small picture of the positive relationships that American oil and gas professionals—and companies—are realizing throughout the African continent. It's a picture of mutual respect and cooperation, and it's something we need to see more of.

I have been so blessed to have worked under great American oilmen who took a keen interest in me and mentored me, including:

- Jeff Mitchell, Senior VP and COO, Vanco Energy Company

- Gilbert Yougoubare, Vice President of Africa, Vanco Energy Company

- Bob Erlich, Partner and Executive Director, Upstream, Cayo Energy LP

- Mark Romanchock, now Principal Geologist, Samsara Geosciences

- Todd Mullen, Interim CEO, EVP & General Counsel, PanAtlantic Exploration Company

- Bill Drennen, President and CEO of WTD Resources, LLC

- H. Daniel (Danny) Hogan, General Manager, LUKOIL International Upstream West

- Ronald Wallace, exploration and development specialist

- Bruce Falkenstein. Manager, License Management – Joint Operations and Compliance, LUKOIL Overseas Offshore

- And the irreplaceable Gene van Dyke. A true pioneer and trailblazer.

Even when I went rogue, they always knew how to rein me in and guide me to find my best self. They shaped my thinking about oil and gas. I hope many young Africans will get the privilege to work with men like this. No-nonsense guys, hard to please, who never had a problem with me wearing cowboy boots or being country. They had my back and were always there to support me during the most difficult times.

We need American oil and gas companies to continue operating in African communities and to continue hiring African people, purchasing from African suppliers, and partnering with African companies. And we need companies willing to share knowledge, technology, and best practices, businesses that are willing to be good players and form positive relationships in the areas where they work.

Doing this remains very much in the interest of the American companies. They can reap tremendous financial rewards here.

It's up to us, as African community members, leaders, and business representatives, to do as much as possible to encourage

American oil and gas companies to launch, continue, and grow African operations.

The Shale Revolution and the New Normal

In 2005, U.S. oil production had been in decline for 3 decades and was only totaling about 5.2 mbo/d. Imports, meanwhile, came to about 10.1 mbo/day. The country's natural gas production had peaked at 22.6 tcf in 1973 and was at 18.1 tcf in 2005. Alarm bells about a pending "natural gas crisis" were sounding.

Enter hydraulic fracturing. For roughly 15 years, Texas oilman George Mitchell had been trying to realize a profit from this process, a decades-old technique also known as "fracking." It calls for sending a high-pressure injection of water, chemicals, and sand into shale deposits to release trapped oil and gas. In the late '90s, his company, Mitchell Energy, started seeing success fracking natural gas. Gradually, other companies started following their lead. Fracking, combined with horizontal directional drilling (HDD) and other technologies, was making it possible for producers to access oil and gas resources that once were considered impractical to exploit.[4]

It was a game-changer. Between 2005 and 2015, U.S. natural gas production grew 50 percent, making the U.S. the world's largest natural gas producer.[5]

U.S. crude oil production surged during the same time period, reaching 9.43 mbo/d by 2015. It went on to reach an all-time high of 11 mbo/d by 2018.[67]

While the U.S. oil and gas industry took a hit around 2014, when oil prices started to plummet, shale oil and gas producers remained resilient. Having surpassed Russia in October 2018 as the world's largest crude oil producer, the U.S. is now an energy exporter for the first time in 65 years.

While I'm happy for my American friends in the petroleum industry, the shale boom is not necessarily good news for African oil exporters. In the years leading up to the shale boom, the U.S. had been one of three primary markets for African crude petroleum, along with China and India. In fact, American refineries along the East Coast were configured to process West Africa's sweet Bonny Light, which has particularly good gasoline yields, making it important to the auto-centric U.S. However, between 2004 and 2013, the volume of African crude petroleum sent to the U.S. dropped nearly 70 percent. If U.S. oil continues to flood the market, oil exports from Africa to the U.S. may stop altogether. This would cause serious concern for African countries like Angola and Nigeria that rely heavily on oil exports for government revenues. This trend underscores the critical importance of capitalizing on oil and gas revenue, throughout the supply chain, to diversify African countries' economies.

The shale boom has also affected the presence of American oil and gas companies in Africa: Many major U.S. players, including Hess, Conoco, Anadarko, Apache, Devon, and Pioneer, have exited or drastically reduced their footprint in Africa to become major U.S. shale players. There has been both a pull and push factor for U.S. energy companies retreating from Africa: a combination of increasingly attractive U.S. onshore shale opportunities and the perception of higher risk in Africa. U.S. domestic shale plays are perceived as a huge, proven resource with lower geological and political risk.

Meanwhile, in Africa, exploration success rates have fluctuated, and the great promise from African oilfields like Ghana's Jubilee hasn't been fully realized. Several developments, including LNG plants in Angola, Mozambique, and Tanzania and the offshore Egina oilfield in Nigeria, saw large cost overruns and delays. A few countries, including Uganda and Mozambique, introduced capital gains taxes on transactions. There has also been unrest in Libya, which has had an impact on some of the producers there, and South Sudan oil operators have been feeling the pinch of U.S. sanctions. The oil price downturn and bank cutbacks on lending have had a negative impact as well.

U.S. oil companies have a long history in Africa, most notably the two supermajors, ExxonMobil and Chevron. While these players have remained, over the past 5 to 10 years, independent American E&P companies continued to move out of Africa and shift their attention to domestic shale plays. This period also saw a number of U.S. independents and IOCs choosing to allocate capital to locations such as Brazil, Guyana, the U.S. Gulf of Mexico, and Mexico—regions with either more transparent politics, better fiscal terms, higher quality of geology, or better recovery volume per well.

Smaller explorers have also disappeared, either because they had been unsuccessful with exploration or struggled to obtain funding. Examples include Erin Energy (which had changed its name from Camac Energy in 2015) and PanAtlantic (formerly Vanco). On the other hand, VAALCO Energy has continued to push for a play in Africa by hiring Thor Pruckl, executive vice president, international operations. The company, which is focusing on the Etame Marin in Gabon and Block P in Equatorial Guinea, still has a strong appetite for Africa and a knack for good marginal assets. Noble and Marathon are really the only remaining mid-cap U.S. E&Ps with a presence in Africa.

This trend to abandon foreign E&P projects isn't limited to Africa, though. U.S. companies have pulled out from other regions where they were historically big players, most notably from the North Sea. Conoco, Marathon, Chevron, ExxonMobil, EOG Resources, and Hess have all sold down or out completely over the last few years.

As I mentioned earlier, the common perception is that U.S. shale is less risky and has better economics than an oil and gas development in Africa. However, as with any comparison, it is often not that simple.

Fundamentally, it is more expensive to extract oil from shale than from conventional reservoirs, mostly because you have to stimulate the shale reservoir through fracking to enable oil to flow. Therefore, conventional onshore production from high-quality reservoirs should be more economical to produce. Offshore production is another story, however. The cost of drilling an offshore well is many times that of an onshore well, even including fracking. Clearly, then, the productivity of the well offshore has to be better to be able to match the economics.

This suggests that if U.S. shale was the holy grail, U.S. shale companies should have consistently performed well, especially coming out of the oil price downturn. That was not always the case. Although fundamentally the economics of production are strong in the U.S., shale has been plagued by issues such as bottlenecks from the high level of production as well as some quality issues and disappointments related to the producibility of the plays.

Although U.S. production has seen a resurgence in recent years, not all shale-focused companies have performed well, and investors have taken issue with the lack of cash generation. There has also been increased pressure on executive remuneration and targets, with high general and administrative costs seen at a lot of companies. Since 2007, energy companies have spent $280 billion more than they generated from operations on shale investments, according to one study. A number of companies have gone into bankruptcy but then reemerged. Companies drill their lowest cost/best return prospects first, meaning that they expect a deterioration in the quality of the well results over time as well as a decline in long-term capital efficiency. There also are perceptions that fracking is harmful, uses too much water, contaminates the groundwater, emits carcinogenic chemicals, and causes earthquakes.

The Risks

There's no denying that operating in Africa represents a number of very real risks for American companies. We need to be aware of these risks so we're better positioned to mitigate them (when possible) and better prepared to have honest conversations with American companies interested in operating here.

In general, E&P companies can expect to face geological, fiscal, governmental, operational, economic and political, infrastructure, gas monetization, funding, and service company risks, among others.

Let's take a closer look at geological risk, which can be broken into the categories of exploration, appraisal, development, and production.

Exploration risk: For shale plays, there is not much in the way of exploration risk: Most of them have already been discovered. Lots of conventional wells have historical data that mitigates risk.

Exploration risk is much more of a factor in newer frontier areas or under-drilled regions—in other words, most of Africa. Comparing the pre-drill chances of success with exploration success rates over the last few years shows that companies, in general, have overstated the chance of success by failing to correctly analyze the pre-drill risk.

Companies also appear to overestimate the chance of finding oil and find gas instead, which is a very different value proposition. With greater investor and industry scrutiny and tighter purse strings, we'd expect success rates to increase as companies only drill their best prospects.

Appraisal risk: Again, appraisal risk is more of an issue for new discoveries rather than for shale plays. And investors tend to focus more on exploration risk than this important area.

There are two issues here:

First, once a discovery has been made, it must be appraised. And that appraisal must be funded. Some companies may not have thought that far ahead. If the size of the discovery calls for drilling, say five test wells, the company immediately is facing a large funding need.

An example of the market response to this was when LEKOIL made a potential discovery of more than 500 mmboe called Ogo in Nigeria. Company stock went down on the day of the announcement because it would need to raise equity for subsequent appraisal.

Second, substantial risk can remain even after the initial discovery. There have been discoveries that appeared commercially viable after the first well, only to end up being questionable after hundreds of millions have been spent. Examples include Paon/Saphir off the coast of Côte d'Ivoire and Chissonga in Angola.

Development risk: This impacts both shale and conventional projects.

In the U.S., the development risk is more likely to be related to bottlenecks and unforeseen cost inflation. Offshore, there have been countless projects over the last decade that have come online later and cost more than expected. Companies may put in contingencies, but in most cases, their development costs still surged far above what they were prepared for.

However, more recent developments have resulted in better performance as companies have realized and addressed some of the issues they've come up against in the past, and the service market has loosened. Many more recent developments have actually come onstream ahead of time and below budget.

Production risk: Another underestimated risk is that once a field starts production, it doesn't produce at the expected rates. Production disappointment is an issue that has plagued offshore developments. The risk is considered lower for shale, but there have been a number of cases where production failed to meet expectations there, too.

According to a Westwood Energy study, half of on stream oil and gas fields are not producing to expectations; about 70 percent of the fields that had only limited appraisal were found to underperform versus the development plan.

There is **geological risk** with shale too: Production may underwhelm on issues such as rising gas/oil ratios (gas production increases relative to oil production over time) and interference between wells that have been drilled too closely together, meaning less oil is recovered per well. Combined with many areas of potential bottlenecks, increasing costs mean that—despite all the hype surrounding shale—acceptable returns aren't necessarily being generated, and it appears that a number of shale plays are reaching a plateau in productivity and efficiency gains.

Perhaps more than geological risk, it's **political risk** that keeps investors and oil and gas companies away from many African countries. This can include expropriation, civil disorder, revolution, unilateral imposition of new taxes and royalties, imposition of export controls or withdrawing licenses for export or import, exchange control restrictions, and other factors that reduce the value of the oil and gas venture. Investors worry a lot about political risk, which frankly, is one of the most difficult to quantify because it often is a wildcard.

In many countries, there is the risk of a black swan event, such as a coup, completely changing the landscape. That, in turn, could impact a company's contract—or create the need for a new one. Although companies can take comfort in most contracts being covered under international law, and arbitration being an option, the years it takes to complete arbitration could well wipe out a company's equity value (such was the case of Houston E&P company Cobalt International Energy Inc. in Angola).[8]

Companies also face the risk of dealing with a bureaucracy, especially in frontier regions, which often causes things to take much longer than expected, including obtaining official approvals to proceed with projects. Government approval also is needed, in most cases, for a transfer of assets. It was the government veto of an asset sale that prevented ExxonMobil from buying Kosmos' Ghana assets.

Another risk that has reared its head recently is countries **arbitrarily imposing capital gains taxes on asset sales**, erasing the company's ability to profit from the transaction. With a production sharing contract, the terms are set and generally enforceable through international arbitration, so these contracts are rarely broken by host governments. Tax and royalty contracts can be exposed to changes in corporate tax rates.

An area of particular concern for U.S. companies is the risk is **getting caught up in corruption issues**, either directly or indirectly. The reputational damage and potential fines may mean that companies simply don't want to take the risk at all, whatever the reward. Several companies operating in Africa, including Cobalt and Weatherford International, have been investigated under the U.S. Foreign Corrupt Practices Act (FCPA).[9] U.S.-based Och-Ziff Capital Management Group and two executives settled charges in 2018 related to the use of intermediaries, agents, and business partners to pay bribes to high-level government officials in Africa for energy investments. Och-Ziff agreed to pay $412 million in civil and criminal matters, and CEO Daniel Och agreed to pay $2.2 million to settle charges against him.[10] BP was recently the subject of a BBC documentary about "suspicious payments" to the Senegalese president's brother.[11]

Other factors that are important to the risk equation are investor sentiment toward a region or country. There may also be specific reasons for investors to be skeptical about a particular country, from recent exploration failures to failed M&A transactions.

The risks for shale production are very different from the challenges faced by a deepwater development. While there is still exploration and appraisal risk, as I said, most of the main U.S. plays have now been discovered, and the focus is more on the delineation and production of existing plays. The cost of appraisal is much lower, which allows companies to reduce the geological risk relative to an offshore play. Production disappointment is a risk but comes from different issues: the risk of interference between wells from too-tight spacing, under-estimating decline rates (b-factor), or underestimating the increase in gas/oil ratio over time.

Political risk obviously still exists in the U.S. but is much less of an issue from U.S. investors' point of view. Spillage is a risk, especially given harsh U.S. penalties, but the risk of a major incident is lower onshore. There are a large number of services and consumables required for shale production, and with a large amount of production concentrated in one area, there is the risk of constraints either inhibiting production or pushing up costs. Areas of concern have included:

- Water handling
- Natural gas liquids processing capacity
- Rig availability
- Completion equipment
- Sand
- People

Encouraged by the master limited partnership (MLP) boom, most companies outsource their midstream requirements, which means that midstream assets trade at much higher multiples. There are two key risks associated with this. First, if companies have committed to take-or-pay agreements in a low-price environment and production is curtailed, they could be stuck with the pipeline fee. Second, companies that make these agreements in a high-price environment could find they can't get access to pipeline capacity.

Realities in the Field

Africa holds a vast amount of discovered oil and gas resources. Over the last decade, there has been a phenomenal amount of gas discovered in Mozambique, Tanzania, Senegal, Mauritania, and Egypt.

New oil discoveries have been much harder to come by. There has been a lack of large oil discoveries in West Africa since the Jubilee oil field found in 2007. Jubilee, Ghana's first commercial oil discovery, initially was estimated to contain 3 bbo representing $400 million in revenue for its first year of production and $1 billion after that. Companies jumped on the bandwagon, with dozens of "Jubilee look-alike" fields being targeted from Morocco down to South Africa. At least 50 wildcat wells have been drilled since that time with the only notable success coming from the SNE Deepwater Oilfield in Senegal (however, ConocoPhillips, the U.S. company involved in this discovery, chose to exit). This is not just an African phenomenon: Exploration success rates, especially for oil, have been very poor over the last five years with a low rate of commercial frontier exploration success and resulting high finding costs.

SNE Deepwater Oilfield

The SNE project in Senegal has been all about potential. As for returns, they're still on the horizon.

The oilfield is estimated to hold both oil and natural gas—an estimated 2.7 billion barrels of recoverable oil reserves. However, the actual value creation has been disappointing so far.[12]

Senegal Hunt Oil obtained the exploration license for SNE in 2005. FAR Limited shot seismic in 2007, and by 2009, $21 million had been spent. Cairn/Conoco farmed in, and the field was discovered in 2014.

By late 2018, Cairn, which has a 40 percent stake in the field, had capitalized the equivalent of $460 million of gross spending; with 2019 capital expenditures, Cairn will have spent $500 million to get to the final investment decision on 200 mmboe net 2C or $2.5 boe (undiscounted). First oil is expected in 2022, and peak production is estimated at 100,000 bbl/d.[13]

Woodside paid Conoco $430 million for a 35 percent stake in the field in 2016, or around $2.2/bbl based on the 560 mmbbl cited by Woodside at the time. Conoco only made a $138 million gain on the sale. Another way to look at it, assuming an optimistic 1/5 success rate for Conoco's exploration globally, Conoco will have invested $1.4 billion on exploration for a $138 million gain—only a 10 percent return. However, this was in a low oil price, buyer's market.[14]

Nevertheless, integrated operators are realizing they need to replenish inventory, meaning transactions are likely to increase. And exploration success rates should improve as operators are now more capital disciplined and more likely to drill only their best wells.

What's more, exploration costs have fallen dramatically in the last few years, as the cost of service provision such as rig rates has come down, the efficiency of drilling has improved (higher spec rigs and high grading of crews), and drilling is being conducted in more favorable conditions (e.g., avoiding high pressure, high temperature, or ultra-deepwater plays). Where a few years ago it wasn't uncommon for an exploration well in Angola to cost more than $250 million, deepwater exploration wells in West Africa being are now being drilled for less than $50 million. For example, Ophir's Ayame well in Côte d'Ivoire cost $20 million.

It is still possible, based on recent deals/equity market valuations, to buy oil resources at a discount, compared to costs in recent years.

According to Drillinginfo.com, Africa saw 247 exploration wells spudded (initiated) in 2018, representing 19 percent of the year's worldwide total, the same as the year before.[15] However, onshore drilling in Algeria and Egypt accounted for 78 percent of this activity, with Algerian NOC Sonatrach alone spudding 76 wells.

In 2014, 67 deepwater new-field wildcats were spudded offshore Africa, representing 33 percent of the total worldwide. In 2016, however, the number fell to just 12, or 14 percent, figures that held nearly steady in 2017 and 2018.

However, the news is starting to appear more promising: nine deepwater discoveries have been made since the beginning of 2018. These include discoveries by Eni in Angola (Kalimba, Afoxé, and Agogo)[16] and by Total in Congo (Ndouma) and offshore South Africa (Brulpadda).[17] Also, during this period, according to Westwood Global Energy Group, there were some high-profile failures in West Africa, including Kosmos' Requin Tigre-1 offshore Mauritania, FAR's Samo-1 offshore The Gambia, and two probably non-commercial pre-salt discoveries at Boudji-1 (Petronas) and Ivela-1 (Repsol) offshore Gabon.[18]

Frontier drilling looks set to increase through 2019 and into 2020, and Total is expected to drill its first wells in Mauritania/Senegal, at the Jamm-1 and Yaboy-1 wells offshore Senegal and Mauritania, respectively. Kosmos, carried by BP, will drill the large Orca prospect, which is reported to have 13 tcf in-place potential. Elsewhere on the margin, Svenska is expected to drill the Atum-1 prospect offshore Guinea Bissau, and Eni is expected to continue its exploration campaign in block 15/06 offshore Angola.[19]

Projections for exploration capital expenditures in Africa are also looking up following a drop of 71 percent between 2014 and 2017, according to Rystad. An initially slow and then robust recovery at a compound annual growth rate (CAGR) of 18 percent over the next 12 years is projected.

African exploration acreage awards have increased significantly in recent years. In 2017, 840,000 square kilometers were awarded, followed by 490,000 square kilometers in 2018, and 340,000 square kilometers as of the first quarter of 2019. That makes Africa the most popular region globally for new acreage among operators.[20]

Exploration Prospects in Africa

Until recently, Angola has been viewed as a relatively unattractive investment destination. Its fiscal terms have been some of the harshest in Africa, and the costs are high due to local content requirements. Exploration in the much-hyped pre-salt basin turned out to be a costly failure, and new developments have stalled. However, reforms by President João Lourenço—intended to increase transparency and make exploration easier—have captured the interest of E&P companies around the globe.

Cameroon is an established, yet underexplored, oil province. The perception is that Cameroon has great potential for natural gas E&P, with more recent exploration for larger oil targets having failed. There has been some offshore exploration over the last five years, but the results have been relatively disappointing and, where successful, generally encountered wet gas.

The Republic of Congo is a mature province, so it doesn't offer much in the way of exploration potential. However, Eni's offshore Nene discovery is one of the biggest in West Africa in recent years. Congo is now an established producer of more than 300,000 bbl/d with significant onshore and offshore production. In October 2016, Congo ratified a new hydrocarbons code, overhauling its oil and gas industry.

Ghana is a poster child for successful frontier exploration and development, with current production reaching around 214,000 bbl/d.[21]

Kosmos Energy discovered commercial quantities of oil and gas in Ghana in 2007. The Jubilee field was developed in less than 3.5 years, reaching first oil in December 2010. Ghana has also successfully developed gas for the domestic market. Although exploration fizzled out during its three-year-long maritime border dispute with Côte d'Ivoire—which was resolved in 2017[22]—there's plenty of promise. Companies like Tullow and Kosmos still see near field and exploration potential to extend production plateaus and increase reserves, and new companies have come in to explore. Ghana is one of the more stable nations in the region, with a good record of power changing hands peacefully.

Given the large number of unsuccessful wells and the failure to make the Paon discovery work, market sentiment on Côte d'Ivoire's exploration potential is not favorable. Côte d'Ivoire has a small existing oil industry with about 33,000 bbl/d of production.[23] The lack of success from deepwater exploration, represented by a number of non-commercial discoveries, has seen notable players such as Anadarko, African Petroleum, Exxon, Ophir, Lukoil, and Oranto exit. Still, it is encouraging to see recent entries by Eni and BP/Kosmos as well as re-entry by Tullow.

In Mauritania, the country's tertiary potential had been scarred by the compartmentalized, Miocene-aged Chinguetti discovery, where production has now ceased. Kosmos has had some huge gas discoveries, despite its thesis of finding oil, cementing the market's view that Mauritania is more of a gas province. Given the amount of gas found so far, further gas is unlikely to be commercialized, so the oil story needs to work to get interest back.

Morocco was viewed as an area with great promise by a number of companies and investors, but following a string of dusters (most recently Eni/Chariot), with little encouragement, interest levels have fallen, and many companies have exited. Morocco still has some of the world's best fiscal terms. The potential of a domestic gas market or easily getting gas to Europe are the key positives. There are diverse play types, including offshore Cretaceous fan, Jurassic carbonates, and U.S. Gulf of Mexico-type salt diapir plays.

Nigeria is Africa's largest oil producer. The inability of the Nigerian government to pass a new hydrocarbon law and the resulting regulatory uncertainty continues to hold back investment in new capital-intensive development projects and has reduced the appetite for deepwater exploration. Other issues are disruption to pipelines/bunkering, state operator delays and inefficiency, delays in liftings/payments, and partner risk. Onshore and offshore exploration efforts in Nigeria have been directed towards the tertiary Niger-Delta petroleum system.

Although the dry holes a few years ago have tarnished Namibia from an investor standpoint, it was interesting to see some previous Namibian skeptics (lack of proven source, reservoirs, and traps; plus those that thought it was a gas province) taking an interest in exploring there. In April 2019, ExxonMobil announced plans to increase its exploration acreage there. Namibia has a good operating environment and existing infrastructure (deepwater port/logistics hub) at Walvis Bay. Along with its long-established regulatory regime set in a politically stable environment, Namibia's legal framework and oil and gas code, in general, are considered to be investor-friendly. There have only been about 15 wells drilled to date. It has an attractive fiscal regime.

Senegal has been a rare positive exploration story over the last few years, given the SNE and Tortue discoveries, which should be online in the early 2020s. Senegal joined the Extractive Industries Transparency Initiative (EITI) in 2013. The Petroleum Code was reformed in 2016 to support transparent development of the oil and gas industry, and Senegal unveiled a new petroleum code in 2019.

It is one of West Africa's more politically and economically stable countries, and it has had a functioning democracy since its independence from France in 1960. President Macky Sall, a geologist and geophysicist, came to power in 2012 and won another five-year term in 2019. Senegal has a fairly attractive production sharing contract-based fiscal regime.

Fiscal Terms

Fiscal terms have a significant impact on the economics of a development. The type of contract that companies opt for is important. Let's look at production sharing contracts compared to tax and royalty contracts.

Production sharing contracts:

- Generally, are less sensitive to capital expenditures and oil prices than tax and royalty contracts.
- U.S. fiscal terms are attractive, but royalties can be high.
- Tax terms will vary by country.
- The terms are generally enforceable through international arbitration; contracts are rarely broken by host governments.

To look at the impact of fiscal terms on deepwater developments in Africa, we can use the assumptions above and only vary the fiscal terms to see how the countries stack up from a profitability standpoint.

For example, let's say a company is developing a 500 mboe field (90 percent oil) in West Africa at $60/bbl Brent, with an adjustment of $10/boe for capital expenditures and $10/boe for operating expenses. We have compared this scenario to a similarly sized U.S. shale oil development in the prolific Permian Basin. The Permian Basin is considered a major driver of U.S. (and North American) upstream and midstream profits.

Although it is the same size, the Permian Basin development likely has less oil than the African site, and we assumed a $7/boe adjustment for capital expenditures and an $8/boe adjustment for operating expenses.

On an un-risked basis, the net present value per barrel available from a West African deepwater development is better than a U.S. shale project.

Put another way, if there were no difference in risk, a company would be more likely to invest in a West African deepwater project than a U.S. shale project.

The realized value is higher in West Africa because, in the U.S., the amount of crude produced is lower (there are more gas and natural gas liquids associated with shale). The African project also gets a bigger discount (based on the supply of crude oil from shale), even though we assume that the gas has zero value in West Africa for the purposes of this comparison. Operating costs are slightly lower in the Permian, as are development costs—although many more wells are required. The total cash flow on an undiscounted basis is much higher in West Africa, but also further out, which is why the higher the discount rate, the more punitive it is on deepwater. The government's take is slightly lower for an average West African development, as we assume a 32.5 percent royalty off the top in the Permian. The break-even oil price at the wellhead is similar for both, but given the $8/bbl discount realized that we assume for the Permian, the break-even is higher.

There have been many deepwater developments that have taken over five years to progress from final investment decision to first oil. However, companies are now opting for simpler, cheaper offshore oilfield designs, which are quicker to implement than bespoke solutions and more cost-effective. Companies also have the option of breaking their investment into phases, so that later phases can be funded out of cash flow and be de-risked by previous phases. Shortening the development cycle by one year reduces break-even prices by 10 percent on average.

One of the most significant perceived advantages that a shale development has over a deepwater development is that the pace of development can be altered to suit the commodity price environment. In theory, rigs can be added and removed in a matter of months (but this can pose logistical and cost challenges). However, the ability to reduce capital expenditures to match cash flow is only of some value to companies that need a return on the huge amounts they paid for acreage in the first place.

The quality of the resource is still a major factor in determining costs. Development costs have come down through a combination of lower service costs, simpler/phased developments, and standardization. Cost inflation is unlikely to rear its head soon offshore, but we did see some in U.S. onshore.

At $60/bbl Brent, the price realization per boe from a standard West African offshore development is around 30 percent higher than from a U.S. shale oil development. Historically, heavier crudes traded at a wide discount, but given rising U.S. light supply (WTI) and declining heavy (from such sources as Venezuela and Mexico), U.S. crude may continue to trade at a discount. The revenue per boe is much higher for an average offshore development, even compared to U.S. shale plays with high outputs of oil, such as those in the Permian and Bakken Formation.

Let's assume a $60/bbl Brent price with a $5/bbl Brent-WTI spread, a $3/per thousand cubic feet (mcf) Henry Hub (HH) price and natural gas liquids trading at 35 percent of WTI (i.e., $19/bbl). For a shale development that is approximately 70 percent black oil, the realization per boe is only $42/boe.

An offshore development in Africa, meanwhile, would realize $54/boe if we assume it was 90 percent oil, and all the gas produced was re-injected or produced for free. Crude pricing depends on the quality of the crude (e.g., API/sulfur), but location is important, too—and in general, West Africa crudes of similar quality trade close to Brent or at a premium.

In the U.S., given the relative oversupply of WTI, it trades at a discount to Brent despite being of a higher quality. There are further in-basin differentials, which is the cost of getting the crude to the WTI delivery point at Cushing. Most shale plays have a large amount of natural gas liquids/condensate, for which pricing is very weak in the U.S. (roughly 35 percent of WTI), as there is an oversupply, and in many cases, ethane is "rejected" and sold as natural gas instead. Gas pricing in the U.S. is also relatively weak (around $3/MMBtu) and unlikely to go much higher in the future, given the large amount of associated gas that can be produced, almost regardless of price, and the economic incentive to produce is coming all from oil.

In West Africa, gas monetization varies by country—and even by regions within a country. In most cases, the discovery of gas is viewed as a hindrance rather than a positive. The various options are generally flaring, re-injection, production to shore either into a gas grid or dedicated facility (power plant/petrochemical facility), into onshore LNG or floating LNG.

The ability to obtain funding for offshore developments outside the U.S. is harder and more expensive than for U.S. onshore companies, given the perceived higher level of risk and the higher liquidity in the U.S. market. The source of funds for many companies came from private equity over the last few years, but with it comes the expectation of high returns (about 20 percent), making funding projects more expensive. Sustained higher oil prices should bring the cost of funding down and open up equity markets again.

Over the last few years, it has been hard for companies to get farm-outs executed for pre-FID discovered resources, and the deals that have been done were generally at low prices and certainly at a discount to fair value. Asset liquidity is much lower outside the U.S.: A smaller pool of buyers means that companies operating in Africa often have to accept less than fair value. Although the U.S. has a much bigger liquidity pool to draw on for raising both debt and equity, the market has been reluctant over the last year to fund oil companies, so there have been very few equity raises or IPOs to force the companies to live within cash flow.

A Look at Returns

I've presented a frank look at the risks American companies face, both in Africa and in the U.S.

But those risks do not negate the opportunities that Africa offers for American companies to earn significant returns on their investments.

The factors that help determine a return can be categorized into three basic elements:

- The cost of getting hold of an asset (oil and gas mineral rights, oilfield license, etc.).

- The revenue obtainable from the oil and gas produced.

- The cost of production.

In terms of these elements, African assets have an advantage over U.S. assets. That's because it's generally cheaper to obtain assets in Africa. Plus, the revenue that can be obtained from the assets, in many cases, is higher, and the cost of production (in costs and taxes), in many cases, is cheaper.

There are costs associated with getting access to an asset, which is an important and often-overlooked component of its valuation. In the U.S., to be able to get hold of an asset or resource, you will have to pay full price, given a large buyer universe. Resources in Africa can generally be obtained for less than fair value, certainly in the current market, which is largely because of lack of buyers and a much less competitive market than the U.S. (although risk, of course, plays a part).

The revenue generation from an asset is determined by whether it is primarily oil or gas. Oil is much easier to monetize, given the ease of transportation and a liquid global market. Oil assets in Africa generally will generate a significantly higher price than the equivalent oil in the U.S., as the U.S. is suffering from logistical constraints and oversupply of shale oil.

Therefore, there is the potential to realize a 10 to 15 percent higher price from oil produced in Africa—which could result in a big difference in a company's return.

Gas is more difficult to monetize and is dependent on the location and market. There is the potential in Africa to realize better prices for gas than in the U.S., where, again, oversupply keeps a lid on pricing (less than $3/MMBtu). In Africa, there is the possibility in many countries to use gas to replace existing higher-cost fuel, such as diesel, for power generation, and another route to market is through LNG.

The cost of production involves the cost to bring the asset online (capital expenditure), the cost to operate the asset (known as operating costs or lifting costs), and the tax payable (royalties, taxes, etc.). The costs are largely dependent on the type of asset and geology. Some of the Nigerian onshore oil plays, for example, have a very low cost per barrel relative to the U.S., due to the lower costs associated with onshore production, the prolific nature of the wells, and a lower transportation cost. Tax rates vary dramatically across Africa and even vary within a country. There are several countries with very favorable tax terms, which unsurprisingly are the countries with little or no oil production, such as South Africa and Morocco.

Around five years ago, if a company made a discovery, the market would not only give the company credit for the discovery but would also give credit for the other identified, analogous prospects that would have been de-risked (Tullow is a good example of this). This is perfectly valid, and if exploration comes back into vogue, we should see it happening once again. However, the reason that the market stopped ascribing future value was that the E&P companies promised a number of follow-on discoveries ("Jubilee lookalikes") that never materialized (e.g., Anadarko's so-called "string of pearls" of expected discoveries up and down the Gulf of Guinea coast). In order to benefit fully from this, companies need to have blocked up a large amount of contiguous acreage, which is much easier to do in frontier regions.

What We Can Do

Of course, honestly acknowledging our risks is one thing. It's also vitally important to minimize them as much as possible. Andrew Skipper, head of Hogan Lovells' African practice, summed it up nicely in a 2018 article in *African Law & Business.*

"We know the need for government to work with private sector in Africa to attract more foreign direct investment (FDI). We know that to do that, we need to create policy and regulate consistently in a modern way (for example, to deal with the growing number of fintech and entrepreneurial start-ups). There also needs to be a focus on building and strengthening institutions, eliminating corruption, and becoming a more transparent and educated nation."[24]

These factors—transparency, stability, and good governance in particular—are of great importance to U.S. companies. An American friend and long-time industry exec with vast experience in Africa once told me that he would happily pass on a million-dollar oil field if he felt the local government was unstable or unreliable. Government stability, he has found, plays a huge role in determining whether a county is likely to honor contracts if and when new leaders take power.

Basically, African governments that want to foster American oil and gas activity need to look at their country from the perspective of American investors. When companies do their due diligence, what are they going to find? Does the government have a demonstrated track record of stability? Of honoring foreign contracts? American companies have plenty of other investment destinations around the world and in their own backyard. To compete for those investments, governments need to ensure that their fiscal terms are attractive and contract sanctity is strong.

A few other points:

- Risk sharing is another way to incentivize investment. Look at Norway's model of paying for almost 80 percent of exploration costs.

- Also important, and often overlooked, is the ease of operating and investing in African countries. Even if fiscal terms are good, fighting through excessive government red tape and approval processes puts companies off.

- The ability to transfer assets is important, too. Companies want to know they'll be able to monetize their assets in the future without capital gains taxes.

Countries that have put the right framework in place need to actively market their country as an investment destination and specify why their oil and gas sector is an attractive place to invest. Countries such as Equatorial Guinea have done a good job of getting the word out about what they have available.

Of course, some factors are outside of governments' control. They need catalysts to be positive. Catalysts include higher oil prices (which have already materialized at the time of this writing), some major exploration successes, and a return of some M&A activity. For example, major exploration success in Guyana has led to more investment in the country and surrounding acreage. Discoveries have been made by ExxonMobil and Hess, and now other North American companies, including Kosmos, Apache, Eco Atlantic Oil & Gas, JHI Associates, and CGX Energy, are looking to invest there.

A Long-Term Relationship

During the U.S.-Africa Business Forum in 2014, President Barack Obama made a case for the United States to develop strong economic ties to Africa. Fostering those connections, he maintained, would be good for all involved.

"We don't look to Africa simply for its natural resources; we recognize Africa for its greatest resource, which is its people and its talents and their potential," Obama told the African leaders gathered. "We don't simply want to extract minerals from the ground for our growth; we want to build genuine partnerships that create jobs and opportunity for all our peoples and that unleash the next era of African growth."[25]

Among the initiatives described by Obama during the Washington, D.C.-based forum was his "Doing Business in Africa" campaign to promote American exports in Africa, and the Power Africa initiative to help bring electricity to more Africans.

Under President Trump, there is Africa enthusiasm in his Assistant Secretary of State for African Affairs, Tibor Nagy, who has served in Ethiopia, Guinea, Nigeria, Cameroon, Togo, Zambia, and the Seychelles during his 32 years as a diplomat. Nagy is known for being a champion of American values and has pushed to build partnerships that promote better health, jobs, skills, education, opportunity, and security with Africa.

During a speech at the University of the Witwatersrand in Johannesburg in June 2019, Nagy announced the recently passed BUILD Act, which doubles the U.S. government's investment capital from $29 billion to $60 billion and will enable Washington's ability to make equity investments in African companies.

Washington also has unveiled the "Prosper Africa" Initiative to increase two-way trade and investment between America and Africa, Nagy said. "Prosper Africa will help us expand the number of commercial deals between U.S. and African counterparts and promote better business climates and financial markets on the continent."[26]

As of this writing, Washington continues to support the Africa-related initiatives established by the George W. Bush and Obama administrations. That includes Power Africa, Feed the Future, and PEPFAR, the successful U.S. initiative to fight HIV/AIDS.

It would be fair to say that Washington today is more focused than ever on policies that "put America first." But we are seeing signs that American leaders, political and military, still understand that fostering good relations with Africa is very much in the interest of the United States. Having good relations with African countries promotes American security. Economic ties with African countries contribute to economic growth in the U.S.

I believe the effort to strengthen, and fully harness, Africa's petroleum resources will span many years, and we will see many leaders and political stances guide America's actions. As Africans, it would be wise to encourage and welcome positive engagements as much as possible while, as Washington does, remaining mindful of the needs of and best decisions for our countries.

More Powerful Together: African Energy and American Ingenuity

Africa is a potential energy powerhouse, to be sure—but many parts of the continent lack the infrastructure and resources necessary to capitalize on that potential. Through game-changing partnerships with U.S. companies, we can address Africa's power issues and do truly amazing things.

Here are just a few examples of what can happen when African energy and American ingenuity join forces:

- Denver-based Pioneer Energy is working on solutions to help curb gas flaring in Nigeria and Equatorial Guinea. These efforts have largely been spearheaded by Ann Norman, Pioneer's General Manager, sub-Saharan Africa. Norman has been a champion of Africa's energy sector, and she has actually moved to Nigeria to play a more active role in the country's energy industry.[27]

- In June 2019, two U.S.-based companies, New York's Symbion Power and California's Natel Energy, announced a collaboration that would bring hydroelectric power to under-served African communities. Symbion Power is also investing in a Kenyan geothermal plant.[28]

In addition, programs like the U.S. government-sponsored "Power Africa" initiative encourage private-sector companies to help develop African energy, build up Africa's power grid, and improve infrastructure in rural African communities. Here are just a few of the many participants:

- Citi, a U.S.-based, global financial institution, has pledged to provide capital, industry expertise and advising, and even payment systems to make it easier to do business in Africa.

- General Electric "intends to provide technology based on a variety of fuel sources as appropriate for each project, including solar, wind, and natural gas, to deliver the power, and support partners in arranging financing for these projects."

- The United States Energy Association is promoting the growth of the African energy industry by sponsoring events and promoting trade and investment opportunities for U.S. companies interested in African energy.

U.S.-based alternative energy companies such as NextGen Solar, dVentus Technologies, and NOVI Energy are working to develop sustainable energy in Africa.[29]

COVID-19
AND ITS IMPACT ON THE WORLD ECONOMY

18

HOW WE'LL RECOVER
FROM COVID-19

In January 2020, South Sudan had ambitious goals for its oil industry: The Ministry of Petroleum was aiming to bring its current production level, about 190,000 bbl, up to 200,000 bbl/d by year-end, and to 350,000 by 2025. When the ministry set those targets, there was more at stake than keeping state-run Nilepet in business and attracting new investors: For South Sudan, oil production represents a promising pathway from years of civil war and extreme poverty toward stability, economic growth and diversity, and a better life for residents.

But, as was the case for many countries, South Sudan's plans for 2020 and the reality it experienced have turned out to be two very different things.

The COVID-19 pandemic essentially brought the global economy to an abrupt and painful halt by the end of the first quarter of this year. Governments ordered people to stay home to prevent the spread of the virus. Businesses were forced to close or dramatically change the way they operated. Schools and places of worship closed their doors. Lockdown policies varied by country, but, for the most part, the effects were the same: Entire economies were being shut down. The oil and gas sector was hit particularly hard. With huge swaths of the population staying at home, business travel canceled, and commercial and industrial transport down, demand for petroleum products plunged, and with them, so did oil prices.

So, instead of celebrating new levels of production this year, South Sudan's petroleum industry has simply been trying to stay afloat. As of late July, oil production had dropped from 190,000 to 170,000 bbl. The pandemic also has delayed the commissioning of South Sudan's 8,000 bbl/d Safinat refinery and led the Ministry of Petroleum to postpone a planned licensing round for more than 14 onshore blocks until 2021.

"We experienced prices that had never been there before, and we are running at a loss, along with private operators," Awow Daniel Chuang, the undersecretary in the Ministry of Petroleum, told Bloomberg in July. "We have been affected much more than others because South Sudan, being a new country just emerging from war, has a lot of challenges."

That said, South Sudan isn't giving up on its economic goals, nor are Africa's other oil-producing countries, which are also dealing with decreased production, delayed projects, job losses, and shrinking economies.

I'll be honest, COVID-19 has been a nightmare, and I believe we're going to see more difficulties before we're through.

But I also believe that throwing up our hands and simply letting this economic devastation decimate Africa's oil and gas industry is ill-advised. There are actions that can be taken, from tax breaks to new government regulations, that will help much-needed international oil companies (IOCs) move forward with planned projects and encourage them to do more business in Africa when the pandemic is over. South Sudan isn't the only African country that stands to benefit from thriving oil and gas operations. As I will explain throughout this book, the strategic use of Africa's natural petroleum resources can open the door to prosperity and stability for everyday Africans across the continent. We can't let that opportunity slip away, and we don't have to.

Africa's Ailing Petroleum Industry

To better understand COVID-19's impact on the global oil industry in general, and Africa more specifically, let's look at oil prices. In 2019, the international benchmark, Brent crude, was averaging around $64 a barrel, about $6 higher than 2018 levels. In early 2020, however, the supply-and-demand balance that influences prices took two major hits. First, we had the Saudi Arabia-Russia oil war, when both countries abandoned previously agreed-upon OPEC+ production limits and flooded the global market with crude at the worst possible time. By April 2020, Brent crude prices had plunged below $20 a barrel, their lowest level since February 2002.

A new OPEC+ agreement implemented in May helped stabilize oil prices to some degree—Brent, for example, was trading for about $45 a barrel in mid-August—but the oil industry has continued to feel COVID-19's dramatic impact on demand.

What has that looked like in Africa? Well, for one thing, between reduced production and lower prices, African countries—many of which rely on oil revenue for much of their budgets—are experiencing significant drops in oil revenue. Collectively, the continent's oil-dependent economies could lose up to $65 billion in income. The result has been cuts in government spending, increased debt obligations, and job losses.

Look at Africa's top-three oil producers: Nigeria, Angola, and Algeria.

In Nigeria, 57% of government revenues come from oil, and oil makes up 80% of the country's exports. Earlier this year, the government predicted its economy would contract by 5.4%. "This comes at a time when fiscal resources are urgently needed to contain the COVID-19 outbreak and stimulate the economy," a World Bank report states. "Meanwhile, the pandemic has also led to a fall in private investment due to greater uncertainty, and is expected to reduce remittances to Nigerian households."

Angola relies on oil for 90% of total export revenues. Between April and May alone, the value of its oil exports dropped by nearly 50%. In another frustrating development, as this book describes, Angola recently put a new royalty and tax regime in place to attract IOCs and boost declining production. And while I am certain those efforts will yield long-term benefits—and other African governments should follow Angola's lead—production will continue to decline in the short term while demand for oil is low.

Like Angola, Algeria derives 90% of its export revenue from oil, which funds 60% of the country's budget. In May, Algeria's federal government said it would have to cut its 2020 budget by 50%. Mansour Kedidir, an associate professor at the Higher School of Economics in Oran, is calling for economic stimulus measures, from lower interest rates and tax cuts to government-funded infrastructure development. Otherwise, Keddir said, a "Pandora's box will be opened" accompanied by "riots, irredentism, religious extremism."

Also problematic is that one of the impacts of the oil downturn we're experiencing today is its potential to hurt the petroleum industry tomorrow. Rystad, an energy consultancy based in Norway, predicted in April that 50% of the licensing rounds scheduled around the world would be canceled this year. "The unlikely upcoming lease rounds represent around 54%—a worrisome sign for global exploration. A number of factors together make these rounds unlikely to go ahead, including the oil-price drop, a global cut in investments by almost 20%, a lack of skilled manpower due to the COVID-19 pandemic,

fiscal regimes that are proving unattractive in the current environment, and a lack of interest among potential participating companies,"
Rystad's senior upstream analyst Aatisha Mahajan said.

In Africa, in addition to licensing round cancellation in South
Sudan, rounds in Côte d'Ivoire, Algeria, Tanzania, Senegal, Somalia,
Liberia, Ghana, Equatorial Guinea, Angola, and Nigeria may go on
the back burner in 2020, Rystad said.

Rystad also is projecting an increase in stranded resources in Africa.
"Non-OPEC countries account for the lion's share of 'lost' recoverable
resources, with more than 260 billion barrels of undiscovered oil now
more likely to be left untouched, especially in remote exploratory
areas," said Rystad Energy's head of analysis, Per Magnus Nysveen.

Another COVID-19 side effect likely to impact the sector's growth:
Midstream development is at risk. Pipeline operations throughout the
continent have been halting or delaying avoidable projects. "With
uncertainty looming large on the prospective projects, pipeline companies are compelled to make tough decisions to keep operations
running," said oil and gas analyst Haseeb Ahmed of UK-based data
analytics firm, GlobalData. Ahmed cited suspended construction on
the 1,980-kilometer Niger-Benin pipeline project, which was expected
to be completed in 2021.

One Problem After Another

How are COVID-19 and the oil industry downturn impacting
African countries that import petroleum products? Well, lower oil
prices are certainly better news for them than they are for petroleum
exporters, but not necessarily enough to offset COVID-19's negative
economic impact. Sectors from manufacturing to tourism are taking a
hit. "Lockdowns and border closures have caused immense hardships,
particularly on those that depend on informal employment, such as

vendors or small-scale farmers and traders," the World Bank recently reported.

Even energy-importing countries that had growing economies before the pandemic are struggling this year. In Zambia, for example, the economy was projected to grow 4% at the start of the year; now, it's expected to shrink 5% because of the double blow of COVID-19 and drought last year. COVID-19 has hurt the country's manufacturing and mining industries and cut tourism revenue.

In South Africa, which implemented the strictest pandemic lockdowns in Africa, economic activity is projected to contract 7.2% in 2020. The International Monetary Fund (IMF) reported that the most affected sectors are construction, personal services, trade, catering, hospitality, transport, storage, and communications. The manufacturing and mining industries have come to a complete halt.

Businesses in Survival Mode

Not only is the petroleum industry downturn impacting countries across Africa—and the world—it's also creating tough times for oil and gas companies, from international majors to independent, indigenous operations.

This is how Austin Avuru, CEO of independent Nigerian oil and gas firm Seplat Petroleum, explained the company's plans to reduce operational spending this year. "Overall, our target is to get close to a neutral cash flow position in 2020. So the main target of our budget restructuring is to be able to survive FY 2020, with the hope that during 2021 prices will climb back, and we will manage to resume our planned investments. Meanwhile, in 2020 the key word is survival."

International oil companies seem to have a similar perspective. Eni and Total, both very active in Africa, are each cutting back on 2020 E&P projects by 25%. And next year, Eni has said, it likely will cut its investments from $2.5 billion to $3 billion. Since Eni is Africa's leading oil producer—it extracted about 1.13 million bbl/d of crude in the third quarter of 2019—that is troubling news.

And Eni and Total are not alone. A number of companies, simply striving to get through the downturn, have been postponing or canceling investments.

In June 2020, at least 13 major projects awaiting final investment decisions were under threat, from Shell's $10 billion deepwater Bonga Southwest Aparo oil and gas project off the coast of Nigeria to Aker Energy's Pecan Field project offshore Ghana. In Senegal, the Sangomar offshore oil project, sanctioned in January, is now facing delays. And in Angola, BP's Platina Field Development and its Palas, Astaea, and June (PAJ) projects could be delayed. There's also a possibility that the Zinia 2 Development, an Angola-based Total/ExxonMobil project, will be postponed.

The 13 projects' combined losses could reduce African oil production by as much as 200,000 barrels a day for the next 5 years, and eventually lead to cuts of more than a million barrels a day, Rystad predicted.

Time for Treatment

With African livelihoods and businesses in jeopardy, not to mention major oil and gas projects that have the potential for far-reaching economic benefits, it's time for decisive action. And I'm convinced that responsibility falls to Africa's government leaders. They need to act now, not only to get Africa through the hardships COVID-19 is inflicting but also to safeguard our path to a better future. That's why I worked with the African Energy Chamber's leadership to develop our Call to Action, a commonsense energy agenda for Africa that we released in late April 2020. In it are 10 recommendations for helping Africa recover—and ultimately, thrive. Most were developed with the goal of cooperating with IOCs so we can break the pattern of postponed and canceled projects in Africa.

Here's a summary of what we're proposing.

Exploration and Extensions of Product Sharing Contracts (PSCs): A 24-month extension on all exploration projects would make it possible for companies to reschedule drilling projects that have been put on hold or canceled. We need to be realistic. It is very difficult to have drilling during lockdowns, curfews, and airport closures.

Work Programs Adjustments: Waiving some of exploration companies' work program commitments is the kind of tangible support we need to show to ensure healthy, long-term business relationships and resumed E&P activities as soon as possible. Instead of putting companies in a difficult position, we should offer flexibility.

Petroleum and Natural Gas Fiscal Regimes: Now more than ever, it's vitally important that governments take steps to provide transparency, predictability, and consistency through regulatory and fiscal policies. What's more, we're calling for stronger public-private conversations about revising fiscal terms within PSCs, especially for contracts over producing areas and fields where operating costs are higher. By providing better fiscal terms, governments will allow operators to meet their commitments and continue to raise capital. Africa must remain competitive to survive. Gone are the days when Nigeria competed for oil and natural gas investment against Algeria and Angola. Today, new players like Senegal, Mozambique, and Uganda are giving the bigger players a run for their money. We face an even bigger challenge with Suriname and Guyana, where fiscal regimes and enabling environments for doing business are more competitive, helping them attract more capital.

Go Bold on Tax Relief for Services Companies: To preserve employment within the services industry, which represents a majority of the sector's jobs, the Chamber is calling for a series of tax relief and deferral measures. These include reducing and/or waiving income taxes on service companies for at least two years, along with giving service companies the option of meeting their income tax obligations in installments.

Financial Support and Patient Capital with Banking: The banking sector and financial institutions must look at providing no-interest loans and loan guarantees to local service companies that have ongoing projects and commitments with foreign majors. We also recommend a single window or special program to facilitate foreign exchange, which would make international transfers easier and local companies more competitive.

Cutting Non-operational Fees: The Chamber urgently requests a reduction in social fees and other fees due to the state, such as surface rental fees or fees related to training funds. Corporate social responsibility (CSR) expenditures, for instance, should be reduced according to a company's level of operations and be cut by 50% for services companies, 40% for exploration companies, and 20% for producing companies. In addition, the obligations for local small-to-midsized enterprises (SMEs) to execute social projects should be suspended until 2022.

Promotion of Upstream Investments: African states should actively promote joint ventures on current farm-in projects. The extension of exploration periods, along with the revision of PSCs' fiscal terms, would strengthen farm-in and farm-out opportunities across the continent. Africa is competing aggressively for exploration dollars against very attractive regions such as the Middle East and the Americas, and its environment needs to become more attractive to ensure capital injections and technology transfers.

Incentives to Critical Infrastructure Projects: Beyond the upstream sector, the Chamber believes governments should offer the necessary state support and government incentives to critical infrastructure projects in the midstream and downstream industries, including refining and LNG projects.

Regional Content Development: The Chamber is calling for a commonsense approach to local content. Governments should review local content regulations and revise or drop inefficient requirements. More importantly, the time has come for African jurisdictions to harmonize their local content regulations and push forward an African regional content approach that will encourage joint ventures and regional expansion within the upstream and services industries. Women's empowerment must be at the front and center of the new approach.

Subsidies Removal: The timing is perfect for subsidy reforms across the continent. The Chamber is encouraging all governments to follow the steps of Nigeria and remove fuel subsidies when applicable. This will allow the saving of several billions of dollars a year and provide better macroeconomic stability for African economies to recover.

As I've said, the oil and gas industry will only work for Africans when we set fair policies and treat oil and gas companies as partners who drive our progress.

Market-Driven Local Content and Making Energy Attractive:
We have to embrace local content more; we have to be ready.
For example, those operating in the Republic of the Congo or
Equatorial Guinea can't move people in or out. They are going to
require locals to do the job and keep the platforms and fields going.
And if they want to bring in expats or services, it might be too
expensive. This creates an urgent need to empower skilled Africans
and implement programs to bring them back home.

Local companies have to be ready. They can't just play the game of
setting up a company and taking commissions from international
players. That has to stop: African companies have to become more
accountable and responsible during these moments. That is the only
way forward. We must move away from being agents and towards
being entrepreneurs. This is how we will survive the next phase of
oil and gas; local content has to have a major role in it. We need a
corrective course.

The Chamber is very focused on seeing incentives put in place.
Countries cannot legislate and regulate themselves to prosperity. They
cannot continue to tell international companies that they must do A,
B, C, and D. It is all about sticks and carrots. On top of that, you
cannot love new jobs but hate those who create them.

We need rules that create changes. So, we proposed a tax incentive for services companies that will train, prepare, and qualify locals
to replace expats. We might see some revenue being lost today, but
in the long term, this will create local taxpayers. We will have more
contracts being created and more services offered locally. This is
what we see as the future of local content. Of course, there have
to be some regulations, and they have to be carefully worded and
drafted to fit within the market and ensure that market forces work
with them.

So, we look for the fundamentals of local content such as training and development. We can look at how Oman, Nigeria, and Ghana have been able to do something in that area and learn from them. When we talk about procurement contracts and domestic supply chains, we need to look at what has *not* worked in the past.

We like to have rights, but what about responsibilities? Governments have a responsibility to set up fundamental frameworks like education. We cannot expect the IOCs to be the ones who are going to train, develop, and prepare our people to serve the industry. It is not their job; we have to set up our education and ensure schools are ready and competitive globally. Once that base is established, every African child can compete. It is about rights and responsibilities.

We celebrate the implementation of the African Continental Free Trade Agreement, but it cannot come without African content. In a small country like Gabon or Equatorial Guinea, when companies can't find qualified people, they immediately go to Europe or the U.S. to source talent. We need to think in terms of African content: If a company can't find staff in the local community, it should look within Africa. We can't be people that do not employ, promote, and contract Africans to compete for projects around Africa.

We also have to consider the role of Black women in local content. While they represent 40–50% of the African population, only 5% of workers in Africa's oil and gas industry are Black women. This is a time for us to make a paradigm shift. For the Chamber, there is no real, local content without a concrete role for women in oil and gas.

Women should be at the forefront of African oil and gas. Women have proven to be better managers and employees and more ethical workers, and they deserve a great place in Africa's energy industry. This industry is not just about prices and stocks; it is about being a catalyst for our economy to become what we dream of.

Many of the old white males that championed the industry are retiring, and young people need to be brought into the industry. However, young people are not looking at working at Exxon or Chevron, but rather for Amazon or Google. If the industry doesn't act, it will lose talent. This is a chance for Africa to succeed by bringing in young Africans, who are already more technology-driven and who will be able to shape the oil industry of the future. The industry of old is gone—it is not going to be oil and gas, but the *energy* industry.

Infusion of Job Opportunities

Even during the pandemic, we should still be striving to connect trained, qualified Africans with well-paying oil and gas sector jobs: There may be fewer positions available in Africa at the moment, but many are still out there.

That's why the Chamber, in addition to releasing our Call to Action, has launched an energy jobs portal. Our goal is to make sure that local jobs are filled by local people. We also want to play a role in helping African energy markets bounce back as quickly as possible after the COVID-19 crisis by providing a free, reliable pipeline to qualified talent.

The portal will help local and international companies find local employees across 30 skill sets in the oil, gas, power, and renewable energy sectors. And the Chamber will operate and vet job postings to prevent fraud.

As I said when we launched the portal, local content has always been the number one priority of the African Energy Chamber when advocating for an energy industry that works for Africans and builds sustainable business models.

Approaching Our Energy Transition Wisely

Almost immediately after COVID-19 infected the global petroleum industry, I started hearing calls to use the oil industry downturn as an opportunity to usher in a new era—one where petroleum products are phased out and replaced with sustainable energy sources.

And, as I've said numerous times, I agree that protecting our environment is of great importance. When the timing is right, I'm convinced that Africa's energy transition will be a positive one for everyday Africans.

That said, despite the difficulties COVID-19 has created for the oil and gas industry, it is still very much alive. Forcing its premature death means the end of its potential to create economic growth. What's more, Africa desperately needs its natural gas resources to address widespread energy poverty. Currently, about 840 million Africans, mostly in sub-Saharan countries, have no access to electricity. That's why this book advocates so strongly for gas-to-power initiatives. Instead of flaring gas and exporting Africa's abundant natural gas reserves, we need to use that gas to power electricity generation. Not only would the increased access to reliable energy contribute to better health and safety for everyday Africans, but it would also provide a necessary piece of the puzzle when it comes to growing African economies. Businesses, schools, organizations—they all need energy to thrive and grow.

As I recently told The Energy Year, this has been a tough time, but we are resilient people, and I firmly believe that we can come out of this stronger. I don't see this pandemic as a time to bury heads in the sand; instead, it is an opportunity to start planning our comeback and determining how we can make Africa better and stronger.

19

LIGHTS OUT: REFORMING AFRICAN POWER GENERATION MONOPOLIES AND TRANSITIONING TO THE FUTURE

I T IS NEARLY IMPOSSIBLE to overestimate the impact of power reliability on economic, industrial, social, or even cultural development in modern-day life. Electricity powers everything: It lights our nights; it fuels every economic activity; it connects us with the world. It is very possible that you are reading the electronic version of this book on an electricity-powered device.

Unfortunately, for many Africans, electricity is not something one can rely on. Hundreds of millions of people in Africa, particularly those living in remote rural locations throughout the continent, are disconnected from the national grid. But the problem of power reliability is not solely geographic in nature. Even for Africans connected to national power grids, living without power is a constant. Many of Africa's networks are old, dilapidated, and poorly maintained. Breakdowns are common. Trust in electric providers is low: In some places, people simply do not subscribe to electric service, or they refuse to pay. Many choose to make illegal connections to the grid, further pressuring the network and eroding the supplier's revenue, which in turn makes it even harder to fund improvements to the network.

The situation is definitely not ideal. The result of this situation is clearly seen, for instance, in South Africa, even if it is the biggest economy and boasts one of the highest rates of access to electricity in Africa.

In March 2019, South Africa's state-owned power utility, Eskom, was forced to repeatedly implement load shedding on its network, leaving the country very much in the dark. A number of factors were behind this event, including plant breakdowns, lack of diesel reserves, and even weather-related damage on the country's power connection to Mozambique, which could have helped with power supply. It was a combination of events that South African President Cyril Ramaphosa described as a "perfect storm," against which there was little to be done.[1]

While we can all agree that it was a particularly challenging blend of factors, the truth is that blackouts are commonplace in South Africa. Crumbling infrastructure networks, a lack of investment in mainte-nance, poor management, corruption, over-staffing—the list of rea-sons goes on, but the consequences are very real.

The situation in the continent's southern tip is particularly dire, as Eskom, responsible for 95 percent of the country's power production, is on the brink of going bust under the gigantic amount of debt it has accumulated, but I will get to that in a minute.

Power failures are not just inconvenient. They effectively stop a country from producing and jeopardize an enormous amount of wealth. Hospitals without power risk lives; industries and services come to a standstill. The African Development Bank estimates that inadequate electricity supply costs sub-Saharan Africa approximately two percentage points of GDP growth every year.[2] This might be an often-used figure, but one worth repeating. In a continent so much in need of economic development to improve the quality of life of its people, this is a dire reality.

A 2019 report by the World Bank places the average accessibility to power across the African continent at 43 percent, less than half of the world average of 88 percent. That amounts to around 600 million people without access to power. To say there is room for improvement is perhaps the year's biggest understatement.[3]

But why is it that the power networks across Africa seem so unreliable and limited in reach? I suggest it is not simply a matter of how many resources are allocated to infrastructure development, but that it has something to do with the very nature of power utilities in Africa.

Traditionally, power generation, transmission, and distribution infrastructure have been state-owned. This was the case in Europe, North America, and pretty much everywhere else in the world, as the sheer size and cost of setting up a network made the national budget the only budget that could afford to build power stations, hundreds of substations, kilometers of power lines, and connecting all of this to people's homes. Monolithic, vertically integrated companies were responsible for every aspect of the network, including pricing.

That, however, is no longer the case. Step by step, utilities around the world have been unbundled into smaller, more specialized operations that are easier to monitor, manage, and sustain. In most places, the network has been privatized, promoting the optimization of services and reducing costs. Most places, but not in sub-Saharan Africa. That needs to change.

Fixing SSA's Power Utilities

In 38 out of 48 sub-Saharan countries, the power sector is completely under state control. In most of the other 10, states have allowed some space for private sector participation, but that remains mostly limited. Most of them suffer from the same problems of inefficiencies and aging infrastructure. The problem is that most, if not all, of the states controlling these companies lack the capital to invest in improving and expanding their power networks.

This comes at great cost to the country's economy and its people. These are capital-intensive, long-term investments that tend to clash with the short-term priorities of political leaders. Further, despite their monopolistic nature, these companies consistently lose money. According to a World Bank study on 39 power utilities across Africa, only those in Uganda and the Seychelles manage to recover their operational and capital costs, and only 19 recovered just their operational costs. Under this setup, these companies are bound to accumulate debt and never provide reliable services to the population, remaining a burden to the state.

Much of the problem arises from the fact that these companies are too big, too opaque, and too stretched out to be able to correct inefficiencies. Further, nation states become so dependent on these monolithic institutions that they are considered "too big to fail," as President Ramaphosa described Eskom. In February 2019, the South African government announced budget support of $1.55 billion for Eskom. The troubles the company has found itself in since then assure that further contributions will be necessary to save the company. Eskom is currently nearly $30 billion in debt, which is about 10 percent of South Africa's GDP.[4]

Now, the South African economy contracted 3.2 percent in the first quarter of 2019. That was partially due to reduced economic activity caused by the load shedding Eskom implemented as it strove to protect the national grid from collapse. Less value created means less tax revenue for the state, which will make the burden of bailing out Eskom even higher, but not as high as having the national grid collapse.

The national budget deficit will almost certainly largely surpass initial estimates, at the peril of South Africa's last investment-grade credit rating. Losing it would probably initiate a quick outflow of investment.

Basically, the South African government finds itself a hostage of its national power company. This is an unsustainable situation, to say the least. The answer here lies in unbundling: Separating power generation from transmission and distribution immediately facilitates management and makes it easier to identify the problems within the network. It also means that if a company is at the brink of collapse, it would be a smaller company and much easier for the state to help back to its feet. This is exactly what President Ramaphosa promised to do back in February. However, considering the strong opposition from South Africa's powerful workers' unions, who fear layoffs, it is uncertain if he will be able to move forward with the process.

Unfortunately, Eskom is just one in a myriad of national power utilities across the continent facing serious challenges. SEGESA in Equatorial Guinea, NEPA in Nigeria, and many others fail to provide adequate services to their customers. Eneo, in Cameroon, just announced in June a series of power cuts and reductions of energy supply due to mounting debt. In Ghana, mounting energy sector debt of $2.2 billion has restrained network expansion for years.[5] Even as I write these words, São Tomé e Príncipe has just endured a five-day blackout as the country lacked the fuel reserves to power its minuscule power generation facilities. Fortunately, there also are examples in the continent that offer positive lessons.

The Ugandan and Kenyan Lesson

A few sub-Saharan countries have already moved forward with unbundling their power utilities. Uganda represents a particularly enlightening example of what the unbundling and progressive privatization of the power generation sector can do for power accessibility and reliability. In 1999, the Ugandan power network was on the verge of collapse, with old and under-maintained infrastructure struggling to serve even the small amount of people connected to the network. The government chose to take a stand, enacting one of the most comprehensive and complex liberalization efforts seen in any African power sector.

As some states have chosen to do before and after, Uganda unbundled its national utility in generation, transmission, and distribution, choosing to retain state control over the transmission network—a sector where public interest tops commercial viability. The process was complex and not without flaws, but private sector actors quickly started to emerge in the form of independent power producers (IPPs), actively contributing to bringing relief to a hydro-based national grid that struggled with drought.

A comprehensive regulatory framework was established to manage the transition in the sector, with an independent authority charged with overseeing licensing and pricing, while a specific entity was created to deal with rural electrification. The result of this transformation was a considerable increase in the country's generation capacity, efficiency improvements, loss reduction, and increased access.

This is particularly evident in Umeme, Uganda's fully privatized power distribution network. After being taken over by private equity partner, Actis, in 2009, and following a restructuring and expansion strategy based on governance strengthening, operational improvements, community outreach, and funding facilitation, Umeme's dilapidated network saw an outstanding change. Its customer base expanded from 292,000 in 2005 to over 1 million in 2017. The company expanded most of its customer base on a prepaid basis, which helped increase revenue collection from 80 to 99 percent in the same period. Energy losses, through improvements in the network, were reduced from 38 to 17.5 percent, and by securing consistent revenue and investor confidence, the company was able to invest half a billion dollars in the network's improvement and expansion.[6] These outstanding results in the span of a decade are rare across the African continent but are representative of what can be achieved through tight regulation in tandem with liberalizing the market and fomenting competition and efficiency.

This by no means implies that there have not been power generation problems in Uganda, which continues to have one of the world's lowest rates of electricity penetration. Further, privatization processes like the one that is taking place in Nigeria, where the government has also chosen to retain control over the transmission sector, represent cautionary tales of the need for expertise and solid regulatory and implementation frameworks to fulfill reform plans.

Despite efforts to reform and liberalize its power network, Nigeria's issues with performance evaluation, changes in political leadership, and overall unpreparedness for the whole transition are undermining privatization's ability to improve the power sector. As a result, the country remains underserved by its power network, utilizing less than half of its already insufficient installed capacity and suffering considerable network losses. Companies, and the people who have the resources for it, have become accustomed to directing a considerable part of their budgets to fueling their own expensive diesel backup generators, just so they can remain in business. The privatization processes in Uganda and Nigeria have fallen short, but their potential to bring about meaningful, positive changes remains.

Another important example can be seen in Kenya. In the 1990s, Kenya's power network went through an extensive unbundling and liberalization process. Also dominated by hydropower generation, years of drought showed the limitations of the country's aging power network and forced the government to invest in costly emergency thermal generation to compensate for lost production. In order to minimize public investment and under the reformed legal framework, independent power producers entered the Kenyan market in the early 2000s while the government continued to invest in its own new generation infrastructure. The government also segregated generation, which is the responsibility of the Kenya Electricity Generation Company and a growing number of IPPS, and created the Kenya Electricity Transmission Company (Ketraco), which handles transmission and infrastructure development.

While the semi-privatization of the generation sector brought great relief to the network, Ketraco's leaner and more project-focused structure managed to build 1,000 kilometers of transmission infrastructure in its first 6 years of existence, a considerable improvement when compared to the 3,200 kilometers built in Kenya between 1956 and 2008. The network extension allowed for a number of new generation projects to be connected to an ever-expanding grid. A favorable investment attraction framework, coupled with a feed-in-tariff (FiT) system that gave producers long-term off-taking contracts at fixed prices, gave the private sector the confidence it needed to continue to invest in the network. As a result, electricity access in Kenya saw a quick rise from 32.1 percent in 2008 to 63.8 percent in 2017. Today, it is well on its way to universal electricity access by making use of private investments and international aid programs.[7]

By presenting these examples, I am not cherry picking. It is no secret that South Africa has also opened its market to IPPs, but today they represent less than 5 percent of the country's output, and Eskom's overall control of the market has largely disincentivized investment. Across the continent, we have examples of unbundling and privatization efforts that remain mainly unsuccessful. However, that has mostly to do with the lack of an investment-conducive environment and transparency, which has kept investors at bay.

Let's be honest; Africa will never achieve its full potential if it cannot power its industries, services, or even its households. This excerpt from the 2015 "Power People Planet" report by the Africa Progress Panel paints a clear picture of this very issue within the energy sector:

"Far too much public finance is wasted on inefficient and inequitable energy subsidies. Governments spend $21 billion a year covering utility losses and subsidizing oil-based products, diverting resources from more productive energy investments. Africa's poorest households are the unwitting victims of one of the world's starkest market failures. We estimate that the 138 million households comprising people living on less than $2.50 a day are spending $10 billion annually on energy-related products, such as charcoal, candles, kerosene and firewood. Translated into equivalent cost terms, these households spend around $10/kWh on lighting, which is about 20 times the amount spent by high-income households with a connection to the grid for their lighting."

The report further states, "current energy-sector investment levels are just $8 billion a year, or 0.49 percent of (Africa's) gross domestic product (GDP). This is inadequate. We estimate the investment financing gap for meeting demand and achieving universal access to electricity is around $55 billion, or 3.4 percent of Africa's GDP in 2013."[8]

Estimates on exactly how much capital is necessary to achieve universal access by 2030 vary anywhere from $50 to $90 billion a year. For every year that does not meet the yearly target, the average for the closing deadline becomes larger. What seems abundantly certain is that African governments do not possess the capital to make these investments on their own, neither are vertically integrated national utilities prepared to maximize the benefits of those investments. Private sector and international cooperation will have a fundamental role in fulfilling this potential, while governments will not only promote and facilitate investment in the power sector but also oversee, regulate, and enforce laws on performance, investment, and pricing that are both just and sustainable.

Transitioning Into the Future

Africa is an energy-rich continent in every way imaginable, but mostly, our energy focus has been on oil and gas exploits. Foreign investment in the continent's energy sector is overwhelmingly dominated by capital flooding into hydrocarbons exploration and production. Dependency on this type of energy has resulted in considerable wealth for oil-rich countries, but considerable costs for those with no oil, gas, or coal reserves. It has also, to a greater extent, shaped the history of Africa over the last 100 years.

While I personally believe that the oil and gas industry has a tremendous potential to fuel economic development and raise hundreds of millions out of poverty, we must not ignore the change of times and what that means for the energy industry worldwide.

An energy transition is taking place across the world and also in the African continent. Concerns regarding hydrocarbon usage, carbon dioxide (CO_2) emissions, and growing evidence of climate change dominate energy debates today and are mirrored in the expanding investments made in renewable energy worldwide. I do not mean to engage in a debate on why Africa should be concerned about CO_2 emissions when we are responsible for so little of it, compared to other regions of the world. My concern is with the lives of the people in the continent and the economies they live in. Within that context, there are a number of arguments to support a progressive, consistent, and strong transition into a greener energy matrix.

After all, Nigeria, the continent's biggest oil producer, is a net importer of oil products and still dramatically fails to provide reliable power to its citizens—a paradoxical situation that can be seen in most oil-producing countries across the continent. For those that do not possess these resources, importing oil and gas to power their economy comes at huge costs to the taxpayer and economic growth.

So, I propose that it is worth exploring other options.

In recent years, the collapsing prices of solar and wind power, coupled with improvements in storage capabilities and changing consumer behavior, have triggered a paradigm shift in the world's energy sector, which is progressively moving from carbon-based power to cleaner forms of energy. In that regard, again, Kenya provides a perfect example of the potential of these technologies to provide power for Africans everywhere. Faced with the aforementioned struggles with its dependency on hydropower, and forced to resort to thermal-based emergency generation using heavy oil, Kenyan leaders have taken unparalleled steps. Endowed with ample geothermal resources in the Great Lakes region, Kenya has invested in extensive geothermal power generation over the last decade, which today places it in the top 10 geothermal power producers worldwide. Today, geothermal power generation accounts for nearly 50 percent of the country's grid capacity, with hydropower remaining the second-biggest source of energy at 30 percent.

The Lake Turkana wind farm, the largest such facility in Africa, came online in October 2018. It now single-handedly represents 11 percent of the country's energy matrix. Thermal power production now stands at 13 percent while the government is progressively phasing out long-term power purchase agreements made during emergency periods. A number of developments in solar should come online in the coming years, which will considerably add to this network's green sources. What's more, Kenya has one of the biggest numbers of micro-grid systems on the continent, a cost-efficient solution that uses renewable energy in remote locations to power communities without the need for onerous connections to the national grid. As the network expands, Kenya is expected to reach 80 percent electricity access by 2022 and an astonishing 100 percent renewable energy sufficiency by 2020.[9]

How did Kenya become a global leader in renewable energy? The country found itself in dire need of energy security following severe droughts that hampered economic growth. The government's comprehensive master plan to deal with this issue focused on locally available resources (geothermal energy) and commercial feasibility, while promoting the involvement of the private sector through policy. The FiT system I mentioned earlier provided price security, while the specifically created Geothermal Development Company was responsible for exploration and drilling for geothermal power, which dramatically reduced operational risk and facilitated private sector involvement in production and generation. Discriminatory policies, including tax breaks, were established to benefit investments in renewable forms of energy; extensive training programs have come to produce a vast and highly qualified workforce in the renewable energy sector; strong independent entities were created to monitor the sector and implement regulation, and extensive use of international funding programs was made.

In sum, none of these opportunities are unique to Kenya. True, geothermal resources are not available everywhere, but most of Africa has solar exposure that is adequate for power generation, not to mention wind, hydro, and other forms of clean power generation.

Please keep in mind that Kenya is a country on the verge of becoming an oil and gas exporter, with extensive oil and gas reserves found in its territory in recent years. I am not saying that oil and gas are to be ignored, but that within the process of energy transition that the world is going through, African countries would be wise to diversify their sources of power and make use of the most economically and environmentally sustainable sources of power available to them.

Today, Kenya is nearing power independence, with a diverse energy matrix that reduces risk while keeping prices relatively low. And while Kenya's example is extreme, most African countries have the resources to at least, in part, follow suit. Many have made endeavors into this sector already, from the Senergy solar plant in Senegal to the Mocuba solar power plant in Mozambique and the Lusaka solar plant in Zambia.

For those countries where renewable energy resources are not as abundant or economical, a low-carbon economy can also be developed around less polluting and abundant resources, namely natural gas, which provides outstanding economic opportunities across the continent that I have already covered extensively in this book.

One thing is certain, though: Africa will never fulfill its true potential until access to reliable power is widespread, and that can only be attained once we have functional, well-funded, transparent power utilities that make use of new technologies and solutions and that partner with the private sector to promote the continent's ability to power itself in a sustainable manner. And the time for that is now.

Innovation is Key

"Technological leapfrogging" is not a new concept, but it is one that is very relevant for the current state of the African power sector. The idea that we can benefit from more efficient technologies developed in other parts of the world to leap over certain inner stages of progress towards a more efficient future is nothing short of appealing.

We witnessed such advances with China's industrialization process: Despite starting much later than Europe or the United States, Chinese industry developed in a much shorter span of time as it benefitted from advanced and efficient technologies. Solutions driven out of necessity, like the ethanol industry in Brazil, developed following the oil supply crisis of the early 1970s, are great examples of how innovation towards more efficient and cleaner solutions can contribute to qualitative jumps in certain industrial sectors.

In this sense, Africa is in a prime position to take advantage of emerging and proven technologies in the power generation sector. We have witnessed this phenomenon in other industries, like telecom, where most African nations avoided heavy investments in a nationwide telephone system, moving directly to mobile phones. Beyond simply replicating existing technologies, some African nations can take advantage of their own unique landscapes to even step further into the future than the rest of the world.

One of the most interesting potential applications of new technologies within the energy sector could be the combination of single standing photovoltaic (PV) panels connected in a network and managed through a blockchain system. Put simply, individuals not connected to the national power grid could, for instance, place a PV panel on their rooftop and produce their own energy. In order to overcome the need for expensive storage solutions, these individuals could be connected to a local network of other energy-producing individuals and trade energy, buying and selling from the network when necessary. The trades would utilize a decentralized ledger system, which would record the balances of each individual energy producer and translate those balances in the form of a cryptocurrency that could then be exchanged for government services or other types of goods. This sort of solution could have an incredibly large impact in the effort to bring power to remote areas, bypassing the need to invest in major transmission connections to centralized power generation facilities.

The fact is, African nations with a considerable portion of their population disconnected from the national power grid could make the transition to decentralized micro-power markets much more quickly than those with more consolidated markets in other parts of the world.

This system could result in the rapid electrification of rural areas across Africa, and guarantee a certain level of energy security, without the need to wait for national utilities to have the resources to invest in network expansion.

If the explosive growth in the number of mobile phones across Africa is any indication, with many countries registering more consumers for mobile subscriptions than connecting people to the power network, decentralized power systems could spread very quickly throughout the continent and respond to the needs of those living in areas where power access remains economically infeasible.

This is just one example from a myriad of new solutions being developed every day in the energy sector that African leaders and entrepreneurs would do well to evaluate and consider, as they present a unique opportunity to propel the continent forward.

What About Big Oil?

For many oil-based economies across Africa, transitioning into a low-carbon power generation matrix might not always seem like the most obvious option. In many places, a shift from heavy oil to natural gas for power generation would already present a much more functional, cost-efficient, and cleaner option. But does this transition affect the future of the oil industry itself, which sustains so many economies across the continent?

At least for the next few decades, oil is not going anywhere. While a deceleration in demand growth has been notable in recent years, crude oil will continue to sustain economic development for many decades to come. We cannot ignore the transformations taking place around us, however, and it is clear that oil and gas companies are very well aware of the shifting tide that seems to be closing in, a transformational moment dubbed "peak oil," when global demand is expected to start diminishing effectively.

For now, the shift has happened mostly in the power generation sector. Transport remains overwhelmingly dependent on oil products, and even if light electric vehicles become widespread, there is still no viable solution to replace oil-based products for heavy-duty trucking or maritime and air transportation. Further, demand for plastics, fertilizers, and other oil and gas-based products is expected to continue to rise in the coming years. There are several opportunities to adjust and adapt to the realities of the future, and oil and gas companies have taken the cue of the changing landscape.

Over the last couple of decades, most oil and gas operators have progressively invested in research and development in new forms of energy. The majority of the majors have been diligently diversifying their portfolio from mostly oil assets into a larger natural gas portfolio, which is seen as having a much more sustained growing demand in the future than oil. More recently, some have also made the shift towards investing in renewable power generation, mainly solar and wind power. A couple have even changed their names to project what is a change in their corporate profile, from an "oil and gas company" (IOC) to an "energy company." The Norwegian Statoil rebranding as Equinor is a perfect example of this shift in the industry.

Particularly in Europe, these companies have been positioning themselves to follow the market trends and technologies and remain dominant in every energy field. Some, like BP and Shell in the 1990s, have suffered from stepping into immature technologies that did not prove investment-worthy, but as the sector matured, the risk of early entry was reduced.

So far, these moves have been cautious. The most bullish within the majors regarding the renewable energy market, Shell, still dedicates less than 10 percent of its annual investment budget to renewables, but the trend is definitely growing amongst the industry's main players. Beyond the economics of this issue, oil and gas companies will be fundamental actors in the fight for environmental sustainability and climate change mitigation. In the words of the secretary-general of OPEC, Mohammad Barkindo, in June 2019, "the oil and gas industry is an instrumental part of the fight against climate change." He went on to say, "We believe that oil and gas are part of the solution to climate change and the solution lies in technology, appropriate policies and corporate decisions."[10]

Much more can be done by oil and gas companies in the field of resource management and environmental impact mitigation. Across Africa, many governments have also pushed local and foreign players to adjust to less harmful practices. In Nigeria, for instance, the efforts to ban gas flaring and utilizing the resource for power generation are a well-known example of those policy initiatives, albeit with limited success.

Synergies between oil and gas players and African policymakers will be fundamental in optimizing the continent's energy transition into low-carbon economies while ensuring financial sustainability.

Energy—Not Oil and Gas—Companies

I've been talking a lot about private players entering the energy market and harnessing the opportunities for more reliable and sustainable energy security. But who are these private players? Surely, there are many companies that have specialized in new technologies and forms of clean energy that could have a big interest in tapping into these mostly under-explored African markets. For that to happen, governments must build attractive and conducive business environments to facilitate foreign and local investment in these industries. Fundamentally, policies have to be defined to train and prepare the workforce to be able to participate in this transformation, much like what happened in Kenya. Tax and pricing frameworks have to be well-defined to allow for the growth in competition among producers as well as promoting affordable rates for consumers.

All this is true and tested, and a fundamental part of the future of the African energy sector and its economic development as a whole. From an investment perspective, sub-Saharan Africa remains a frontier market when it comes to renewables, with only around 10 percent of its energy coming from green sources, compared to about 25 percent globally.[11] But I propose that the transition from high-carbon to low-carbon economies will involve much more traditional actors than many would expect: the very same oil and gas companies that now operate in Africa's main oil and gas hotspots. After all, these companies are already well-established players with solid market knowledge, understanding of the legal framework and the political system, and the capital and the know-how to push forward with endeavors of this size.

Obviously, a cultural shift will also be necessary within these oil and gas players for a successful transition to take place: there are differences between the business models of producing oil and power. And the corporate world, particularly within the framework of the African experience, never looked kindly on utilities. But the shift is happening, as this excerpt from a Financial Times article from November 2018 illustrates:

"Total has said it is 'allergic' to the word utility even as it builds a retail energy business in France while sidestepping the regulated market. It bought US solar company SunPower, power vendor Lampiris, battery specialist Saft and took an indirect stake in EREN Renewable Energy before acquiring French electricity retailer Direct Energie for €1.4bn this year. This has enabled it to develop a portfolio of gas-fired and renewable energy power plants."

Across Europe, oil and gas majors like Repsol or Shell already have electric vehicle charging stations in their pumps, produce renewable energy equipment, and have large portfolios of natural gas production. Equinor has bet considerably on offshore wind farms. BP, within its "Beyond Petroleum" slogan, has acquired solar company Lightsource, electric vehicle charging network Chargemaster, and battery company StoreDot.

These are decisive moves towards the greener future of the energy sector. The question for us is: How can we bring and promote these sorts of synergies in Africa?

Where Do Africans Stand?

Right now, we stand way in the back—for several reasons. And we will continue to fall behind until we answer some critical questions:

How can we expect to foster development and promote investment in our power generation sectors if our power networks continue to be bundled up in inefficient, opaque, politicized, and under-funded companies?

Why would foreign investors want to participate in a system that so often fails to produce revenue, where national utilities so commonly fail to pay their debts or fulfill their obligations?

If we don't adapt to this changing world, we will be left behind.

Today, Africa has been presented with a unique opportunity. The fact that our power network is underdeveloped leaves us with fewer legacy issues, opening the door to new solutions and technologies. I have already extensively covered the endless challenges that unreliable power supply presents to an economy, particularly in a growingly digitized world. We need to shift gears and adjust.

We need to unbundle and streamline our power utilities, making them leaner, more adaptable to the needs of the market, and more manageable.

We need to create the conditions for independent power producers to come in and contribute to growing access to power through efficient, clean, and affordable solutions.

We need to create the conditions to attract investment and give certainty to the private sector. I don't mean just international companies, but for African entrepreneurs.

We need to empower local players to tap into this growing market and participate in this energy transition, too—and for that, we need qualified personnel, training programs, promotion policies, access to equipment, and fiscal benefits for the development and deployment of new technologies.

We need to promote knowledge exchange amongst African nations and further integration of the different power pools in the continent, so we can draw on each other's' strengths and guarantee energy security. We need to draw on our international partners and IOCs, which are becoming energy companies. They possess the know-how and capital to invest in this sort of infrastructure.

And finally, we need capable and strong leaders who understand the fundamental relevance of the shifts taking place in the world and the need to position African nations to take advantage of these changes.

Africa has an extraordinary potential for growth in this sector, which, in turn, will propel more general economic growth through clean, affordable, and reliable power. The question is, will we take this opportunity or again be left behind in the world's march forward?

20

CONCLUDING THOUGHTS

NIGERIAN BILLIONAIRE BENEDICT PETERS made headlines in early 2019 when the United Kingdom-based Foreign Investment Network (FIN; www.foreigninvestmentnetwork.com) presented him with its prestigious Icon of the Year Award,[1] which recognizes outstanding achievements within the upstream, midstream, and downstream sectors of Africa's petroleum sector. FIN, a financial consultant for developing economies, recognized Peters for his significant contributions to oil and gas development in Africa. Twenty years after he launched his company, Aiteo Group, Peters has transformed it from a small downstream operation to an integrated energy conglomerate with major investments in hydrocarbon exploration and production.

Equally important, the oil and gas wealth that Peters has accumulated is doing immeasurable good in the lives of everyday Africans. Aiteo is making sizeable, ongoing donations to nonprofit organizations like FACE Africa, which is devoted to providing sub-Saharan Africans clean water. His nonprofit organization, the Joseph Agro Foundation, addresses unemployment and water shortages by creating job opportunities for farmers. And don't forget the hundreds of local jobs and business opportunities that his company's operations create.

As far as I'm concerned, this is the kind of activity, the kind of positive change, that Africa's petroleum resources can be and should be unleashing across the continent: job creation, capacity building, and the empowerment of Africans.

Of course, gigantic companies and billions of dollars are not pre-requisites for oil and gas to fulfill their potential for good in Africa. Operations that function on a much smaller scale than Aiteo are making a meaningful difference. Look at what Egoli Gas has been able to accomplish in Johannesburg, South Africa.

- The private natural-gas distribution company is a job creator: As of 2018, it employed 113 people, and as the company expands beyond Johannesburg, it will offer even more open-ings and training opportunities for area residents.

- The company supports the local economy by purchasing from and partnering with South African businesses, from the IT ser-vice provider that allows Egoli to monitor its pipeline network to equipment suppliers.

- Egoli generates tax revenue for government, which can, in turn, be used to expand infrastructure, finance education, and invest in South Africa's long-term economic growth and well-being.

While the natural gas it distributes comes from another African coun-try, Mozambique, Egoli is making a difference in its community. And I'm convinced that its example, like the many examples in this book, demonstrates that strategic oil and gas operations can, without a doubt, contribute to a stable, economically vibrant Africa in ways that no foreign aid could hope to achieve.

It is possible to break the resource curse. And as I write these final thoughts, I have even more evidence to support my point. In fact, during the brief period I've spent writing these chapters, I've seen encouraging developments throughout the continent.

One of the most exciting announcements has been by French multinational oil and gas company, Total, which announced in February 2019 a massive natural gas discovery off the southern coast of South Africa: roughly 1 billion bbl equivalent in gas and condensate resources.[2]

This is the first major deepwater discovery off South Africa's coast. Not only does it represent a tremendous opportunity to meet domestic natural gas needs, but it will also be a massive driver of the kinds of economic activity I've been talking about: domestic job and business opportunities, natural gas monetization, and further diversification.

As I said after the announcement, we can only hope that this discovery will be a catalyst for policymakers to work on creating an enabling business environment for exploration and drilling activities in South Africa. And we have every reason to be optimistic: South Africa is already working on new legislation on oil and gas exploration.

The South African discovery is huge—and it's only one of many important announcements to surface while I've been writing.

In the areas of good governance and transparency, Uganda announced in early 2019 that it would join the Extractive Industries Transparency Initiative (EITI) to minimize petroleum revenue mismanagement. EITI requires the disclosure of information from throughout the extractive industry value chain, from the point of extraction to how revenues make their way through the government and to the public.[3] By joining, Uganda is making a solid commitment to transparent governance.

And Uganda is not an outlier; it's one of 24 African countries in EITI. What's more, within weeks of Uganda's announcement, both Benin and Senegal adopted new petroleum codes of their own.

"Benin's new petroleum code will allow us to regulate access to exploration blocks; improve governance and transparency thanks to a clear institutional framework; and implement measures to promote hydrocarbon upstream activities," said Benin Parliament member André Biaou Okounlola, who initiated his country's new code draft.[4]

Senegal's new codes, updating laws drafted in 1998, emphasize transparency, local content, and block licensing.[5]

In the area of strategic collaboration, Nigerian Minister of State for Petroleum Resources Ibe Kachikwu has announced that Nigeria will mobilize oil and gas producers throughout the continent, on the platform of the African Petroleum Producers Organization, to raise up to $2 billion to finance energy projects across the continent. I applaud this initiative, and the strategic use of petroleum resources, to meet Africa's critical energy needs.

Zambia and Angola, meanwhile, are in the early stages of a $5 billion oil project that will lead to the construction of a shared petroleum pipeline. The two countries signed a memorandum of understanding in November 2018 that allows them to trade in oil and gas, a wisely calculated move that will defray the costs of importing unrefined oil. Currently, Zambia spends more than $1 billion annually to import petroleum products. The Southern African country also wants to stabilize produce prices, which now are subject to the ups and downs of the turbulent international oil market.

"Government's target is to lower the prices of fuel in the country and sourcing the commodity from nearer oil-rich countries like Angola was one of the reasons to put up a pipeline," said Mathew Nkhuwa, Zambia's Energy Minister, in January 2019. "We are committed to ensuring that it comes on stream soon, probably in two years' time."[6]

Another exciting example of strategic cooperation is the Nigeria-Morocco Gas Pipeline, which will supply natural gas to at least 15 countries in West Africa. The project feasibility study was completed in January 2019, and a preliminary engineering study is underway now. "This pipeline will help in the industrialization of these countries," said Maikanti Baru, group managing director of the Nigerian

National Petroleum Corporation. "It will also meet the needs of consumers for heating and other uses. We see gas as a fuel to take Africa to the next level."[7]

Well said, Maikanti. I couldn't agree more.

These are only a few of many promising collaborations announced while this book was coming together. I'm also excited about the technical assistance cooperation agreement that the African Energy Chamber has entered with the Ministry of Petroleum of the Republic of South Sudan. Our chamber will be mobilizing South Sudan's capacity-building efforts, investing in energy access initiatives, and helping the country develop reforms that create an enabling environment for oil investors.

South Sudan is East Africa's only mature oil producer. It's in the best interests of the region to rally around the country's efforts to build a sustainable hydrocarbons sector. It, in turn, will provide a pillar for the development of East Africa's entire energy value chain.

I should mention that I've been extremely impressed with the tremendous efforts being made to revamp and restart oil fields in South Sudan, thanks to the pragmatic approach of the country's former Minister of Petroleum Ezekiel Lol Gatkuoth and current Minister Awow Daniel Chuang. In late 2018 and early 2019, production resumed at the Toma South and Unity oilfields for the first time since the civil war halted activity there five years earlier. And as I write, work to restore the Al-Nar, Al-Toor, Manga, and Tharjiath oilfields is moving forward at full steam.

I respect Minister Gatkuoth's commitment to continued collaboration between the oil industries of Sudan and South Sudan.

"We call for a measured, methodical approach to make sure the industry continues to develop, that our people can rely on employment from the petroleum industry, and that our nations can continue to depend on this resource," he said in April 2019, days after Omar al-Bashir was removed from power in Sudan. "This is the superglue that binds our common destinies and ensures peaceful progress together."[8]

South Sudan also has remained determined to provide investors with an enabling environment to invest and do business. And that strategy is yielding significant fruit. In May 2019, South African state-owned oil company, Strategic Fuel Fund (SFF), signed an exploration and production-sharing agreement with South Sudan for Block B2, the second such agreement to be signed in the nation's post-independence history. It includes productive parts of South Sudan's Muglad Basin.[9] My firm was the lead negotiator.

This is a brilliant deal that will not only boost the oil sector, but also promote peace and stability within the country. The future outlook for exploration in South Sudan and Block B is huge, with prospective resources into the billions of barrels. The potential discoveries can be quickly and cheaply integrated into existing infrastructure. I am also impressed by the deal's commitment to local content, dedication to hiring citizens of South Sudan, and investment in education. Education is likely going to do more to strengthen the overall economy than anything else the government can do. South Sudan's ability to attract, retain, and leverage energy investment is key for inclusive and sustainable economic growth.

There have been other exciting developments as well. In the area of infrastructure, Côte d'Ivoire's refinery, Société Ivoirienne de Raffinage (SIR), has secured €577 million (USD 660 million) in debt financing to enable modernization work on its 76,300-bbl/d operation in the Vridi district of Abidjan.[10] In addition to allowing the refinery to reduce the interest rate on existing debt, re-financing will allow SIR to upgrade its refinery and production processes, expand its business, and, hopefully, create more jobs.

In the area of training opportunities, Japanese firm MODEC Production Services Ghana JV Limited (MPSG) launched a six-month oil and gas training program for Ghanaian nationals in February 2019. Sixteen participants are lined up to train in Floating Production Storage and Offloading operations. After completing the course, the graduates will share what they've learned with other Ghanaians in the oil and gas sector.[11]

The news out of Angola while I've been writing this book has been especially encouraging. In the last year alone, Angolan NOC Sonangol launched its "Regeneration Program" focusing on restructuring the company and streamlining Angola's oil industry. The country also has developed new tax laws, created a regulatory framework designed to encourage investment in marginal oilfields, and announced plans to develop a larger, highly trained petroleum workforce between 2019 and 2023. "Being a capital-intensive sector and technologically highly developed, the added value for the sustainable and economic development of Angola will be all the more relevant if it is obtained with the growing incorporation of a qualified Angolan workforce," said Diamantino Azevedo, Angola's minister for mineral resources and petroleum.

Angola's efforts to create an efficient, sustainable, and transparent oil and gas industry have not gone unnoticed by the global community and have already yielded increased interest among IOCs. When OPEC Secretary General Mohammad Sanusi Barkindo visited the country for the first time, he praised Angola's hard work: "We congratulate the government's heroic efforts to reform the industry. These are the right reforms at the right time."[12]

I am not being overly optimistic. Good things really are happening across the continent, and the petroleum industry is the common denominator.

And, no, I have not shut my eyes to the challenges we face in Africa. But I am saying this: Africa is faced with challenges, NOT insurmountable obstacles. There is so much we can accomplish; I've given you proof.

Let's not stop there. Why not work together—fight together—to harness the transformative power of oil and gas for our continent?

ENDNOTES

Chapter One: It's High Time for African Oil and Gas to Fuel a Better Future for Africans

[1] Frankie Edozien, "In Nigeria, Plans for the World's Largest Refinery," The New York Times, October 9, 2018, https://www.nytimes.com/2018/10/09/business/energy-environment/in-nigeria-plans-for-the-worlds-largest-refinery.html

[2] "Dangote Refinery Will Transform, Diversify Nigeria's Economy – Director," The Eagle Online, October 31, 2018, https://theeagleonline.com.ng/dangote-refinery-will-transform-diversify-nigerias-economy-director/

[3] "The World Bank In Chile," The World Bank, April 10, 2019, https://www.worldbank. org/en/country/chile/overview

[4] Martina Mistikova, "Opportunities for Service Companies in Chile's Copper Sector, BizLatinHub, November 20, 2018, https://www.bizlatinhub.com/opportunities-chile-copper-sector/

[5] Sean Durns, "Four Countries that Beat the Resource Curse," Global Risk Insights, April 22, 2014, https://globalriskinsights.com/2014/04/four-countries-that-beat-the-resource-curse/

[6] "Mining for Development: Leveraging the Chilean Experience for Africa," Meeting report of a round table organized by the African Minerals Development

Centre (AMDC), United Nations Economic Commission for Africa (ECA) and Chilean Embassy in Ethiopia, June 19 and 20, 2017, https://issuu.com /africanmineralsdevelopmentcentre/docs/amdc_-_chile-africa_meeting _report_

[7]"Yes Africa Can: Success Stories from a Dynamic Continent," The World Bank Group, Africa Region, http://siteresources.worldbank.org/AFRICAEXT/Resources /258643-1271798012256/Botswana-success.pdf

[8]"Ranking of Countries with Highest Per Capita Income (1966), Classora, September 8, 2015, http://en.classora.com/reports/s30614/ranking-of-countries -with-highest-per-capita-income?edition=1966

[9]"BIH Profile," Botswana Innovation Hub, 2019, http://www.bih.co.bw/bih -profile/

[10]"Science and Technology in Botswana," The Mt. Kenya Times, September 11, 2017, https://mtkenyatimes.co.ke/science-technology-botswana/

[11]Paula Ximena Meijia and Vincent Castel, "Could Oil Shine like Diamonds? How Botswana Avoided the Resource Curse and its Implications for a New Libya," African Development Bank, October 2012, https://www.afdb.org/fileadmin /uploads/afdb/Documents/Publications/Could%20Oil%20Shine%20like %20Diamonds%20-%20 How%20Botswana%20Avoided%20the%20 Resource%20Curse%20and%20its%20 Implications%20for%20a%20New %20Libya.pdf

[12]"Gas Set to Shine as African Nations Wake up to Potential," The National, September 4, 2018, https://www.thenational.ae/business/energy/gas-set-to-shine -as-african-nations-wake-up-to-potential-1.766717

[13]"BP Statistical Review of World Energy," BP, June 2018, https://www.bp .com/content/dam/bp/business-sites/en/global/corporate/pdfs/energy-economics /statistical-review/bp-stats-review-2018-full-report.pdf

[14]"Western Supermajors in New Scramble to Tap Africa's Under-Explored Oil & Gas Resources," Africa New Energies, September 13, 2018, https://www.ane.na /news/opinion/western-supermajors-in-new-scramble-to-tap-africas-under-explored -oil-gas-resources/

[15]Willis Krumholz, "Petroleum Powerhouse: Why America No Longer Needs the Middle East," The National Interest, April 29, 2019, https://nationalinterest.org /feature/petroleum-powerhouse-why-america-no-longer-needs-middle-east-55012

[16]Cameron Fels, "Trump's Africa Strategy and the Evolving U.S.-Africa Relationship," Woodrow Wilson International Center for Scholars, April 19, 2019, https://africaupclose.wilsoncenter.org/author/cameron-fels/

Chapter Two: It's Up to Africans to Fix Africa

[1]Brian Adeba, "How War, Oil and Politics Fuel Controversy in South Sudan's Unity State," African Arguments, August 5, 2015, http://africanarguments.org /2015/08/05/how-war-oil-and-politics-fuel-controversy-in-south-sudans-unity -state-by-brian-adeba/

[2]"South Sudan Country Profile," BBC News, August 6, 2018, http://www.bbc .co.uk/news/world-africa-14069082

[3]"South Sudan Welcomes First International Law Firm," Global Legal Post, April 19, 2017, http://www.globallegalpost.com/big-stories/south-sudan-welcomes -first-international-law-firm-99184828/

[4]"South Sudan Oil & Power 2018 Evaluation," Africa Oil & Power, November 2018, https://africaoilandpower.com/wp-content/uploads/2018/11 /SSOP_Evaluation.pdf

[5]Corey Flintoff, "Is Aid to Africa Doing More Harm Than Good?" National Public Radio, December 12, 2007, https://www.npr.org/2007/12/12/17095866 /is-aid-to-africa-doing-more-harm-than-good

[6]Dambisa Moyo, Dead Aid: Why Aid Is not Working and How There Is a Better Way for Africa, 2009. https://books.google.com/books/about/Dead _Aid.html?id=-gYxhXHj OckC&printsec=frontcover&source=kp_read_button #v=onepage&q&f=false

[7]Shakira Mustapha and Annalisa Prizzon, Africa's Rising Debt: How to Avoid a New Crisis, October 2018, https://www.odi.org/sites/odi.org.uk/files/resource -documents/12491.pdf

[8]John Gallup, Jeffrey Sachs, and Andrew Mellinger, 1999, "Geography and Economic Development," https://www.researchgate.net/publication/233996238 _Geography_and_ Economic_Development

[9]"Financing the End of Extreme Poverty," September 2018, https://www.odi.org /publications/11187-financing-end-extreme-poverty

[10]Indermit Gill and Kenan Karakülah, Sounding the Alarm on Africa's Debt, April 6, 2018, https://www.brookings.edu/blog/future-development/2018/04/06 /sounding-the-alarm-on-africas-debt/

[11]"In Five Charts: Understanding the Africa Country Policy and Institutional Assessment (CPIA) Report for 2017," The World Bank, September 12, 2018, https://www.worldbank.org/en/region/afr/publication/in-five-charts-under standing-the-africa-country-policy-and-institutional-assessment-cpia-report -for-2017

[12]Charlotte Florance, "22 Years After the Rwandan Genocide, Huffington Post, April 7, 2016, https://www.huffingtonpost.com/to-the-market/22-years-after-the -rwanda_b_9631032.html

[13]Thabo Mphahlele, "ICF Report Hails Major Improvements in Africa's Business Environment, BizNis Africa, September 5, 2016, https://www.biznisafrica.com /icf-report-hails-major-improvements-in-africas-business-environment/

[14]Jim Morrison, "The "Great Green Wall" Didn't Stop Desertification, but it Evolved Into Something That Might," Smithsonian, August 23, 2016, https://www.smithsonianmag. com/science-nature/great-green-wall-stop -desertification-not-so-much-180960171/

Chapter Three: A Place at the Table: Africa and OPEC

[1]BP Statistical Review of World Energy 2019, https://www.bp.com/en/global /corporate/energy-economics/statistical-review-of-world-energy/downloads.html

[2]"OPEC Share of World Crude Oil Reserves, 2017," Organization of the Petroleum Exporting Countries, 2019, https://www.opec.org/opec_web/en/data_ graphs/330.htm

[3] BP Statistical Review of World Energy 2019, https://www.bp.com/en/global/corporate/energy-economics/statistical-review-of-world-energy/downloads.html

[4] "Equatorial Guinea Exports," Trading Economics, n.d., https://tradingeconomics.com/equatorial-guinea/exports

[5] "Keynote Address by OPEC Secretary General at the APPO CAPE VII Congress and Exhibition," Organization of the Petroleum Exporting Countries, April 3, 2019, https://www.opec.org/opec_web/en/5475.htm

[6] Paul Burkhardt, "Equatorial Guinea Expecting $2.4 billion Oil Investment," Bloomberg, November 5, 2018, https://www.bloomberg.com/news/articles/2018-11-05/equatorial-guinea-is-said-to-expect-2-4-billion-oil-investment

[7] "Equatorial Guinea Set for Upsurge in Offshore Drilling," Offshore, December 11, 2018, https://www.offshore-mag.com/drilling-completion/article/16803408/equatorial-guinea-set-for-upsurge-in-offshore-drilling

[8] Matt Piotrowski, "OPEC: New And Improved?" The Fuse, January 24, 2018, http://energyfuse.org/opec-new-improved/

[9] Vladimir Soldatkin, "Russian Oil Output Reaches Record High in 2018," Reuters, January 2, 2019, https://www.reuters.com/article/us-russia-oil-output/russian-oil-output-reaches-record-high-in-2018-idUSKCN1OW0NJ

[10] NJ Ayuk, "An African Perspective: No Good Will Come from NOPEC," Africa Oil & Power, July 22, 2018, https://africaoilandpower.com/2018/07/22/an-african-perspective-no-good-will-come-from-nopec/

[11] "OFID Governing Board Approves New Loans and Grants to Boost Socio-Economic Development," The OPEC Fund for International Development, June 17, 2013, http://www.ofid.org/FOCUS-AREAS

[12] Dennis Lukhoba, "How OPEC Can Give the Republic of the Republic of Congo More Power in the International Fuel Market," Footprint to Africa, May 2, 2018, http://footprint2africa.com/opinions/opec-can-give-republic-republic-congo-power-international-fuel-market/

[13]Tim Daiss, "Can Any Country Dethrone Qatar As Top LNG Exporter?" Oilprice . com, February 23, 2019, https://oilprice.com/Energy/Natural-Gas/Can-Any -Country- Dethrone-Qatar-As-Top-LNG-Exporter.html

[14]Dania Saadi, "Quicktake: Why Is Qatar Leaving OPEC?" The National, December 4, 2018, https://www.thenational.ae/business/energy/quicktake -why-is-qatar-leaving-opec-1.798742

Chapter Four: Empowering Women for a Stronger, Healthier Oil and Gas Industry

[1]Caroline McMillan Portillo, "Check out the most inspiring quotes from Emma Watson's UN speech," Bizwomen, September 24, 2014, https://www.bizjournals .com/bizwomen/news/out-of-the-office/2014/09/check-out-the-most-inspiring -quotes-from-emma.html?page=all

[2]Carly McCann, Donald Tomaskovic-Devey, and M.V. Lee Badgett, "Employer's Responses to Sexual Harassment," University of Massachusetts Amherst: Center For Employment Equity, December 2018, https://www.umass .edu/employmentequity/employers-responses-sexual-harassment

[3]Felix Fallon, "Oil & Gas Gender Disparity: Positions and Prospects for Women in the Industry," Egypt Oil & Gas, May 10, 2018, https://egyptoil-gas.com/features /oil-gas-gender-disparity-positions-and-prospects-for-women-in-the-industry/

[4]"Report Indicates Oil and Gas Sector Still A Mans World," PCL Group, January 2016, http://www.portlethen.com/index.php/archives/1068/

[5]Amanda Erickson, "Women Poorer and Hungrier than Men Across the World, U.N. Report Says, The Washington Post, February 14, 2018, https:// www.washingtonpost.com/news/worldviews/wp/2018/02/14/women-poorer -and-hungrier-than-men-across-the-world-u-n-report-says/?noredirect=on&utm _term=. f5f8261a7476

[6]"Wangari Maathai Quotes," BrainyQuote, n.d., https://www.brainyquote.com /authors/wangari_maathai

[7]"Women's Economic Empowerment in Oil and Gas Industries in Africa," African Natural Resources Center of African Development Bank, 2017, https://

www.afdb.org/fileadmin/uploads/afdb/Documents/Publications/anrc/AfDB _ WomenEconomicsEmpowerment_V15.pdf

[8]Magali Barraja and Dominic Kotas, "Making Supply Chains Work for Women: Why and How Companies Should Drive Gender Equality in Global Supply Chains," BSR, November 19, 2018, https://www.bsr.org/en/our-insights/blog-view /gender-equality-global-supply-chains-companies

[9]Andrew Topf, "Top 6 Most Powerful Women In Oil And Gas," OilPrice.com, July 29, 2015, https://oilprice.com/Energy/Energy-General/Top-6-Most-Powerful -Women-In- Oil-And-Gas.html

[10]Katharina Rick, Iván Martén, and Ulrike Von Lonski, "Untapped Reserves: Promoting Gender Balance in Oil and Gas," World Petroleum Council and The Boston Consulting Group, July 12, 2017, https://www.bcg.com/en-us/publications /2017/energy-environment-people-organization-untapped-reserves.aspx

[11]Kwamboka Oyaro, "Corporate Boardrooms: Where Are the Women?" AfricaRenewal, December 2017/March 2018, https://www.un.org/africa renewal/magazine/december- 2017-march-2018/corporate-boardrooms-where- are-women

[12]"The Oil Industry's Best Kept Secret: Advice from Women in Oil and Gas," Offshore Technology, February 20, 2019, https://www.offshore-techno logy.com/features/the-oil-industrys-best-kept-secret-advice-from-women-in-oil -and-gas/

[13]Lebo Matshego, "Innovative Ways to Empower African Women," Africa .com, October 12, 2017, https://www.africa.com/innovative-ways-to-empower -african-women/

[14]"Asanko Gold Launches Women in Mining Empowerment Initiative," Africa Business Communities, October 24, 2018, https://africabusinesscommunities.com /news/ghana-asanko-gold-launches-women-in-mining-empowerment-initiative/

[15]Gerald Chirinda, "What Can Be Done to Economically Empower Women in Africa?" World Economic Forum, May 8, 2018, https://www.weforum.org /agenda/2018/05/women-africa-economic-empowerment/

[16]"How Africa Is Preparing for the Future with STEM," Higher Life Foundation, March 20, 2018, Educationhttps://www.higherlifefoundation.com/how-africa -is-preparing-for-the-future-with-stem-education/

[17]Unoma Okorafor, "STEM Education for Young Girls in Africa," indi-egogo campaign, https://www.indiegogo.com/projects/stem-education-for-young -girls-in-africa#/

[18]"Interview: Marcia Ashong, Founder, TheBoardroom," Africa Business Communities, August 3, 2018, Africahttps://africabusinesscommunities.com/features /interview-marcia-ashong-founder-the-boardroom-africa/

[19]James Kahongeh, "Breaking Barriers in Oil and Gas Sector," Daily Nation, June 8, 270 2018, https://www.nation.co.ke/lifestyle/mynetwork/Breaking-barriers -in-oil-and-gas-sector/3141096-4601382-13rhc91z/index.html

[20]"African Best Oil & Gas Analyst of the Year (Rolake Akinkugbe)," FBN Quest, November 15, 2018, https://fbnquest.com/awards/african-best-oil-gas-analyst -of-the-year-rolake-akinkugbe/

[21]LinkedIn Profile: Rolake Akinkugbe-Filani, https://www.linkedin.com/in /rolakeakinkugbe/?originalSubdomain=uk

[22]"Executive Team," Tsavo Oilfield Services, https://www.tsavooilfieldservices .com/about-us/team-2/

[23]Toby Shapshak, "How a Doctor Helped Turn a Lagos Swamp into a Sustainable Trade Zone," Forbes, December 12, 2018, https://www .forbes.com/sites/tobyshapshak/2018/12/12/how-a-doctor-helped-turn -a-lagos-swamp-into-a-sustainable-trade-zone/#374e2c393d3ᵉ

[24]Profile: Althea Eastman Sherman, Oil & Gas Council, https://oilandgascouncil .com/event-speakers/althea-eastman-sherman/

[25]"Ceremony of the Oil & Gas Awards 2014 in Malabo," Official Web Page of the Government of the Republic of Equatorial Guinea, September 22, 2014, https:// www.guineaecuatorialpress.com/noticia.php?id=5687&lang=en

Chapter Five: Abundant, Accessible, Affordable: The "Golden Age" of Natural Gas Shines in Africa

[1]"World Energy Outlook 2011," International Energy Agency, June 6, 2011, https://webstore.iea.org/weo-2011-special-report-are-we-entering-a-golden-age

[2]"Filling the Power Supply Gap in Africa: Is Natural Gas the Answer?" Ishmael Ackah Institute of Oil and Gas Studies, University of Cape Coast, 2012, https://papers.ssrn. com/sol3/papers.cfm?abstract_id=2870577

[3]"How Hard Has The Oil Crash Hit Africa?" Global Risk Insights, November 23, 2016, https://oilprice.com/Energy/Energy-General/How-Hard-Has-The-Oil-Crash-Hit- Africa.html

[4]Jonathan Demierre, Morgan Bazilian, Jonathan Carbajal, Shaky Sherpa, and Vijay Modi, "Potential for Regional Use of East Africa's Natural Gas," Sustainable Development Solutions Network, May 2014, https://energypolicy.columbia.edu/sites /default/files/Potential-for-Regional-Use-of-East-Africas-Natural-Gas-SEL-SDSN.pdf

[5]"World Energy Outlook 2018," IEA, http://www.worldenergyoutlook.org /resources/energydevelopment/africafocus/

[6]Jude Clemente, "Oil And Natural Gas Companies Could Be Heroes In Africa," Forbes, September 9, 2016, http://www.forbes.com/sites/judeclemente/2016/09/29 /oil-and-natural-gas-companies-could-be-heroes-in-africa/#5911074f5ca0

[7]"World Energy Outlook 2006," IEA, https://www.iea.org/publications /freepublications/publication/cooking.pdf

[8]International Energy Agency: Sustainable Development Goal 7 https://www.iea .org/sdg/electricity/

[9]Jonathan Demierre, Morgan Bazilian, Jonathan Carbajal, Shaky Sherpa, and Vijay Modi, "Potential for Regional Use of East Africa's Natural Gas," Sustainable Development Solutions Network, May 2014, https://energypolicy.columbia.edu/sites /default/files/Potential-for-Regional-Use-of-East-Africas-Natural-Gas-SEL-SDSN.pdf

[10]"Natural Gas-Fired Electricity Generation Expected to Reach Record Level in 2016," U.S. Energy Information Administration, July 14, 2016, https://www.eia.gov /todayinenergy/detail.php?id=27072

[11]"Gas-Fired: The Five Biggest Natural Gas Power Plants in the World," Power Technology, April 14, 2014, http://www.power-technology.com/features /featuregas-fired-the-five-biggest-natural-gas-power-plants-in-the-world-4214992/

[12]David Santley, Robert Schlotterer, and Anton Eberhard, "Harnessing African Natural Gas A New Opportunity for Africa's Energy Agenda?" The World Bank, 2014, https://openknowledge.worldbank.org/bitstream/handle /10986/20685/896220WP0P1318040Box0385289B00OUO0900ACS.pdf ?sequence=1&isAllowed=y

[13]"Gas-to-Power: Upstream Success Meets Power Sector Growth," Africa Oil & Power, March 11, 2016, http://africaoilandpower.com/2016/11/03/gas-to-power/

[14]Simone Liedtke, "Diversified Fuel Source Required to Fuel Local Facilities," Engineering News, February 3, 2017, http://www.engineeringnews.co.za/article /diversified-fuel-source-including-natural-gas-required-to-fuel-local-facilities -2017-02-03/rep_id:4136

[15]NJ Ayuk, "Using African Gas for Africa First," Vanguard, March 18, 2018, https://www.vanguardngr.com/2018/03/using-african-gas-for-africa-first/

[16]NJ Ayuk, "Using African Gas for Africa First," Vanguard, March 18, 2018, https://www.vanguardngr.com/2018/03/using-african-gas-for-africa-first

[17]Sylivester Domasa, "Tanzania: Natural Gas Find Saves 15 Trillion," Tanzania Daily News, October 10, 2016, https://allafrica.com/stories/201610110332 .html

[18]Babalwa Bungane, "Tanzania Becoming an Energy Exporter," ESI Africa, April 11, 2016, https://www.esi-africa.com/news/tanzania-becoming-an-energy-exporter

[19]"Mozambique: SacOil to construct natural gas pipeline," ESI Africa, March 2, 2016, https://www.esi-africa.com/industry-sectors/generation/mozambique -sacoil-to-construct-natural-gas-pipeline

[20]Anabel Gonzalez, "Deepening African Integration: Intra-Africa Trade for Development and Poverty Reduction," statement to the World Bank, December 14, 2015, http://www.worldbank.org/en/news/speech/2015/12/14/deepening-african -integration-intra-africa-trade-for-development-and-poverty-reduction

[21]"Liquefied Natural Gas (LNG)," Shell, n.d., http://www.shell.com/energy -and-innovation/natural-gas/liquefied-natural-gas-lng.html

[22]KPMG International, "Unlocking the supply chain for LNG project success," 2015, 272 https://assets.kpmg/content/dam/kpmg/pdf/2015/03/unlocking-supply -chain-LNG-project-success.pdf

[23]Derek Hudson, David Bishopp, Colm Kearney, and Alistair Scott, "East Africa: Opportunities and Challenges for LNG in a New Frontier Region," BG Group PLC, December 2018, https://www.gti.energy/wp-content/uploads/2018/12/1-4-Derek _ Hudson-LNG17-Paper.pdf

[24]African Review, Regional Gas-to-Power Hubs 'a Win-Win for Africa', January 5, 2017 http://www.africanreview.com/energy-a-power/power-generation /regional-gas-to-power-hubs-a-win-win-for-africa

[25]Jude Clemente, "Oil And Natural Gas Companies Could Be Heroes In Africa," Forbes, September 9, 2016, http://www.forbes.com/sites/judeclemente/2016/09/29 /oil-and-natural-gas-companies-could-be-heroes-in-africa/#5911074f5ca0

[26]World Energy Outlook 2018," IEA, http://www.worldenergyoutlook.org /resources/energydevelopment/africafocus/

[27]Babatunde Akinsola, "Trans-Saharan Pipeline Project Begins Soon," Naija 247 News, February 12, 2017, https://naija247news.com/2017/02/12/trans -saharan-pipeline-project-begins-soon/

[28]Rosalie Starling, "WAPCo Considers Pipeline Expansion," Energy Global World Pipelines, May 12, 2014, https://www.energyglobal.com/pipelines /business-news/12052014/wapco_considers_pipeline_expansion_324/

[29]Emmanuel Okogba, "African Energy Chamber (AEC): Africa's Energy Industry Finally Has an Advocate," Vanguard, June 5, 2018, https://www.vanguardngr .com/2018/06/african-energy-chamber-aec-africas-energy-industry-finally -advocate/

Chapter Six: Monetizing Natural Resources: Successes, Lessons, and Risks

[1]Anslem Ajugwo, "Negative Effects of Gas Flaring: The Nigerian Experience," Journal of Environment Pollution and Human Health, July 2013, http://pubs.sciepub.com/jephh/1/1/2/

[2]"Eyes on Nigeria: Gas Flaring," American Association for the Advancement of Science, n.d., https://www.aaas.org/resources/eyes-nigeria-technical-report/gas-flaring

[3]Kelvin Ebiri and Kingsley Jeremiah, "Why Nigeria Cannot End Gas Flaring in 2020: Experts," The Guardian, May 6, 2018, https://guardian.ng/news/why-nigeria-cannot-end-gas-flaring-in-2020-experts/

[4]"Equatorial Guinea Exports," Trading Economics, n.d., https://tradingeconomics.com/equatorial-guinea/exports

[5]Emma Woodward, "Equatorial Guinea Thinks Big on LNG," DrillingInfo, May 18, 2018, https://info.drillinginfo.com/equatorial-guinea-thinks-big-on-lng/

[6]Anita Anyango, "Equatorial Guinea to Construct a Gas Mega-Hub," Construction Review Online, May 28, 2018, https://constructionreviewonline.com/2018/05/equatorial-guinea-to-construct-a-gas-mega-hub/

[7]"Togo and Equatorial Guinea Sign Liquefied Natural Gas Deal, Promote Regional Gas Trade," Ministry of Mines, Industry & Energy and Government of Equatorial Guinea, 273 April 9, 2018, https://globenewswire.com/news-release/2018/04/09/1466764/0/en/Togo-and-Equatorial-Guinea-Sign-Liquefied-Natural-Gas-Deal-Promote-Regional-Gas-Trade.html

[8]"Comparison Size: Qatar," Almost History, 2011, http://www.vaguelyinteresting.co.uk/tag/comparison-size-qatar/

[9]Hassan E. Alfadala and Mahmoud M. El-Halwagi, "Qatar's Chemical Industry: Monetizing Natural Gas," CEP Magazine, February 2017, https://www.aiche.org/resources/publications/cep/2017/february/qatars-chemical-industry-monetizing-natural-gas

[10]Abdelghani Henni, "Geopolitical Issues Lead Qatar to Change Gas Strategy," Hart Energy, September 28, 2018, https://www.epmag.com/geopolitical-issues-lead-qatar-change-gas-strategy-1717376#p=2

[11]David Small, "Trinidad And Tobago: Natural Gas Monetization as a Driver of Economic and Social Prosperity," Ministry of Energy and Energy Industries, 2006, http://members.igu.org/html/wgc2006/pdf/paper/add10639.pdf

[12]Jacob Campbell, "The Political Economy of Natural Gas in Trinidad and Tobago," n.d., http://ufdcimages.uflib.ufl.edu/CA/00/40/03/29/00001/PDF.pdf

[13]Mfonobong Nsehe, "Meet NJ Ayuk, the 38-Year-Old Attorney Who Runs One of Africa's Most Successful Law Conglomerates," Forbes, November 21, 2018, https://www.forbes.com/sites/mfonobongnsehe/2018/11/21/meet-the-38-year -old-attorney-who-runs-one-of-africas-most-successful-law-conglomerates /#37c5cae8466d

[14]"The Monetization of Natural Gas Reserves in Trinidad and Tobago," II LAC Oil and Gas Seminar, July 25, 2012, http://www.olade.org/sites/default/files/seminarios /2_ petroleo_gas/ponencias/14hs.%20Timmy%20Baksh.pdf

[15]Paul Burkhardt, "Africa Enjoys Oil Boom as Drilling Spreads Across Continent," Bloomberg, November 5, 2018, https://www.bloomberg.com/news /articles/2018-11-06/africa-enjoys-oil-boom-as-drilling-spreads-across-the-continent

[16]"Africa's Oil & Gas Scene After the Boom: What Lies Ahead," The Oxford Institute for Energy Studies, January 2019, https://www.oxfordenergy.org/wpcms /wp-content/uploads/2019/01/OEF-117.pdf

[17]"Three Questions with Nyonga Fofang," Africa Oil & Power, October 5, 2016, https://africaoilandpower.com/2016/10/05/three-questions-with-nyonga -fofang/

[18]"Three Questions With Nyonga Fofang," Africa Oil & Power, 2017, https:// africaoilandpower.com/2016/10/05/three-questions-with-nyonga-fofang

[19]"Market Report: Growth in Investment Opportunities Within Africa," Africa Oil & Power, March 6, 2019, https://africaoilandpower.com/2019/03/06 /market-report-growth-in-investment-opportunities-within-africa/

[20]"Baru: Africa Yet to Tap over 41bn Barrels of Crude, 319trn scf of Gas," This Day Live, March 17, 2019, https://www.thisdaylive.com/index.php/2019/03/17/baru-africa-yet-to-tap-over-41bn-barrels-of-crude-319trn-scf-of-gas/

[21]"Angola Crude Oil Production," Trading Economics, n.d., https://trading economics.com/angola/crude-oil-production

[22]"Angola Oil and Gas," export.gov, November 1, 2018, https://www.export.gov/article?id=Angola-Oil-and-Gas

[23]Gonçalo Falcão and Norman Jacob Nadorff, "Angola 2019-2025 New Concession Award Strategy," Mayer Brown, February 27, 2019, https://www.mayerbrown.com/en/perspectives-events/publications/2019/02/angola

[24]Henrique Almeida, "Angola Plots Recovery With Oil-Block Auction, New Refineries," Bloomberg, April 23, 2019, https://www.bloomberg.com/news/articles/2019-04-23/angola-plots-recovery-with-oil-block-auction-new-refineries

[25]Shem Oirere, "Congo Unveils More Enticing Offshore Exploration Opportunities," Offshore Engineering, November 22, 2018, https://www.oedigital.com/news/444302-congo-unveils-more-enticing-offshore-exploration-opportunities

[26]"Equatorial Guinea Primed for Huge Growth as Host of 2019 'Year of Energy'," Ministry of Mines and Hydrocarbons, n.d., https://yearofenergy2019.com/2018/12/11/equatorial-guinea-primed-for-huge-growth-as-host-of-2019-year-of-energy/

[27]"Equatorial Guinea Orders Oil Firms to Cancel Deals with CHC Helicopters," Offshore Energy Today, July 18, 2018, https://www.offshoreenergytoday.com/equatorial-guinea-orders-oil-firms-to-cancel-deals-with-chc-helicopters/

[28]"Gabon Opens 12th Offshore Round, Ends Corporate Tax," The Oil & Gas Year, November 7, 2018, https://www.theoilandgasyear.com/news/gabon-announces-end-of-corporate-tax/

[29]Mark Venables, "Focus Returns to Gabon as Government Relaxes Hydrocarbon Code," Hart Energy, April 3, 2018, https://www.hartenergy.com/exclusives/focus-returns-gabon-government-relaxes-hydrocarbon-code-30915

[30] "Baru: Africa Yet to Tap over 41bn Barrels of Crude, 319trn scf of Gas," This Day Live, March 17, 2019, https://www.thisdaylive.com/index.php/2019/03/17/baru-africa-yet-to-tap-over-41bn-barrels-of-crude-319trn-scf-of-gas/

[31] Macharia Kamau, "Flurry of Exits by Exploration Firms Threatens to Burst Kenya's Oil Bubble," Standard Digital, April 7, 2019, https://www.standardmedia.co.ke/business/article/2001319842/oil-and-gas-companies-exit-kenya-casting-doubt-on-commercial-viability

[32] "Announcement of 2018 Licensing Round, Republic of Cameroon," January 10, 2018, https://www.cgg.com/data/1/rec_docs/3698_Announcement_of_2018_Licensing_ Round_-_Republic_of_Cameroon_-_January_2018.pdf

[33] Sylvain Andzongo, "Cameroon: Franco-British Perenco Plans $12.5-$36.5m in Investment in Bomana Oil Block," Business in Cameroon, February 22, 2019, https://www.businessincameroon.com/hydrocarbons/2202-8874-cameroon-franco-british-perenco-plans-12-5-36-5mln-investment-in-bomana-oil-block

[34] "Victoria Oil and Gas Lifts 2P Reserves Estimate at Cameroon Field," Oil Review, June 4, 2018, http://www.oilreviewafrica.com/exploration/exploration/victoria-oil-and-gas-lifts-2p-reserves-estimate-at-cameroon-field

[35] Evelina Grecenko, "Bowleven Encouraged After Recent Results from Cameroon Assets," Morningstar, October 18, 2018, http://www.morningstar.co.uk/uk/news/AN_1539863495618474800/bowleven-encouraged-after-recent-results-from-cameroon-assets.aspx

[36] Jamie Ashcroft, "Tower Resources to Raise £1.7mln to Support Upcoming Cameroon Drill Programme," Proactive Investors, January 24, 2019, https://www.proactiveinvestors.co.uk/companies/news/213235/tower-resources-to-raise-17mln-to-support-upcoming-cameroon-drill-programme-213235.html

[37] Morne van der Merwe, "Fewer Mergers and Acquisitions Are Taking Place in Africa, Here's Why," CNBC Africa, July 20, 2018, https://www.cnbcafrica.com/news/east-africa/2018/07/20/fewer-mergers-and-acquisitions-are-taking-place-in-africa-heres-why/

Chapter Seven: Job Creation: Making Our Own Multiplier Effect

[1] Gerhard Toews and Pierre-Louis Vezina, "Resource discoveries and FDI bonanzas: An illustration from Mozambique," International Growth Centre, October 26 2017, https://pdfs.semanticscholar.org/539c/e283bb081d2ee05cf26d 5fb10800194f69c5.pdf

[2] Yun Sun, "China's Aid to Africa: Monster or Messiah?" Brookings, February 7, 2014, https://www.brookings.edu/opinions/chinas-aid-to-africa-monster-or -messiah/

[3] "Oil Industry in Singapore," Wikipedia, June 16, 2019, https://en.wikipedia .org/wiki/Oil_industry_in_Singapore

[4] "Oil & Gas Equipment and Services," EDB Singapore, n.d., https://www.edb.gov.sg /en/our-industries/oil-and-gas-equipment-and-services.html

[5] Girija Pande and Venkatraman Sheshashayee, "Why Singapore Needs to Save its Offshore O&G Services Industry," The Business Times, June 19, 2019, https://www.businesstimes.com.sg/opinion/why-singapore-needs-to-save -its-offshore-og-services-industry

Chapter Eight: A "Recipe" for Economic Diversification

[1] Cecile Fruman, "Economic Diversification: A Priority for Action, Now More Than Ever," World Bank Blogs, March 1, 2017, http://blogs.worldbank.org/psd /economic-diversification-priority-action-now-more-ever

[2] Aaron Coseby, "Climate Policies, Economic Diversification and Trade," UNCTAD Ad Hoc Expert Group Meeting, October 3, 2017, https://unctad .org/meetings/en/SessionalDocuments/ditc-ted-03102017-Trade-Measures -Coseby.pdf

[3] Scott Wolla, "What Are the 'Ingredients' for Economic Growth?" Federal Reserve Bank of St. Louis, September 2013, https://research.stlouisfed.org /publications/page1- econ/2013/09/01/what-are-the-ingredients-for-economic- growth/

[4]Bontle Moeng, "Deloitte Africa: The Need for Economic Diversification in the Continent Is High," BizNis Africa, April 25, 2017, https://www.biznisafrica .com/deloitte-africa-the-need-for-economic-diversification-in-the-continent-is -high/

[5]"Botswana Embarks on Economic Diversification Beyond Diamonds," Africanews, 276 November 14, 2016, http://www.africanews.com/2016/11/14 /botswana-embarks-on-economic-diversification-beyond-diamonds//

[6]"Economy of Botswana," Wikipedia, June 9, 2019, https://en.wikipedia.org/wiki /Economy_of_Botswana

[7]"Botswana Economy Profile 2018," IndexMundi, January 20, 2018, https://www . indexmundi.com/botswana/economy_profile.html

[8]"Petroleum Industry in Nigeria," Wikipedia, May 25, 2019, https://en.wikipedia .org/wiki/Petroleum_industry_in_Nigeria

[9]Frankie Edozien, "In Nigeria, Plans for the World's Largest Refinery," The New York Times, October 9, 2018, https://www.nytimes.com/2018/10/09/business/energy -environment/in-nigeria-plans-for-the-worlds-largest-refinery.html?

[10]NJ Ayuk, "Natural Gas: Nigeria's Lost Treasure," How We Made it in Africa, February 9, 2018, https://www.howwemadeitinafrica.com/nj-ayuk -natural-gas-nigerias-lost-treasure/60826/

[11]Onome Amawhe, "Nigeria Is a Natural Gas Nation," Vanguard, January 30, 2018, https://www.vanguardngr.com/2018/01/nigeria-natural-gas-nation/

[12]Nigerian Gas Flare Commercialization Programme, http://www.ngfcp.gov.ng/

[13]"Republic of Congo: Economy," Global Edge, n.d., https://globaledge.msu.edu /countries/republic-of-congo/economy

[14]"Republic of the Congo: GDP Share of Agriculture," TheGlobalEconomy. com, n.d., https://www.theglobaleconomy.com/Republic-of-the-Congo/Share_of _agriculture/

[15]"Republic of Congo: Agricultural Sector," export.gov, July 18, 2017, https:// www.export.gov/article?id=Republic-of-Congo-Agricultural-Sector

[16]Elie Smith, "Haldor Topsoe to Help Build $2.5 billion Congo Fertilizer Plant, Bloomberg, September 18, 2018, https://www.bloomberg.com/news /articles/2018-09-18/haldor-topsoe-to-help-build-2-5-billion-congo-fertilizer -plant

[17]Ernest Scheyder, "In North Dakota's Oil Patch, a Humbling Comedown," Reuters, May 18, 2016, https://www.reuters.com/investigates/special-report /usa-northdakota-bust/

[18]"Equatorial Guinea," U.S. Energy Information Administration, December 2017, https://www.eia.gov/beta/international/analysis.php?iso=GNQ

[19]Emma Woodward, "Equatorial Guinea Thinks Big on LNG," DrillingInfo, May 18, 2018, https://info.drillinginfo.com/equatorial-guinea-thinks-big -on-lng/

[20]"Equatorial Guinea to Construct a Gas Megahub," Africa Oil & Power, May 10, 2018, https://africaoilandpower.com/2018/05/10/equatorial-guinea-to -construct-a-gas-megahub/

[21]"Equatorial Guinea Makes Plans for Gas Mega-Hub," Gambeta News, May 15, 2018, http://www.gambetanews.com/equatorial-guinea-plans-for-gas-mega-hub/

[22]"Equatorial Guinea Economy Profile 2018," IndexMundi, January 20, 2018, https://www.indexmundi.com/equatorial_guinea/economy_profile.html

[23]Jeff Desjardins, "How Copper Riches Helped Shape Chile's Economic Story," Visual Capitalist, June 21, 2017, https://www.visualcapitalist.com/copper-shape -chile-economic-story/

[24]Cecile Fruman, "Economic Diversification: A Priority for Action, Now More Than Ever," World Bank Blogs, March 1, 2017, http://blogs.worldbank.org/psd /economic-diversification-priority-action-now-more-ever

[25]"Chile: 20th Century," Wikipedia, June 26, 2019, https://en.wikipedia.org/wiki /Chile#20th_century

Chapter Nine: Calling All Leaders!
More on Good Governance

[1]"Doing Business 2005: Removing Obstacles to Growth," World Bank, September 8, 2004, http://www.doingbusiness.org/en/reports/global-reports/doing-business-2005

[2]"It's Time for Africa: Ernst & Young's 2011 Africa Attractiveness Survey," Ernst & Young, 2011, http://www.ey.com/za/en/issues/business-environment/2011-africa-attractiveness-survey---fdi-in-africa---africas-true-market-value

[3]"Doing Business 2019: Training for Reform," World Bank, October 31, 2018, http://www.doingbusiness.org/content/dam/doingBusiness/media/Annual-Reports/English/DB2019-report_web-version.pdf

[4]Christopher Adam, "Africa Needs Smart Macroeconomic Policies to Navigate Headwinds," The Conversation, April 25, 2016, https://theconversation.com/africa-needs-smart-macroeconomic-policies-to-navigate-headwinds-58104

[5]Vitor Gaspar and Luc Eyraud, "Five Keys to a Smart Fiscal Policy," International Monetary Fund, April 19, 2017, currently e source, but the link is "ere are the cources:for the government to https://blogs.imf.org/2017/04/19/five-keys-to-a-smart-fiscal-policy/

[6]"Natural Resources for Sustainable Development: The Fundamentals of Oil, Gas, and Mining Governance" (online training module), National Resource Governance Institute, February-April 2016, https://resourcegovernance.org/events/natural-resources-sustainable-development-fundamentals-oil-gas-and-mining-governance

[7]Thomas Scurfield and Silas Olan'g, "Magufuli Seeks the Right Balance for Tanzania's Mining Fiscal Regime," National Resource Governance Institute, January 31, 2019, https://resourcegovernance.org/blog/magufuli-seeks-right-balance-tanzania-mining-fiscal

[8]Efam Dovi, "Ghana's 'New Path' for Handling Oil Revenue," Africa Renewal, January 2013, https://www.un.org/africarenewal/magazine/january-2013/ghana%E2%80%99s-%E2%80%98new-path%E2%80%99-handling-oil-revenue

[9]Harriet Sergeant, "Does Aid Do More Harm Than Good?" The Spectator, February 17, 2018, https://www.spectator.co.uk/2018/02/does-aid-do-more-harm-than-good/

[10]"Addressing Corporate Fraud and Corruption in Africa," Financier Worldwide, August 2012, https://www.financierworldwide.com/addressing-corporate-fraud-and-corruption-in-africa#.W_2ZTpNKhTY

[11]Joe Amoako-Tuffour, "Public Participation in the Making of Ghana's Petroleum Revenue Management Law," October 2011, https://resourcegovernance.org/sites/default/files/documents/ghana-public-participation.pdf

[12]Babafemi Oyewole, Best Practice for Local Content Development Strategy: The Nigerian Experience, https://unctad.org/meetings/en/Presentation/Atelier%20Lancement%20Tchad%20-%20Babafemi%20Oyewole%20-%2026%20nov%202015.pdf

Chapter Ten: Industrialization: Linking Promise to Prosperity

[1]John Anyanwu, "Manufacturing Value Added Development in North Africa: Analysis of Key Drivers," African Development Bank, October 2017, https://www.researchgate. net/publication/320558479_Manufacturing_Value_Added_Development_in_North_ Africa_Analysis_of_Key_Drivers

[2]"Atlas of Sustainable Development Goals 2017: Goal 9," The World Bank, n.d., http://datatopics.worldbank.org/sdgatlas/archive/2017/SDG-09-industry-innovation-and-infrastructure.html

[3]Franck Kuwonu, "Using Trade to Boost Africa's Industrialization," Africa Renewal, August 2015, https://www.un.org/africarenewal/magazine/august-2015/using-trade-boost-africa%E2%80%99s-industrialization

[4]Lisa Friedman, "Africa Needs Fossil Fuels to End Energy Apartheid," Scientific American, August 5, 2014, https://www.scientificamerican.com/article/africa-needs-fossil-fuels-to-end-energy-apartheid/

[5]"Africa Mining Vision," African Union, February 2009, http://www.africaminingvision. org/amv_resources/AMV/Africa_Mining_Vision_English.pdf

[6]Kayode Adeoye, "Upgrading Kainji Dam and Improving Electricity," The Guardian, March 29, 2017, https://guardian.ng/energy/upgrading-kainji-dam-and-improving-electricity/

[7]L. N. Chete, J. O. Adeoti, F. M. Adeyinka, and O. Ogundele, "Industrial Development and Growth in Nigeria: Lessons and Challenges," The Brookings Institution, July 2016, https://www.brookings.edu/wp-content/uploads/2016/07/L2C_WP8_Chete-et-al-1.pdf

[8]Landry Signé and Chelsea Johnson, "The Potential of Manufacturing and Industrialization in Africa: Trends, Opportunities, and Strategies," Brookings Institution, September 2018, https://www.brookings.edu/wp-content/uploads/2018/09/Manufacturing-and-Industrialization-in-Africa-Signe-20180921.pdf

[9]"Lagos Free Trade Zone Woos Singaporean Investors as Existing Investments hit $150M," Business Day, August 2, 2017 https://www.nipc.gov.ng/lagos-free-trade-zone-woos-singaporean-investors-existing-investments-hit-150m/

[10]Anzetse Were, "Manufacturing in Kenya: Features, Challenges and Opportunities," Supporting Economic Transformation, August 2016, https://set.odi.org/wp-content/uploads/2016/09/Manufacturing-in-Kenya-Anzetse-Were.pdf

[11]"Kenya's Industrial Transformation Programme," Ministry of Industry, Trade and Cooperatives, n.d., http://www.industrialization.go.ke/index.php/downloads/282- kenya-s-industrial-transformation-programme

[12]"Industrialize Africa: Strategies, Policies, Institutions and Financing," African Development Bank, November 20, 2017, https://www.afdb.org/en/news-and-events/industrialize-africa-strategies-policies-institutions-and-financing-17570/

[13]"Interview: Ashley Taylor," Oxford Business Group, n.d., https://oxfordbusinessgroup.com/interview/ashley-taylor

Chapter Eleven: Technological Solutions For Oil and Gas

[1]Jaya Shukla, "Banking through Mobile Money Technology in Africa," The New Times, June 18, 2018, https://www.newtimes.co.rw/business/banking-through-mobile-money-technology-africa

[2]"M-Pesa," Wikipedia, June 24, 2019, https://en.wikipedia.org/wiki/M-Pesa

[3]Erik Hersman, "The Mobile Continent," Stanford Social Innovation Review, Spring 2013, https://ssir.org/articles/entry/the_mobile_continent

[4]Sama Tanya, "NJ Ayuk on How Tech can Impact Africa's Oil & Gas Industry," Bequadi, February 7, 2018, https://www.bequadi.com/nj-ayuk-2/

[5]"MOGS Oil & Gas Operations and Projects," n.d., https://www.mogs.co.za /oil-gas-services/operations/oiltainking-mogs-saldanha

[6]Paul Burkhardt, "Africa's Oil Hub Woos Global Traders With New Million-Barrel Tanks," Bloomberg, February 25, 2019, https://www.bloomberg .com/news/features/2019-02-26/africa-s-oil-hub-woos-global-traders-with-new -million-barrel-tanks

[7]Iyabo Lawal, "FUPRE as Bridge Between Education and Innovation," The Guardian, April 25, 2019, https://guardian.ng/features/education/fupre-as-bridge -between-education-and-innovation/

[8]"'At Friburge We Leverage Cutting Edge Technology That Will Significantly Cut Costs And Reduce The Heavy Effects Of Resource Mining On Africa's Bourgeoning Eco System' – Dos Santos," Orient Energy Review, February 2, 2017, https://orientenergyreview.com/uncategorised /at-friburge-we-leverage-cutting-edge-technology-that-will-significantly-cut -costs-and-reduce-the-heavy-effects-of-resource-mining-on-africas-bourgeon ing-eco-system/

[9]Abdi Latif Dahir, "This Documentary Tells the Story of Africa's Longest Internet Shutdown," Quartz, August 6, 2018, https://qz.com/africa/1349108 /cameroons-internet-shutdown-in-blacked-out-documentary/

[10]Abdi Latif Dahir, "How Do You Build Africa's Newest Tech Ecosystem When the Government Shuts the Internet Down?" Quartz, February 3, 2017, https://qz.com /africa/902291/cameroons-silicon-mountain-is-suffering-losses-from-the-countrys -internet-shutdown/

[11]"Rebecca Enonchong: A Heavyweight in African Tech," The World Bank, March 8, 2019, https://www.worldbank.org/en/news/feature/2019/03/08 /rebecca-enonchong-a-heavyweight-in-african-tech

[12]Marriane Enow Tabi, "Rebecca Enonchong: How I Built a Global Tech Business with no Funding—7 Lessons," Journal du Cameroun, January 14, 2019, https://www.journalducameroun.com/en/rebecca-enonchong-how-i-built-a-global-tech-business-with-no-funding%E2%80%8A-%E2%80%8A7-lessons/

[13]Arlene Lagman, "Njeri Rionge, The Serial Entrepreneur," Connected Women, January 17, 2016, https://www.connectedwomen.co/magazine/herstory-njeri-rionge-the-serial-entrepreneur/

[14]"Rolling out the Web to Kenya's Poor," BBC News, May 14, 2012, https://www.bbc. com/news/world-africa-17901645

Chapter Twelve: Oil and Gas Companies Can Help Reshape African Economies

[1]"Interview: Tunde Ajala," Africa Business Communities, October 1, 2018, https://africabusinesscommunities.com/features/interview-tunde-ajala,-executive-director-dovewell-oilfield-services-nigeria/

[2]Derby Omokoh, "Arthur Eze: Nigeria Profile," Oil Voice, October 2, 2017, https://oilvoice.com/Opinion/8804/Arthur-Eze-Nigeria-Profile

[3]Mfonobong Nsehe, "Nigerian Oilman Prince Arthur Eze Builds $800,000 School In South Sudan," Forbes, October 1, 2018, https://www.forbes.com/sites/mfonobongnsehe/2018/10/01/nigerian-oilman-prince-arthur-eze-builds-800000- school-in-south-sudan/#21367c36751b

[4]Ninsiima Julian, "Oranto Petroleum Increases its Support to the Education of Uganda, South Sudan's Communities," PLM Daily, March 11, 2019, http://www.pmldaily.com/news/2019/03/oranto-petroleum-increases-its-support-to-the-education-of-uganda-south-sudans-communities.html

[5]"Sahara Group Canvasses Investments in Emerging Markets at Europlace Forum in Paris," Sahara Group, July 10, 2018, http://www.sahara-group.com/2018/07/10/sahara-group-canvasses-investments-in-emerging-markets-at-europlace-forum-in-paris/

[6]"Sustainability Through Synergy," Sahara Group, 2016, http://www.sahara-group .com/wp-content/uploads/2018/06/Sahara_Group_2016_Sustainability_Report .pdf

[7]"Q&A with Kola Karim," Unity Magazine, n.d., https://unity-magazine.com /qa-with-kola-karim/

[8]Derek Dingle, "Kase Lawal Is One of the Biggest Power Players in Houston's Oil Industry," Black Enterprise, May 17, 2017, https://www.blackenterprise.com /kase-lawal-houston-oil/

[9]Susannah Palk, "Kase Lawal: Not Your Average Oil Baron," CNN, May 19, 2010, http://www.cnn.com/2010/WORLD/africa/05/18/kase.lukman.lawal /index.html

[10]"Oil Company Tradex Does Well in Chad, Equatorial Guinea and the Central African Republic," Business in Cameroon, October 2018, page 9, https://www . businessincameroon.com/pdf/BC68.pdf

[11]Andy Brogan, "Why National Oil Companies Need to Transform," Ernst & Young, April 12, 2019, https://www.ey.com/en_gl/oil-gas/why-national -oil-companies-need-to-transform

[12]"NOC-IOC Partnerships," World National Oil Companies Congress, June 2012, http://www.terrapinn.com/conference/world-national-oil -companies-congress/Data/nociocpartnerships.pdf

[13]"Angola: Total Will Launch a Fuel Retail Network with Sonangol," BusinesWire, 281 December 21, 2018, https://www.businesswire.com/news /home/20181221005176/en/Angola-Total-Launch-Fuel-Retail-Network -Sonangol

Chapter Thirteen:
Following Nigeria's Lead on Marginal Fields

[1]Ejiofor Alike, "FG Sets Bid Round Guidelines for Award of 46 Marginal Oil Fields," This Day, September 18, 2017, https://www.thisdaylive.com/index .php/2017/09/18/fg-sets-bid-round-guidelines-for-award-of-46-marginal -oil-fields/

[2] Dolapo Oni, "Nigeria Targets Local Upstream Players with Marginal Field Round," Petroleum Economist, March 7, 2018, http://www .petroleum-economist.com/articles/upstream/licensing-rounds/2018/nigeria -targets-local-upstream-players-with-marginal-field-round

[3] Chijioke Nwaozuzu, "Marginal Oil Fields Development in Nigeria: Way Forward," Business a.m., August 6, 2018, https://www.businessamlive.com /marginal-oil-fields-development-in-nigeria-way-forward/

[4] "Special Report: Untold Story of How Skye Bank's Bubble Burst," Ripples Nigeria, July 6, 2016, https://www.ripplesnigeria.com/special-skye-bank/

[5] Chijioke Nwaozuzu, "Marginal Oil Fields Development in Nigeria: Way Forward," Business a.m., August 6, 2018, https://www.businessamlive.com /marginal-oil-fields-development-in-nigeria-way-forward/

[6] Elie Smith, "Congo Republic Sees OPEC Admission Opening Up Its Oil Industry," Bloomberg, June 23, 2018, https://www.bloomberg.com/news/articles /2018-06-23/congo-republic-sees-opec-admission-opening-up-its-oil-industry

[7] Viktor Katona, "Can Angola Overhaul Its Struggling Oil Industry?" OilPrice.com, October 29, 2018, https://oilprice.com/Energy/Crude-Oil/Can-Angola-Overhaul -Its- Struggling-Oil-Industry.html

[8] "Angola Facts and Figures," Organization of the Petroleum Exporting Countries, 2018, https://www.opec.org/opec_web/en/about_us/147.htm

[9] Stephen Eisenhammer, "Angola Cuts Tax Rates for Development of Marginal Oil Fields," Reauters, May 22, 2018, https://af.reuters.com/article/investingNews /idAFKCN1IN0SN-OZABS

[10] "Angola: 2019 Licensing Round, Marginal Fields Drive Explorers' Interest," Africa Oil & Power, https://africaoilandpower.com/2018/12/17 /independent-oil-companies-turn-attention-to-angola-2019-licensing-round -marginal-fields-drive-explorers-interest/

[11] Moses Aremu, "Deepwater Fields Define Angola's Oil Wealth in the New Century," Oil and Gas Online, n.d., https://www.oilandgasonline.com/doc /deepwater-fields-define-angolas-oil-wealth-in-0001

[12]"Infrastructure," Sahara Group, n.d., http://www.sahara-group.com/businesses /#infrastructure

[13]"Upstream," Sahara Group, n.d, http://www.sahara-group.com/businesses /#upstream

[14]"Sustainability Through Synergy," Sahara Group, 2016, http://www.sahara -group.com/wp-content/uploads/2018/06/Sahara_Group_2016_Sustainability _Report.pdf

Chapter Fourteen: The Critical Art of Deal-Making: It's Time to Negotiate for a Better Future

[1]"Contract Negotiation and Fiscal Policies in Africa's Extractives Sector," NEPAD, November 5, 2018, https://www.nepad.org/news/contract-negotiation -and-fiscal-policies-africas-extractives-sector

[2]Desmond Davies, "Obasanjo Advises African Leaders to Improve Negotiation Skills," Ghana News Agency, April 19, 2017, http://www.ghananewsagency.org /features/obasanjo-advises-african-leaders-to-improve-negotiation-skills-115788

[3]Richard Harroch, "15 Tactics for Successful Business Negotiations," Forbes, September 16, 2016, https://www.forbes.com/sites/allbusiness/2016/09/16/15 -tactics-for-successful-business-negotiations/#55751d3d2528

[4]Danny Ertel, "Getting Past Yes: Negotiating as if Implementation Mattered," Harvard Business Review, November 2004, https://hbr.org/2004/11 /getting-past-yes-negotiating-as-if-implementation-mattered

[5]"Corporate Responsibility Report," Kosmos Energy, 2015, https://www .unglobalcompact.org/system/attachments/cop_2016/300841/original/Kosmos _ Energy_2015_Corporate_Responsibility_Report.pdf?1468431920

[6]"Senegal," BP, n.d., https://www.bp.com/en/global/corporate/what-we-do /bp-worldwide/bp-in-senegal.html

[7]"Kosmos Energy Welcomes Approval of Inter-Governmental Cooperation Agreement between Mauritania and Senegal," Kosmos Energy, February 12, 2018, http://investors. kosmosenergy.com/news-releases/news-release-details /kosmos-energy-welcomes-approval-inter-governmental-cooperation

[8]"Noble Energy Announces Agreement to Progress Development of Alen Natural Gas, Offshore Equatorial Guinea," May 10, 2018, http://investors .nblenergy.com/news-releases/news-release-details/noble-energy-announces -agreement-progress-development-alen

[9]NJ Ayuk, "Equatorial Guinea's New Flare," Vanguard, June 13, 2018, https:// www.vanguardngr.com/2018/06/equatorial-guineas-new-flare/

[10]Robert Brelsfor, "Uganda Inks Deal for Country's First Refinery," Oil & Gas Journal, April 12, 2018, https://www.ogj.com/articles/2018/04/uganda-inks-deal-for -country-s-first-refinery.html

[11]"Behind the Scenes in Uganda's $4bn Oil Refinery Deal," The Observer, April 17, 2018, https://observer.ug/news/headlines/57478-behind-the-scenes-in -uganda-s-4bn-oil-refinery-deal.html

[12]Edward McAllister and Oleg Vukmanovic, "How One West African Gas Deal Makes BG Group Billions," Reuters, July 12, 2013, https://www .reuters.com/article/bg-equatorial-guinea-lng/how-one-west-african-gas-deal -makes-bg-group-billions-idUSL5N0FA1BE20130712

[13]Oleg Vukmanovic, "Equatorial Guinea in LNG Sale Talks as Shell Deal Winds Down," Reuters, May 11, 2018, https://af.reuters.com/article/topNews /idAFKBN1IC0MV-OZATP

Chapter Fifteen: The Connection Between Energy Security and Social Security

[1]Ahmad Ghaddar, "Libya Port Attack Cut Output by 400,000 Barrels Per Day: NOC 283 Head," Reuters, June 19, 2018, https://www.reuters.com/article/us-libya -security-oil/libya-port-attack-cut-output-by-400000-barrels-per-day-noc-head -idUSKBN1JF180

[2]Ayman al-Warfalli and Shadia Nasralla, "East Libyan Forces Advance Rapidly to Retake Key Oil Ports," Business Insider, June 21, 2018, https://www.businessinsider .com/r-east-libyan-forces-advance-rapidly-to-retake-key-oil-ports-2018-6

[3]"East Libyan Forces Reclaim Key Oil Ports," eNCA, June 22, 2018, https://www .enca. com/africa/east-libyan-forces-reclaim-key-oil-ports

[4]Jan-Philipp Scholz, "Gas Flaring in the Niger Delta Ruins Lives, Business," Deutsche Welle, November 11, 2017, https://www.dw.com/en/gas-flaring-in-the-niger-delta-ruins-lives-business/a-41221653

[5]Leonore Schick, Paul Myles, and Okonta Emeka Okelum, "Gas Flaring Continues Scorching Niger Delta," Deutsche Welle, November 14, 2018, https://www.dw.com/en/gas-flaring-continues-scorching-niger-delta/a-46088235

[6]John Campbell, "The Trouble With Oil Pipelines in Nigeria," Council on Foreign Relations, September 14, 2017, https://www.cfr.org/blog/trouble-oil-pipelines-nigeria

[7]Shadow Governance Intel, "Nigeria's Oil Theft Epidemic," OilPrice.com, June 6, 2017, https://oilprice.com/Energy/Crude-Oil/Nigerias-Oil-Theft-Epidemic.html

[8]Terry Hallmark, "Oil and Violence in the Niger Delta Isn't Talked About Much, but it Has a Global Impact," Forbes, February 13, 2017, https://www.forbes.com/sites/uhenergy/2017/02/13/oil-and-violence-in-the-niger-delta-isnt-talked-about-much-but-it-has-a-global-impact/#422d73284dc6

[9]Bukola Adebayo, "Major New Inquiry into Oil Spills in Nigeria's Niger Delta Launched," CNN, March 26, 2019, https://www.cnn.com/2019/03/26/africa/nigeria-oil-spill-inquiry-intl/index.html

[10]Irina Slav, "Nigerian Army Destroys Major Oil Smuggling Hub," OilPrice.com, April 16, 2019, https://oilprice.com/Latest-Energy-News/World-News/Nigerian-Army- Destroys-Major-Oil-Smuggling-Hub.html

[11]"Market Report: NNPC to Provide Support to the Agriculture Industry," Africa Oil & Power, April 15, 2019, https://africaoilandpower.com/2019/04/15/market-report-nnpc-to-provide-support-to-the-agriculture-industry/

[12]Gege Li, "Harnessing Plants and Microbes to Tackle Environmental Pollution," Chemistry World, March 29, 2019, https://www.chemistryworld.com/research/harnessing-plants-and-microbes-to-tackle-environmental-pollution/3010307.article

[13]Rebecca Campbell, "See How This Non-Profit Is Using the Blockchain to Clean up the Niger Delta," Forbes, January 14, 2019, https://www.forbes.com/sites

/rebeccacampbell1/2019/01/14/see-how-this-non-profit-is-using-the-blockchain-to
-clean-up-the-niger-delta/#2cbb69c53302

[14]Nkosana Mafico, "Using Blockchain Technology to Clean Up the Niger Delta," Huffington Post, October 8, 2017, https://www.huffpost.com/entry /using-revolutionary-technology-to-clean-up-the-niger_b_59d373eae4b 092b22a8e3957

[15]Bukola Adebayo, "Contaminated Lands, Water: New Major Inquiry into Oil Spills in Niger Delta," Vanguard, March 31, 2019, https://www.vanguardngr.com/2019/03/contaminated-lands-water -new-major-inquiry-into-oil-spills-in-niger-delta/

[16]Ian Ralby, "Downstream Oil Theft: Global Modalities, Trends, and Remedies," Atlantic Council Global Energy Center, January 2017, https://www.atlanticcouncil .org/images/publications/Downstream-Oil-Theft-RW-0214.pdf

[17]Terry Hallmark, "The Murky Underworld of Oil Theft and Diversion," Forbes, May 26, 2017, https://www.forbes.com/sites/uhenergy/2017/05 /26/the-murky-underworld-of-oil-theft-and-diversion/#dc609716886ᵉ

[18]"Nigeria Takes Action Against Gas Flaring," Journal du Cameroun, April 3, 2019, https://www.journalducameroun.com/en/nigeria-takes-action-against-gas-flaring/

[19]Samuel Petrequin and Ebow Godwin, "2 Arrested in Togo Soccer Team Attack," CBS News, January 11, 2010, https://www.cbsnews.com/news/2-arrested -in-togo-soccer-team-attack/

[20]Ed Cropley, "Rebels Alive and Kicking in Angolan Petro-Province, Oil Workers Say," Reuters, June 14, 2016, https://www.reuters.com/article /angola-oil-security/rebels-alive-and-kicking-in-angolan-petro-province-oil -workers-say-idUSL8N1952C9

[21]"What's Behind the Surge in Violence in Angola's Cabinda Province?" World Politics Review, September 9, 2016, https://www.worldpoliticsreview.com/trend-lines /19873/what-s-behind-the-surge-in-violence-in-angola-s-cabinda-province

[22]Lucy Corkin, "After the Boom: Angola's Recurring Oil Challenges in a New Context," Oxford Institute for Energy Studies, May 2017, https://www

.oxfordenergy.org/wpcms/wp-content/uploads/2017/05/After-the-Boom-Angolas
-Recurring-Oil-Challenges-in-a- New-Contect-WPM-72.pdf

[23]Matthew Hill and Borges Nhamire, "Burning Villages, Ethnic Tensions Menace Mozambique Gas Boom," Bloomberg, July 1, 2018, https://www.bloomberg .com/news/articles/2018-07-02/burning-villages-ethnic-tensions-menace -mozambique-s-gas-boom

[24]Jordan Blum, "Anadarko's Mozambique LNG Attacked Amid Insurgency, One Contractor Killed," Houston Chronicle, February 22, 2019, https://www.houston chronicle.com/business/energy/article/Anadarko-Mozambique-Attacked-for- First -Time-Amid-13636373.php

[25]Paul Burkhardt and Matthew Hill, "Chevron Gets Treasure, Trouble with Rebel-Hit Mozambique Gas," Bloomberg, April 12, 2019, https://www.bloomberg .com/news/articles/2019-04-12/chevron-reaps-treasure-trouble-in-rebel-hit -mozambique-gas-area

[26]Chris Massaro, "Nigeria Plagued by Ethnic and Religious Violence as Attacks on Christians Rise," Fox News, April 24, 2019, https://www.foxnews.com/world /nigeria-ethnic-religious-violence-christians

[27]Orji Sunday, "Organised Crime Kills More Civilians in Nigeria than Boko Haram," TRT World, April 24, 2019, https://www.trtworld.com/magazine /organised-crime-kills-more-civilians-in-nigeria-than-boko-haram-26143

[28]Brian Adeba, "How War, Oil and Politics Fuel Controversy in South Sudan's Unity State," African Arguments, August 5, 2015, http://africanarguments .org/2015/08/05/how-war-oil-and-politics-fuel-controversy-in-south-sudans-unity -state-by-brian-adeba/

[29]"South Sudan Country Profile," BBC, August 6, 2018, http://www.bbc.co.uk /news/world-africa-14069082

[30]Javira Ssebwami, "South Sudan enters into Agreement with African Energy Chamber to Provide Technical Assistance to its Petroleum Sector," PML Daily, January 31, 2019, http://www.pmldaily.com/business/2019/01/south-sudan -enters-into-agreement-with-african-energy-chamber-to-provide-technical -assistance-to-its-petroleum-sector.html

[31]Abdelghani Henni, "South Sudan: When Oil Becomes A Curse," Hart Energy, July 19, 2018, https://www.hartenergy.com/exclusives/south-sudan-when-oil-becomes-curse-31242

[32]Okech Francis, "South Sudan Sees $2 billion Oil Investments as First Start," World Oil, December 19, 2018, https://www.worldoil.com/news/2018/12/19/south-sudan-sees-2-billion-oil-investments-as-first-start

[33]Nhial Tiitmamer, "South Sudan's Mining Policy and Resource Curse," The Sudd Institute, April 22, 2014, https://www.suddinstitute.org/publications/show/south-sudan-s-mining-policy-and-resource-curse

[34]Nhial Tiitmamer, "The South Sudanization of the Petroleum Industry Through Local Content: Is the Dream within Reach?" The Sudd Institute, October 20, 2015, https://www.suddinstitute.org/publications/show/the-south-sudanization-of-the-petroleum-industry-through-local-content-is-the-dream-within-reach

[35]Wim Zwijnenburg, "South Sudan's Broken Oil Industry Increasingly Becoming a Hazard," New Security Beat, May 2, 2016, https://www.newsecuritybeat.org/2016/05/south-sudans-broken-oil-industry-hazard/

[36]William Charnley, "South Sudan: Post Civil War Instability," Global Risk Insights, March 19, 2019, https://globalriskinsights.com/2019/03/south-sudan-war-peace-deal/

Chapter Sixteen: Managing Oil and Gas Revenue

[1]"Laura FitzGerald, the Bells of the Wells," CNBC, n.d., https://www.cnbc.com/laura-fitzgerald/

[2]Laura FitzGerald, "Women's Oil Business Plan: Removing Your Glass Ceiling," Ilios Resources, n.d., http://iliosresources.com/oil-business-plan/

[3]Rob Wile, "Why Letting an Oil Company Frack in Your Backyard Is Actually an Awesome Idea," Business Insider, October 15, 2012, https://www.businessinsider.com/if-you-want-to-become-a-millionaire-let-an-oil-company-frack-your-backyard-2012-10

[4]David Bailey, "In North Dakota, Hard to Tell an Oil Millionaire from Regular Joe," Reuters, October 3, 2012, https://www.reuters.com/article/us-usa-northdakota -millionaires/in-north-dakota-hard-to-tell-an-oil-millionaire-from-regular-joe -idUSBRE8921AF20121003

[5]"Oil in Nigeria: A Cure or Curse?" Glonal Citizen, August 31, 2012, https:// www.globalcitizen.org/en/content/oil-in-nigeria-a-cure-or-curse/

[6]"Poverty and Crime Flourish in Oil-Rich Niger Delta," PBS News Hour, July 27, 2007, https://www.pbs.org/newshour/politics/africa-july-dec07-delta _0727

[7]Daron Acemoglu and James Robinson, "Is There a Curse of Resources? The Case of the Cameroon," Why Nations Fail, May 16, 2013, http://whynationsfail. com/blog/2013/5/16/is-there-a-curse-of-resources-the-case-of-the-cameroon.html

[8]William Lloyd, "Top 10 Facts About Living Conditions In Cameroon," The Borgen Project, February 19, 2019, https://borgenproject.org/top-10-facts-about -living-conditions-in-cameroon/

[9]Tim Cocks, "Anglophone Cameroon's Separatist Conflict Gets Bloodier," Reuters, June 1, 2018, https://www.reuters.com/article/us-cameroon-separatists /anglophone-cameroons-separatist-conflict-gets-bloodier-idUSKCN1IX4RS

[10]Yusser AL-Gayed, "Oil, Order and Diversification in Libya," Natural Resource Governance Institute, August 12, 2016, https://resourcegovernance.org/blog /three-ways-oil-reliance-has-hit-libya-and-government

[11]Jim Armitage, "Libya Sinks into Poverty as the Oil Money Disappears into Foreign Bank Accounts," The Independent, July 17, 2018, https://www .independent.co.uk/news/business/analysis-and-features/libya-poverty-corruption -a8451826.html

[12]Charles Recknagel, "What Can Norway Teach Other Oil-Rich Countries?" Radio Free Europe, November 27, 2014, https://www.rferl.org/a/what-can-norway -teach-other-oil-rich-countries/26713453.html

[13]Richard Valdmanis, "Debt-Wracked Nations Could Learn from Norway, Prime Minister Says," Reuters, September 25, 2013, https://www.reuters.com/article

/us-usa-norway-stoltenberg/debt-wracked-nations-could-learn-from-norway-prime
-minister-says-idUSBRE98P04D20130926

[14]"Kenya Proposes Transparent, but Risky, New Sovereign Wealth Fund," Natural
Resource Governance Institute, March 6, 2019, https://resourcegovernance.org/blog
/kenya-proposes-transparent-risky-new-sovereign-wealth-fund

[15]Larry Diamond and Jack Mosbacher, "Petroleum to the People, Africa's Coming
Resource Curse—And How to Avoid It," Foreign Affairs, September/October 2013,
http://media.hoover.org/sites/default/files/documents/diamond_mosbacher
_latest3.pdf

[16]Shanta Devarajan, "How to Use Oil Revenues Efficiently: Universal Basic
Income," Brookings, May 30, 2017, https://www.brookings.edu/blog/future
-development/2017/05/30/how-to-use-oil-revenues-efficiently-universal-basic
-income/

[17]Emeka Duruigbo, "Managing Oil Revenues for Socio-Economic Development
in Nigeria," North Carolina Journal of International Law and Commercial Regulation,
Fall 2004, https://scholarship.law.unc.edu/cgi/viewcontent.cgi?referer=https://www
.google. com/&httpsredir=1&article=1781&context=ncilj

[18]Landry Signé, "Africa's Natural Resource Revenue for All: The Alaska Permanent
Fund Dividend Model," Brookings, June 26, 2018, https://www.brookings.edu/blog
/africa-287 in-focus/2018/06/26/africas-natural-resource-revenue-for-all-the-alaska
-permanent-fund-dividend-model/

[19]Svetlana Tsalik, "Caspian Oil Windfalls: Who Will Benefit?" Open Society
Institute, 2003, http://pdc.ceu.hu/archive/00002053/01/051203.pdf

[20]Ujjwal Joshi, "Chad-Cameroon Pipeline Project," June 6, 2013, https://www
.slideshare. net/ujjwaljoshi1990/chad-cameroon-pipeline-project-22545357

[21]Artur Colom Jaén, "Lessons from the Failure of Chad's Oil Revenue
Management Model (ARI)," Real Instituto Elcano, December 3, 2010, http://
www.realinstitutoelcano.org/wps/wcm/connect/8473080041b87f3a9de5f
fe151fccd56/ARI12-2010_Colom_Chad_Oil_Revenue_Management_Model
.pdf?MOD=AJPERES&CACHEID=8473080041b87f3a9de5ffe151fccd56

[22]"Chad-Cameroon Petroleum Development and Pipeline Project: Overview," The World Bank, December 2006, http://documents.worldbank.org/curated /en/821131468224690538/pdf/36569.pdf

Chapter Seventeen: American Ingenuity and Africa Oil and Gas Potential

[1]Shawn Simmons, "Thank a Mentor By Becoming One Yourself," STEAM Magazine, Summer/Fall 2016, https://mydigitalpublication.com/publication/frame . php?i=312844&p=66&pn=&ver=html5

[2]Sarah Donchey, "Women Making a Difference: Shawn Simmons fulfills dream of becoming engineer," Click2Houston.com, February 23, 2018, https://www . click2houston.com/community/women-making-a-difference/shawn-simmons -fulfills-dream-of-becoming-engineer

[3]"Dr Shawn Simmons advises on ExxonMobil's work in Nigeria," Diversity /Careers in Engineering & Information Technology, http://www.diversitycareers .com/articles/pro/06-augsep/managing_exxon.html

[4]Robert Rapier, "How The Shale Boom Turned The World Upside Down," Forbes, April 21, 2017, https://www.forbes.com/sites/rrapier/2017/04/21/how -the-shale-boom-turned-the-world-upside-down/#5cf4192a77d2

[5]Robert Rapier, "How The Shale Boom Turned The World Upside Down," Forbes, April 21, 2017, https://www.forbes.com/sites/rrapier/2017/04/21/how-the-shale -boom-turned-the-world-upside-down/#5cf4192a77d2

[6]"Overview of U.S. Petroleum Production, Imports, Exports, and Consumption," Bureau of Transportation Statistics, https://www.bts.gov/content /overview-us-petroleum-production-imports-exports-and-consumption-million -barrels-day

[7]"U.S. monthly crude oil production exceeds 11 million barrels per day in August," United States Energy Information Administration, November 1, 2018, https://www .eia. gov/todayinenergy/detail.php?id=37416.

[8]"Cobalt in dispute with Sonangol over Angolan assets," Offshore Energy Today, 2017, https://www.offshoreenergytoday.com/cobalt-in-dispute-with-sonangol -over-angolan-assets/

[9]BP And Partner's US$350 million Payments In Corruption-Prone Angola Show
288 Need for U.S. Transparency Rule, Global Witness, August 4, 2014, https://www
. globalwitness.org/en/archive/bp-and-partners-us350-million-payments-corruption
-prone-angola-show-need-us-transparency/

[10]Jonathan Stempel, "Och-Ziff reaches $29 million shareholder accord over
Africa bribery probes," Reuters, October 2, 2018, https://www.reuters.com/article
/us-och-ziff-settlement/och-ziff-reaches-29-million-shareholder-accord-over-africa
-bribery-probes-idUSKCN1MC2DS

[11]"BBC Expose On $10BN Deal Shows BP May Have Been Complicit In
Corruption," Global Witness, June 3, 2019, https://www.globalwitness.org/en
/press-releases/bbc-expos%C3%A9-on-10bn-deal-shows-bp-may-have-been
-complicit-in-corruption/

[12]Daniel Graeber, "More Oil Progress Offshore Senegal," UPI, March 7, 2017,
https://www.upi.com/Energy-News/2017/03/07/More-oil-progress-offshore
- Senegal/9391488887085/

[13]Rick Wilkinson, "Cairn Energy group begins FEED at SNE field off Senegal," Oil
& Gas Journal, December 17, 2018, https://www.ogj.com/exploration-development
/article/17296866/cairn-energy-group-begins-feed-at-sne-field-off-senegaler

[14]Angela Macdonald-Smith, "Woodside Petroleum to pay $565.5m for
ConocoPhillips' Senegal venture,_" _The Australian Financial Review, July 14, 2016,
https://www.afr.com/business/energy/oil/woodside-petroleum-to-pay-5655m-for
-conocophillips-senegal-venture-20160714-gq5b49

[15]Dai Jones, "2018 Global Exploration Activity Stable and 2019 Outlook
Upbeat," DrillingInfo.com, April 4, 2019, https://info.drillinginfo.com/blog/2018
-global-exploration-activity-stable-and-2019-outlook-upbeat/

[16]"Eni announces a major oil discovery offshore Angola," Eni, March 13,
2019, https://www.eni.com/en_IT/media/2019/03/eni-announces-a-major-oil
-discovery-offshore-angola

[17]Dai Jones, "2018 Global Exploration Activity Stable and 2019 Outlook
Upbeat," DrillingInfo.com, April 4, 2019, https://info.drillinginfo.com
/blog/2018-global-exploration-activity-stable-and-2019-outlook-upbeat/

[18]"West African Rig Market: A Slow-Burn Recovery," Westwood Global Energy Group, April 10, 2019, https://www.westwoodenergy.com/news/west wood-insight/west-african-rig-market-a-slow-burn-recovery/

[19]"West African offshore rig market remains subdued," Offshore, April 10, 2019, https://www.offshore-mag.com/drilling-completion/article/16790829 /west-african-offshore-rig-market-remains-subdued

[20]Dai Jones, "2018 Global Exploration Activity Stable and 2019 Outlook Upbeat," DrillingInfo.com, April 4, 2019, https://info.drillinginfo.com/ blog/2018-global-exploration-activity-stable-and-2019-outlook-upbeat/

[21]"Ghana Crude Oil Production," Trading Economics, https://tradingeconomics .com/ghana/crude-oil-production

[22]Ismail Akwei, "Ghana wins three-year maritime boundary dispute case against Ivory Coast," AllAfrica, September 23, 2017, https://www.africanews .com/2017/09/23/ghana-wins-three-year-maritime-boundary-dispute-case -against-ivory-coast//

[23]"Côte D'ivoire Crude Oil Production by Year," IndexMundi, https://www .indexmundi. com/energy/?country=ci&product=oil&graph=production

[24]Andrew Skipper, "Africa 2019 – The Optimist's View," African Law & Business, December 18, 2018, https://www.africanlawbusiness.com/news/8891 -africa-2019-the-optimists-view

[25]Garrett Brinker, "President Obama Speaks at the U.S.-Africa Business Forum," obamawhitehousearchives.gov, August 5, 2014, https://obamawhitehouse.archives .gov/blog/2014/08/05/president-obama-speaks-us-africa-business-forum

[26]Tibor Nagy, "The Enduring Partnership between the United States and South Africa," africanews., June 25, 2019, https://www.africanews.com/2019/06/25 /the-enduring-partnership-between-the-united-states-and-south-africa-speech-by -assistant-secretary-tibor-nagy/

[27]"Ann Norman, Pioneer Energy: 'Africa is open for business,'" Kapital Afrik, March 20, 2019, https://www.kapitalafrik.com/2019/03/20/ann-norman -pioneer-energy-africa-is-open-for-business/

28"Africa: Symbion Power Announces Low-Cost, Mini-Hydro Pilot in Rwanda and Geothermal Plant in Kenya During U.S. 'Prosper Africa' Rollout," AllAfrica, https://allafrica.com/stories/201906200815.html

29Power Africa: Beyond The Grid, Private Sector Partner List, https://www.usaid.gov/powerafrica/privatesector

Chapter Nineteen: Lights Out: Reforming African Power Generation Monopolies and Transitioning To the Future

1"Load shedding: Eskom drops to Stage 2 on Friday 22 March," The South Africa, March 22, 2019, https://www.thesouthafrican.com/news/load-shedding-today-friday- 22-march-2019/

2"Why We Need to Close the Infrastructure Gap in Sub-Saharan Africa" The World Bank, April 2017, https://www.worldbank.org/en/region/afr/publication/why-we-need-to-close-the-infrastructure-gap-in-sub-saharan-africa

3Moussa P. Blimpo and Malcolm Cosgrove-Davies, "Electricity Access in Sub-Saharan Africa: Uptake, Reliability, and Complementary Factors for Economic Impact," Africa Development Forum Series, 2019, https://openknowledge.worldbank.org/bitstream/handle/10986/31333/9781464813610. pdf?sequence=6&isAllowed=y

4Michael Cohen, Paul Burkhardt, and Paul Vecchiatto, "The Only Option for Eskom Is One South Africa Can't Afford," June 18, 2019, https://www.bloomberg.com/news/articles/2019-06-19/the-only-option-for-eskom-is-one-south-africa-can-t-afford

5Julius Yao Petetsi, "Ghana: Minority Expresses Worry Over Energy Sector Debt," AllAfrica, June 21, 2019, https://allafrica.com/stories/201906240402.html

6"Umeme investment in power distribution infrastructure paying off," The Independent, 290 November 22, 2017, https://www.independent.co.ug/umeme-tremendously-contributed-towards-power-distribution/

7Lily Kuo, "Kenya's national electrification campaign is taking less than half the time it took America," Quartz Africa, January 16, 2017, https://qz.com/africa/882938

/kenya-is-rolling-out-its-national-electricity-program-in-half-the-time-it-took-amer-ica/

[8]Africa Progress Panel, "Africa Progress Report 2015, Power People Planet: Seizing Africa's Energy and Climate Opportunities" https://app.box.com/s /kw1za0n3r4bo92a3wfst0wuln216j6pp

[9]"Kenya Launches Africa's Biggest Wind Farm," The East African, July 18, 2019, https://www.theeastafrican.co.ke/business/Kenya-to-launch-africa-biggest-wind -farm/2560- 5202472-m7582y/index.html

[10]Carla Sertin, "Oil and gas industry key to climate change solutions: OPEC Secretary- General Barkindo," OilandGasMiddleEast.com, July 10, 2019, https://www.oilandgasmiddleeast.com/drilling-production/34513-oil-and-gas -industry-instrumental-part-of-climate-change-solutions-opec-secretary -general-barkindo

[11]International Energy Agency, "Africa Energy Outlook: A Focus on Energy Prospects in Sub-Saharan Africa," 2019 https://www.iea.org/publications/free publications/publication/WEO2014_AfricaEnergyOutlook.pdf

Chapter Twenty: Concluding Thoughts

[1]Collins Olayinka and Kingsley Jeremiah, "AITEO Founder Peters Wins FIN African Icon Award," The Guardian, January 31, 2019, https://guardian.ng /appointments/aiteo-founder-peters-wins-fin-african-icon-award/

[2]Tsvetana Paraskova, "South Africa Oil Discovery Could Be a Game-Changer," OilPrice.com, February 10, 2019, https://oilprice.com/Energy/Crude-Oil /South-Africa-Oil- Discovery-Could-Be-A-Game-Changer.html

[3]Kim Aine, "Unganda Joins Extractive Industries Transparency Initiative to Boost Investor Confidence," ChimpReports, January 29, 2019, https://chimp reports.com/uganda-joins-extractive-industries-transparency-initiative-to-boost -investor-confidence/

[4]"Benin's National Assembly Adopts New Petroleum Code," Africa Oil & Power, January 25, 2019, https://africaoilandpower.com/2019/01/25/benins -national-assembly-adopts-new-petroleum-code/

[5] Thomas Hedley, "Senegal's Petroleum Code Moves Towards Final Stage," Africa Oil & Power, January 14, 2019, https://africaoilandpower.com/2019/01/14/senegals-petroleum-code-moves-towards-final-stage/

[6] Jeff Kapembwa, "Zambia, Angola Sign Agreement on Oil and Gas," The Southern Times, January 28, 2019, https://southerntimesafrica.com/site/news/zambia-angola-sign-agreement-on-oil-and-gas

[7] Okechukwu Nnodim, "Nigeria, Morocco Gas Pipeline to Supply 15 Countries," Punch, January 29, 2019, https://punchng.com/nigeria-morocco-gas-pipeline-to-supply-15- countries/

[8] "Oil is the Glue that Binds Sudan and South Sudan," Oil Review, April 16, 2019, 291 http://www.oilreviewafrica.com/downstream/downstream/oil-is-the-glue-that-binds-sudan-and-south-sudan-ezekiel-lol-gatkuoth

[9] Steven Deng, "South Africa's State-owned Oil Company Signs Deal to Explore Highly-prospective Oil Block B2 in South Sudan," AfricaNews.com, May 6, 2019, https://www.africanews.com/2019/05/06/south-africas-state-owned-oil-company-signs-deal-to-explore-highly-prospective-oil-block-b2-in-south-sudan/

[10] Robert Brelsford, "Ivory Coast Secures Loan to Support Refinery Revamp," Oil & Gas Journal, January 14, 2019, https://www.ogj.com/articles/2019/01/ivory-coast-secures-loan-to-support-refinery-revamp.html

[11] "Ghanaians Undergo Oil and Gas Training in Brazil," Ghana Business News, January 31, 2019, https://www.ghanabusinessnews.com/2019/01/31/ghanaians-undergo-oil-and-gas-training-in-brazil/

[12] "Angola Sets Sights on Training and Education to Bolster Oil and Gas Sector," Africa Oil & Power, January 7, 2019, https://africaoilandpower.com/2019/01/07/angola-sets-sights-on-training-and-education-to-bolster-oil-and-gas-sector/